Criminology and Climate

This book explores the role of the insurance industry in contributing to, and responding to, the harms that climate change has brought and will bring either directly or indirectly. The Anthropocene signifies a new role for humankind: we are the only species that has become a driving force in the planetary system. What might criminology be in the Anthropocene? What does the Anthropocene suggest for future theory and practice of criminology? *Criminology and Climate*, as part of Routledge's *Criminology at the Edge* Series, seeks to contribute to this research agenda by exploring differing vantage points relevant to thinking within criminology.

Contemporary societies are presented with myriad intersecting and interacting climate-related harms at multiple scales. *Criminology and Climate* brings attention to the finance sector, with a particular focus on the insurance industry as one of its most significant components, in both generating and responding to new climate 'harmscapes'. Bringing together thought leaders from a variety of disciplines, this book considers what finance and insurance have done and might still do, as 'fulcrum institutions', to contribute to the realisation of safe and just planetary spaces.

An accessible and compelling read, this book will appeal to students and scholars of criminology, sociology, law and environmental studies and provides readers with a basis to analyse the challenges and opportunities for the finance sector, and in particular the insurance industry, in the regulation of climate harms.

Cameron Holley is a Professor at the University of New South Wales Law, UNSW. Cameron works in the areas of environmental law, natural resources law, energy law and water law, with a focus on regulation and governance.

Liam Phelan is a Senior Lecturer at the School of Environmental and Life Sciences, University of Newcastle, Australia. Liam researches and teaches in two areas: environmental studies with a particular focus on complexity and climate change, and higher education policy and practice.

Clifford Shearing holds professorships at the Universities of Cape Town, Griffith and Montreal. The principal focus of Clifford's academic work has been on widening criminology's boundaries, with a primary focus on 'security governance'. His policy and applied work have been concerned with enhancing safety. His research and writing have become increasingly centred on criminology's responses to the challenges of the Anthropocene.

Criminology at the Edge

Over the last few decades, criminology has become known for its rigorous research methods and innovative analyses as well as for the development and testing of traditional and new theories. Criminology, as a science, has become known for its empirical-based theorizing and its dedication to enable this knowledge to contribute effectively to realizing the goal of creating safe and just societies. This interdisciplinary series explores innovative developments and imagined futures within criminology.

The objective of this series is to expand the boundaries of criminology and facilitate, encourage and disseminate the fruits of a thorough and meticulous discussions of the most important emerging trends within criminology. Innovative criminologists will be encouraged to take risks as they imagine a criminology for the 21st Century, and to think outside existing criminological boxes.

Benoit Leclerc
Ross Homel
Clifford Shearing

Griffith University, Australia

The Future of Rational Choice for Crime Prevention
Edited by Danielle M. Reynald and Benoit Leclerc

Criminology and the Anthropocene
Edited by Cameron Holley and Clifford Shearing

Big Data
Benoit Leclerc and Jesse Cale

Criminology and Climate
Insurance, Finance and the Regulation of Harmscapes
Edited by Cameron Holley, Liam Phelan and Clifford Shearing

For more information about this series, please visit: https://www.routledge.com/Criminology-at-the-Edge/book-series/CATE

Criminology and Climate

Insurance, Finance and the Regulation
of Harmscapes

**Edited by Cameron Holley,
Liam Phelan and Clifford Shearing**

Routledge
Taylor & Francis Group

LONDON AND NEW YORK

First published 2021
by Routledge
2 Park Square, Milton Park, Abingdon, Oxon OX14 4RN

and by Routledge
605 Third Avenue, New York, NY 10017

First issued in paperback 2022

Routledge is an imprint of the Taylor & Francis Group, an informa business

British Library Cataloguing-in-Publication Data
A catalogue record for this book is available from the British Library

Library of Congress Cataloging-in-Publication Data
Names: Holley, Cameron, editor. | Phelan, Liam, editor. | Shearing, Clifford D., 1942- editor.
Title: Criminology and climate : insurance, finance and the regulation of harmscapes / edited by Cameron Holley, Liam Phelan, and Clifford Shearing.
Description: Abingdon, Oxon ; New York, NY : Routledge, 2021. | Series: Criminology at the edge | Includes bibliographical references and index. | Identifiers: LCCN 2020035268 | ISBN 9780367192303 (hardback) | ISBN 9780429201172 (ebook)
Subjects: LCSH: Climate change insurance. | Climatic changes--Social aspects. | Criminology--Environmental aspects.
Classification: LCC HG9979 .C75 2021 | DDC 368.1/22--dc23
LC record available at https://lccn.loc.gov/2020035268

ISBN : 978-0-367-68366-5 (pbk)
ISBN: 978-0-367-19230-3 (hbk)
ISBN: 978-0-429-20117-2 (ebk)

DOI: 10.4324/9780429201172

Typeset in Times New Roman
by KnowledgeWorks Global Ltd.

Contents

Illustrations

Figures

Tables

Preface

No single discipline has a mortgage on understanding climate change, let alone its resolution. Instead, climate change is a challenge to be shared across disciplines, and beyond. While it's true enough that we have come to this volume from a criminological perspective, we have done so mindful that the edges or liminal zones between disciplines can be generative sites of important new understanding. As such, the contributions to this volume, even as they are linked by criminology, extend across the social and physical sciences.

The relationship between the insurance industry and the broader finance sector, and climate change, invites more-than-disciplinary inquiry. On the one hand, the finance sector has been a major enabler of the fossil fuel-driven economic activity that, absent mitigation, will likely render the planet uninhabitable. On the other hand, insurance companies – as societies' risk managers – have traditionally constituted a crucial institution in regulating harms. Yet, notwithstanding the potential for playing a crucial role in both mitigating and adapting to climate change, the insurance industry, and much of the broader finance sector, have remained remarkably unengaged with climate change.

Through this volume we have sought to bring together thought leaders from a variety of disciplines to review the role of the finance sector broadly and the insurance industry in particular, as 'fulcrum institutions', to contribute to the realisation of a safe and just climate. We are grateful to the volume's contributors, who have brought their diverse perspectives to bear in shedding light on the intersection of finance, insurance and climate change.

Acknowledgements

We are grateful to Elaine Atkins, Ricky Röntsch and Georgia Regan for their assistance in the preparation of this book. The book was supported by two Australian Research Council Discovery Project grants (project numbers DP170100281 and DP190101584) as well as the Mauerberger Foundation Fund.

Contributors

Megan Bowman is a Reader (Associate Professor) of the School of Law and Director of the Climate Law and Governance Centre at King's College, London. Bowman leads the King's/UN Environment (UNEP) partnership on *Legal Readiness for Climate Finance*. Her work investigates climate-related financial regulation, and legal and regulatory options for countries to mobilise public and private sustainable finance. She also consults to national governments and prominent NGOs on implementing the Paris Agreement. She is a qualified barrister and solicitor of the High Court of Australia and Supreme Court of Victoria.

Mathieu Charbonneau is a Postdoctoral Fellow at the Karl Polanyi Institute of Political Economy, Concordia University (Montreal, Canada). Charbonneau's research focus, from the perspective of institutional economic sociology and public policy, is on climate change and the insurance industry, the governance of organ donation and transplant, workers compensation, the cyber-insurance market, and health and drug insurance.

Sylvia Dorbor is a part of the African Climate and Development Initiative at the University of Cape Town. Dorbor is passionate about global sustainability and hopes to contribute immensely to Africa, and the world at large. Her Honours research focused on renewables energy in the form of biogas and she is interested in the use and adoption of renewable energy sources, so as to reduce global greenhouse gas emissions. Her Master's research focused on the relationship between human influence and drought risk.

Aaron Doyle is Associate Professor at the Department of Sociology and Anthropology, Carleton University (Ottawa, Canada). Doyle has published a number of articles and chapters, and authored, co-authored, or co-edited nine books. A key theme of his work is how public and private institutions govern risks and risky populations.

Louise du Toit is a Postdoctoral Fellow in the Law Faculty of North-West University. Du Toit's research interests broadly include environmental law, energy law, and climate change law and policy (both nationally and globally). She is the assistant editor of *Environmental Law in South Africa* and an admitted attorney of the High Court of South Africa.

Neil Gunningham is a Research Professor within RegNet – the School of Regulation and Global Governance – at the Australian National University, and leads RegNet's Climate Finance Initiative. He is a Fellow of the Australian Academy of Social Sciences and a past Fulbright Scholar. His books include *Smart Regulation* (with Grabosky and Sinclair) and *Shades of Green: Business, Regulation and Environment* (with Kagan and Thornton). His current research is on regulating climate finance, and on the roles of social activism in averting a climate catastrophe.

Cameron Holley is a Professor at the University of New South Wales. Holley works in the areas of environmental law, natural resources law, energy law and water law, with a focus on regulation and governance.

Karl Mallon is the CEO of Climate Risk Pty Ltd. Climate Risk was established in 2005 with the specific mission to compute the costs of climate change risks to society, so that the costs of inaction on emissions could be understood. Climate Risk provided the modelling for the Cross Dependency Initiative's *Second Pass National Assessment.* Mallon is editor and co-author of' *Renewable Energy Policy and Politics: A Handbook for Decision Making* published by Earthscan (London) and a contribution author for 'Practical Adaptation Studies', published by Wiley. Mallon is a founding board member of The Climate Bonds Initiative (London).

David Maslo is an actuary, finance and underwriting Analyst at African Risk Capacity Insurance Company (ARC Ltd). He works in risk management with experience in developing and implementing sovereign risk transfer solutions for natural hazards. He has experience in direct engagement with the private sector, multinational development institutions and country governments in emerging markets for catastrophe risk financing decisions.

Mark New is Director of the African Climate and Development Initiative at the University of Cape Town, and AXA Research Chair in African Climate Risk. He is also a coordinating lead author on the IPCC 6th Assessment Report, responsible for Chapter 17 of Working Group II, Decision Making Options for Managing Risk, and an editor for Global Environmental Change and Environmental Research Letters. He serves on the Science Committees of the World Adaptation Science Programme and the South African Global Change Science Programme. His research has spanned climate change detection, attribution, impacts and adaptation. His recent research has focused quantifying and adapting to the changing risks of damaging climate events in southern Africa, on climate adaptation knowledge systems, and on understanding barriers and enablers to effective climate adaptation responses.

Romaric Odoulami is a Postdoctoral research fellow at the African Climate and Development Initiative, University of Cape Town. Odoulami's PhD research examined the potential impacts of large-scale changes in land cover on climate extremes over West Africa based on a regional climate modelling approach. His current research includes the underlying mechanisms driving the 'Day Zero' drought that caused the Cape Town water crisis in 2017, and on human influence on the drought's likelihood and severity using the science of event attribution. He is also working on testing the concept of using attribution science to quantify changes in risk for agricultural insurance, and therefore insurance cost.

Vanessa Otto-Mentz is a Partner with Deloitte in Amsterdam. She was previously the Head of Strategy for the Santam Group, a board member for the UN Environment's Principles for Sustainable Insurance, and a management committee member for ClimateWise the insurance leaders group hosted by the Cambridge Institute for Sustainability Leadership, and an advisory board member for the Embedding Project at Simon Fraser University. She is a PhD candidate at the University of Cape Town.

Liam Phelan is a Senior Lecturer at the School of Environmental and Life Sciences, University of Newcastle, Australia. Phelan researches and teaches in two areas: environmental studies with a particular focus on complexity and climate change, and higher education policy and practice.

Clifford Shearing is a Professor at the Universities of Cape Town, Griffith, and Montreal. The principal focus of Shearing's academic work has been on widening criminology's boundaries, with a primary focus on 'security governance'. His policy and applied work have been concerned with enhancing safety. His research and writing have become increasingly centred on criminology's responses to the challenges of the Anthropocene.

Nicholas Philip Simpson is a Postdoctoral Research Fellow – Climate Risk Assessment and Management, African Climate and Development Initiative, University of Cape Town. Simpson's current research concentrates on climate risk management through finance, insurance and energy access. His work cuts across the economic spectrum to consider how public and private actors are responding to climate risk. Simpson's other research interests explore the complexity of climate risk and security practices at the interface of climate change and conflict. He is the Chapter Scientist and a Contributing Author to the Africa chapter of the 6th Assessment of the Intergovernmental Panel on Climate Change.

Darren Sinclair is an Associate Professor and DECRA Research Fellow, Institute for Governance and Policy Analysis (IGPA), University of Canberra. Sinclair has published widely on environmental regulation and governance, and on occupational health and safety regulation in the mining industry.

Johan Strumpfer is an Organisational Strategy & Change Consultant, Adjunct Professor, University of Cape Town, Graduate School of Business. Johan Strumpfer focuses on organisation change starting with strategy. He is a (reflective) practitioner who has worked with over 200 organisations in this role in his career, both locally and internationally. He has been responsible for a large number of inhouse leadership development programs for businesses and has taught at postgraduate level, mostly MBAs at a number of different universities. His areas of interest are complexity, large scale systems change, strategy and organisational change implied by strategy. His ontology of organisations is that human populated wholes are fundamentally different from other 'systems'. His concerns are with his granddaughters who will need to live through this climate change catastrophe.

Daniel Wiseman is a lawyer with ClientEarth's Climate Finance Initiative. He currently leads research and advocacy work on the implications of climate change and the zero-carbon transition for legal duties relating to corporate governance, company reporting, and financial law and regulation. Prior to joining ClientEarth, Wiseman worked as a lawyer in the corporate team at a leading independent Australian law firm.

1 Dark clouds

Regulatory possibilities

*Cameron Holley, Liam Phelan,
and Clifford Shearing*[*]

Tomorrow belongs to the people who prepare for it today.

(African Proverb)

This book arises at a time when our skies are dark, and are becoming darker. There is now irrefutable evidence that the temperate era of the last 12,000 years, the Holocene era, is drawing to a close. We are moving towards a series of tipping points that could well bring an end to the nurturing 'ecological assemblages' (Trisos, Merow and Pigot, 2020) and Schumacher's (1973) 'natural capital', which provided humans and many other species with the provision of essential 'ecosystem services' (Farber, Costanza and Wilson, 2002). During this now vanishing era, the earth has been characterised by what Rockström et al. (2009: 1) have termed 'planetary boundaries' that provide a 'safe operating space for humanity'.

The warning that these dark clouds carry with them is that we humans have been, especially since we have begun living in industrial societies, systematically destroying the very basis of our existence – an engagement that Brisman and South (2018) compare with self-cannibalism, autosarcophagy. This autosarcophagy has been, and continues to remain, the consequence of carbon-intensive economies – ways of being, built on fire and the heat it produces (Hartmann, 1999).

Hidden in these dark clouds is the spectre of collapse (Diamond, 2005), a collapse that, as Umair Haque (2019) has recently argued, emerges from the bottom-up. This is a collapse of the biospheric foundations (see also Smil, 2002), upon which humans, as biophysical and social creatures, depend for their existence and upon which they have built their worlds. Yet, despite this complete dependence on these foundations, humans have collectively paid very little, if any, attention to them. The consequences in this

---

[*] Chapter 1 draws on ideas initially presented in Holley, C., Mutongwizo T. and Shearing, C. (2020). 'Conceptualizing Policing and Security: New Harmscapes, the Anthropocene, and, Technology', *Annual Review of Criminology*, 3, pp. 341–358.

'age of collapse', according to Haque (2019), is that 'the bottom [is] depleted, which causes the middle to implode, which takes the top away with it, too'.

Back in 2017, as we began planning this volume, we settled on the term 'harmscapes' to conceptualise the evolution of arrays of intersecting and interacting harms. Climate change is a primary exemplar (Berg and Shearing, 2018: 75): a globally coherent phenomenon that creates myriad diverse harms, manifesting in multiple and connected ways. Climate change harms play out at multiple spatial and temporal scales: spatially, harms range from localised to global scales, and temporally, some harms are immediate, others are delayed, and others again are, from any meaningful human perspective, effectively permanent. Climate change is a change process characterised by non-linear dynamics and threshold effects: as such, impacts can cascade across sectors, and with limited predictability (Duit and Galaz, 2008). The impacts of climate change are dispersed, but uneven. And as with impacts, attribution of climate change, primarily through anthropogenic fossil fuel emissions, is also dispersed and uneven.

Fossil fuels have provided great benefits for contemporary societies, as well as significant costs: as Mitchell notes, '[f]ossil fuels helped create both the possibility of twentieth-century democracy and its limits' (Mitchell, 2009: 399). As such climate change presents a profound challenge to regulatory approaches and frameworks, and one that we use harmscapes to accentuate.

Warnings about climate change, and other environmental catastrophes, that are today at the forefront of our existence, are not new. Indeed, as Bonneuil and Fressoz (2016) have recently spelt out so clearly, they have been articulated for centuries. But they have fallen on deaf ears. Virtually no one has listened, and this remains broadly true today although these warnings are clearer and louder than ever. Rather than heed these increasingly clear warnings of our dark clouds, many political and economic leaders, as they have for some time, continue to treat these very pointed warnings by the very constituency that has enabled our industrial societies to emerge, namely scientists, as the alarmist cries of 'Chicken Littles', making absurd claims that the 'sky is falling' when only an acorn has fallen.

Fortunately, responses and action have begun to emerge and accelerate – for example, varieties of international and domestic environmental laws, regional and state-led reforms, along with civil society litigation against states and companies, and business-led reforms (Dahlmann et al., 2020; Hamann et al., 2020). At the same time, many of today's political and economic leaders across the world, the current president of the United State of America provides perhaps the prime example, continue to claim that the sky has not changed and that it has most certainly not fallen, and that it will not fall any time soon. It is this attitude of fundamental neglect of the foundational nature of ecosystem services that has driven, and continues to drive, contemporary economies – embraced by businesses both big and small. This attitude is finally being challenged by some, including investment-focused businesses – the focus in this volume – by rethinking their foundational dependencies and incorporating this into wider conception of purpose; what Dahlmann et al. (2020) term 'purpose ecosystem'.

The essays in this volume explore the response of businesses to climate change, with a particular focus on the insurance industry and the broader finance industry, industries whose existence is central to the global economy but who had (bar concerns over corporate social licence) historically stayed outside of climate and environmental interventions. It is true that criminology and its green variants have extensively critiqued corporate activities that harm the environment and people (see generally Brisman and South, 2020: 19). However, there is value, we argue, in extending our focus beyond established boundaries and traditional institutions of criminal justice to consider the potential of these private auspices and providers of security (see Brisman and South, 2020: 19). A core reason for our focus is that the finance sector occupies a 'fulcrum position': if it chooses to act in response to the dark warning clouds, it would likely trigger a cascade of activity that could, in short order, bring about an enormous and crucial reshaping shift in the earth system, which might just provide sufficient mitigation to avoid the emergence of a sixth extinction.

At least two drivers are spurring the finance industry to begin to act. First, under Article 2 of the Paris Agreement, the financial sector was championed by the global community as having a central role in enabling the transition to an environmentally sustainable economy in line with global climate targets, and in building global financial resilience to environmental risks (Grünewald, 2020). Vast amounts of finance for climate action was said to be needed to solve climate challenges: finance that only the private sector has the wherewithal to provide (Gunningham, this volume). But scaling up climate finance – for low-carbon infrastructure, renewable energy, energy efficiency, and other mitigation measures – involved transforming a finance sector that had only just begun its journey towards sustainability. This led to call for a 'quiet revolution' (UNEP, 2015; Gunningham, this volume), led partly by financial market regulation and regulators who recognised 'a need for collective leadership and globally coordinated action' (NGFS, 2019: 4).

As this quiet revolution began, business leaders recognised the financial risks of climate change, both physical and transitional in nature (Grünewald, 2020). Directly threatened by the emergence of very tangible and costly impacts of post-Holocene earth system changes, insurance and finance industry leaders, most notably perhaps Carney, the former Governor of the Bank of England, sounded loud and shrill calls for change.

> The stakes are undoubtedly high, but the commitment of all actors in the financial system to act will help avoid a climate-driven 'Minsky moment' – the term we use to refer to a sudden collapse in asset prices… There is a need for [action] to achieve net zero emissions, but actually it comes at a time when there is a need for a big increase in investment globally to accelerate the pace of global growth, to help get global

interest rates up, to get us out of this low-growth, low-interest-rate trap we are in...I don't normally quote bankers, but James Gorman, who is the CEO of Morgan Stanley, said the other day: "If we don't have a planet, we're not going to have a very good financial system." Ultimately, that is true.

(Carney, quoted in Carrington, 2019)

Perhaps recognising that they 'can't wish away systemic risks', and that 'in the end, a small investment up front can save a tremendous cost down the road' (Carney, quoted in Gill, 2020) the financial and insurance industry have been motivated to change. By 2020, the 'quiet revolution' in climate finance was, in fact, no longer quiet or niche, but defined by an explosion of sustainable finance-related tools and initiatives driven by private banks, other finance actors, and public and private partnerships (Mancini and Van Acker, 2020: 10). There are now more than 390 policy and regulatory climate finance measures implemented at national, sub-national, and regional levels (Mancini and Van Acker, 2020: 25).

These developments, albeit briefly covered here, reveal an emerging practice of finance and insurance businesses as governors of global environmental security, a fact that led us to pursue this book on criminology and climate.

Criminology, climate change, and the role of private securities

In the global climate change context, criminology is arguably at a crossroads. Globally, we are beginning to rethink safety and security in biophysical terms, which poses a challenge for criminology as an area of enquiry whose fundamental topic has been safety and security (Shearing, 2015). Recognising that security itself is an idea that arguably cannot be constrained into a single discipline (Zedner, 2009: 10; Ngoc Cao and Wyatt, 2016: 415), the joining of environment and security (once common only in international relations' geopolitical focus on environmental impacts upon states, see Brauch, 2008: 31; Chalecki, 2013: 4) has come to include broader understandings, such as legal scholar Hulme's (2009: 25) explanation of the term as capturing 'the environment's ability to impact on human security and man's ability to impact on the stability and viability of the biosphere'. Similar definitions can be found in green criminology (e.g. see Shearing's (2015: 261) description of environmental security as an umbrella term for 'water security', 'energy security', 'food security', and 'climate security') and in international relations (e.g. see Dalby's (2002: 60) description of 'developing an economic system that reduces dependence on a single resource, a dynamic system that can accommodate change'.

The rise of environmental security concerns (see Dalby, 2002; Chalecki, 2013), prompted vociferously by climate change, has seen criminologists begin to ask what criminology could be, and should be, in this Anthropocene age (see e.g. contributions in Holley and Shearing, 2018). While answers to the question are being explored, the growth of private actors in climate governance may in fact provide rich ground for criminologists to till. As many readers will know, private security provision has in fact been a long, rich, and debated issue in criminology.

Traditionally, the governance of security in criminology (sometimes termed 'policing' – see Stenning and Shearing, 2015) referenced activities – particularly activities by government agencies – intended to maintain rule-based relationships with respect to property and the integrity of persons, (prevention) and to respond to breaches of these relationships once they have occurred (law enforcement). For many criminologists, there was typically an acceptance, and indeed an embracing, of a Maitland-esque conceptualisation, which argued that the only way to enhance the delivery of public goods like safety, to be enjoyed by all, was to ensure the advance of state institutions (Maitland, 1885).

However, during the mid-20th century, evidence of a sizable private police/policing industry began to emerge (see for example, Kakalik and Wildhorn, 1977; Spitzer and Scull, 1977) albeit these claims of pluralisation of policing were initially resisted. Today, this private sector policing (including its 'low' and 'high' variants (Brodeur, 1983; O'Reilly, 2015)) tends to be termed private security in deference to the conception that 'policing' was an exclusively 'police' activity (however, for an example of the re-emergence of the term 'private policing', see Sparrow, 2014). Certainly, some consider private security as a regressive development, a 'tainted trade' (Thumala, Goold and Loader, 2011) undermining the trajectory of a long, and indeed noble, history of the governance of security becoming increasingly more inclusive (see for example, Loader and Walker, 2007 and more recently Loader and White, 2017). While such debates continue, a burgeoning of research on private security has subsequently emerged to account for its development (for example, Jones and Newburn, 1998).

Around the same time, parallel developments between what was happening with respect to the governance of security were also occurring in a wider field of the provision of public services (Osborne and Gaebler, 1993; Rhodes, 2007) as well environmental protection under signs of market-based instruments, light-handed regulation, voluntarism, and ecomodernisation (see generally Holley, 2017). Even so, the emergence of private security, as an institution for providing safety, has arguably been so significant that, in many contexts and locations, it now surpasses the public police institution several times over, both with respect to the number of agents employed and the cost of security provision. Berg and Howell (2017: 4–5 with internal references omitted) provide some numbers to illustrate the situation in South Africa and Liberia:

> multinational conglomerates such as G4S reportedly operates in 24 African countries employing approximately 120,400 people. South Africa hosts the largest (known) numbers of private security companies

and employees on the continent – both per capita and in terms of raw numbers. In 2015/2016, there were over 8692 security companies and approximately 488,666 registered and active private security employees in South Africa compared to 151,834 police officers in the South African Police Service (excluding civilians) and members of the armed forces. In other words, compared to the state security apparatus, private security outnumbers the public police by 3 to 1.... private security is one of the fastest growing industries. In Liberia, for instance, the private security industry reportedly doubled its revenues between 2004 and 2011, while in South Africa, private security has gone from an industry worth 600 million (USD44 million) in 1986 to current estimates of it being worth 60 billion Rand (USD4 billion).

With the growth of such a large industry, regulation of private security has understandably come to focus on attempting to ensure that the industry operates within legal parameters and that minimum standards are maintained, both as a protection to customers and to ensure that the activities of the industry, when engaging persons who are threatening to harm or have harmed the peace of their employers, are done within legal boundaries (see e.g. Berg, 2003; Button, 2007; Abrahamsen and Williams, 2011).

As the 'web' of regulated security assemblages has grown (Brodeur, 2010; Abrahamsen and Williams, 2011), traditional police have become one node among many within a nodal security delivery landscape (Johnston and Shearing, 2003). Within this framing, the central issues of securing security have become who does what, in what context, under whose auspices, and how various nodes relate to each other as they engage in the provision of safety. In Brodeur's (2006: ix) words, this pluralisation of security 'does away with the single stuff mythology'. This has given rise to new research agendas that have embraced the study of both public and private auspices and providers of security governance (Berg, Nakueira and Shearing, 2014), an area which has relevance to the emerging private provision of environmental security for our planet.

Environmental security, finance, and insurance

As with many polycentric governance systems, the range of finance and insurance practices that are emerging evidence diverse definitions of 'climate', 'green', and 'sustainable' finance, an array of public and private funding sources, a multitude of objectives, and a multiplicity of implementation channels (public, private, and civil society implementers), often with varying priorities (energy, forests, urban infrastructure) (Lundsgaarde, Dupuy and Persson, 2018: 3). Phelan et al. (2020, 2011), for instance, highlight various pathways of action in insurance, ranging from largely adaptive approaches aimed at increasing insurers' capacity to accommodate the climate risks faced by their policyholders; 'weakly mitigative', meaning that they provide for some mitigation, but on a very limited scale; and few pursing 'divest and decline' actions by insurance industry described as 'strongly mitigative'.

Such diversity of responses from finance and insurance companies in this challenging context is not necessarily 'bad' (Lundsgaarde, Dupuy and Persson, 2018), but they do represent an emerging challenge for thinking about and responding to the governance of our shared environmental security, how it might and should be organised, and who can and should be delivering public goods as the field of climate governors continues to broaden and decentre. The still-nascent generation of practices and thoughts on these issues points us in useful, and sometimes contradictory, directions, with which theoretical and empirical scholarship is slowly grappling (Wood et al., 2019). Ideas and theories both outside (Braithwaite and Drahos, 2000; De Búrca, Keohane and Sabel, 2014; Wood et al., 2019) and inside criminological scholarship (Ericson and Carriere, 1994; Nel, Shearing and Reyers, 2011; Hall and Farrall, 2013: 126–127; Herbstein et al., 2013; South, 2015: 273; O'Malley, 2018) have begun to explain, understand, and reform the role of private actors in governance, global finance, and insurance industry, and this edited book seeks to add to the endeavour.

The chapters in this book explore:

- sites of optimism and innovation in the role of the private finance industry as environmental security actors;
- how to enhance the activities of these private governors; and
- the implications of these trends for the private provision of security.

Each of the chapters adopts a somewhat different take in exploring these questions, and here we provide a brief overview of each chapter, with an eye to their collective reactions to these three issues.

Otto-Mentz and Strumpfer, in 'Co-creating sustainable risk futures: a role for insurers', begin by acknowledging the role insurance plays as society's safety net. Insurers manage risk by transferring and pooling risk, and communicate risk levels to consumers through insurance pricing and contract conditions. However, in practice, insurance coverage is often not comprehensive, leading to gaps in protection, particularly in the face of disasters. In response, 'protection gap entities' have evolved: consortiums of public and private entities established to build resilience against disaster risk. Initiatives of this kind underscore the importance of cooperation in risk management. Otto-Mentz and Strumpfer argue that climate change now presents a challenge that exceeds the insurance industry's capacity to manage financial risk and build resilience, and cooperation is now not only desirable, but essential. Otto-Mentz and Strumpfer call for collaboration amongst diverse organisations in order to manage problems that are 'too big' to be managed by a single entity. With this in mind, they cast their gaze beyond the financial sector to an illustrative historical case study of co-creation through the Durban Functional Region Forum in South Africa.

Drawing on the lessons from that case study, Otto-Mentz and Strumpfer argue that insurers could – and should – play a key role in facilitating collective efforts at risk management through opening their strategy processes, but that the key to success for initiatives' in this vein will be their broader societal engagement.

Gunningham, in 'Crime, regulation and climate finance', explains – bluntly – that 'humanity is on a trajectory to destroy the habitability of our planet and to precipitate the largest mass extinction of species in the last 65 million years'. He does so in order to bring focus to the needed development of rules to foster and govern climate finance flows. On any assessment, effectively mitigating climate change calls for tremendous amounts of finance – at least scores of trillions of dollars for low-carbon infrastructure, renewable energy, energy efficiency, and other mitigation measures in the near future. Finance at this scale is available in the private sector, but the sector itself is new in its attention to sustainability, and lacks a tried and tested architecture for operating in this new arena. With reference to the 2008 Global Financial Crisis, Gunningham points out that underregulated financial markets can cause catastrophic social and economic harm, and argues the case for new and effective financial market regulation. However, even as there are varied approaches available to effective regulation there are challenges, and Gunningham reviews key approaches. Effective mitigation of climate change will call for action extending beyond the financial sector – other economic instruments such as a price on carbon will have roles to play as well. Gunningham leaves readers with a broader question: can a rapid transition to a low-carbon economy be achieved 'within the strictures of capitalism'.

Sinclair, in 'Speak loudly and carry a small stick: Prudential regulation and the climate, energy and finance nexus', argues that government action will be insufficient for preventing dangerous climate change, and that the financial sector has a role to play in achieving a transition to a low-carbon economy. While civil society has long sought to change societal norms about the desirability or otherwise of investment in fossil fuels, it is only more recently that finance sector regulators in Western countries have begun to craft policy responses to climate change framed as a risk to financial order and stability. These regulatory responses by states are, in Sinclair's view, still 'nascent', and Sinclair assesses their impacts and limitations, as well as their possible futures. New regulatory responses focused on financial stability offer some prospects for leveraging the financial sector as environmental security actors, but Sinclair notes that these approaches remain 'very tentative indeed', where a much more muscular approach is called for.

Charbonneau and Doyle, in 'The contradictory roles of the insurance industry in the era of climate change', bring focus to the dual role the insurance industry plays in both creating and managing climate risk – the insurance industry is, after all, central in fossil fuel-driven economic growth, and generates revenue from two primary sources tightly wound through the economy: underwriting and investments. The authors note insurers' market-based initiatives that increase their capacity to assume risks serve as adaptation measures as climate risks increase. One is reinsurance – insurance for insurers – which enables insurers to transfer risk to a larger pool within the industry. Another is to sell insurance-linked securities, in order to transfer risk beyond the industry entirely, and onto larger equity markets. Charbonneau and Doyle also note the existence of insurance schemes for climate-implicated weather risks that draw on private and state actors. These measures are effective adaptations to climate change, but do not contribute to climate change mitigation. Ultimately, even as some insurers are taking steps in the right direction, Charbonneau and Doyle question the potential of – private – insurance actors to drive effective change, and instead look to nation states to drive transition, through public policy and international collaboration.

Mallon and Phelan, in 'Quantifying changing climate risks and built environments in Australia: Implications for lenders, insurers and regulators', bring attention to the quantification of climate risks. Their chapter analyses the recent report *Climate Change Risk to Australia's Built Environment: A Second Pass National Assessment*, published by Cross Dependency Initiative, a risk analysis company that provides infrastructure risk analysis and quantification for governments and utilities in Australia and internationally. That climate change exacerbates some weather risks is not controversial and is a well-understood output of global-scale climate models. However, quantifying climate-exacerbated weather risks at local scale is more challenging. Coastal inundation, forest fires, riverine flooding, and other risks all present significant and growing risks to build environments in Australia. In this chapter, Mallon and Phelan offer a brief 'tour' of the quantification method and challenges by way of framing the challenges changing climate risk profiles present to key stakeholders in property: insurers, lenders, and the regulators of insurers and regulators. Mallon and Phelan argue that increased transparency about long-term risks to property is essential to support informed decision-making about effective climate change adaptation investment.

du Toit, in 'The influence of government regulation on insurers' responses to climate change', begins by noting that some larger, mostly European insurers have in recent years begun to exclude coal (and to a much more limited extent, some other fossil fuels) from their extensive investment portfolios. A smaller subset has taken a further step, and begun to exclude coal from the underwriting side of their business too. Even as the number of insurers involved is small, this is a significant development: insurers have long been subject to calls from civil society to respond strongly to climate change, i.e., with the intent to mitigate climate change, rather than the more limited ambition of adapting to it. The reasons for insurers' decisions are surely complex. Nevertheless, in this chapter, du Toit seeks to explore the particular role of governments' and regulators' in influencing insurers' decisions to divest from coal. du Toit notes that insurers with coal exclusion policies tend to be domiciled in states that have stronger rather than weaker regulatory responses to climate change, including France, Norway, the Netherlands, and the United Kingdom. There are other drivers for insurers' coal exclusion policies, including stranded asset risk and reputation risk, and du Toit reviews these also. du Toit concludes that while no single driver is determinative, government regulation is significant and suggests further opportunities for government regulation to strengthen insurers' responses even further. This is likely essential, given du Toit noting that corporations generally – including insurers – are 'ill-suited' to addressing climate change.

Simpson, in 'Insurance in the Anthropocene: Exposure, solvency and manoeuvrability', provides an important case study of strategic decision-making within an African insurer seeking to navigate three key challenges facing the industry and its regulators: climate risk exposure, solvency, and manoeuvrability. The insurer has operations across 35 countries – 32 in Africa and 3 in Asia – and its short-term division is engaging currently in understanding, responding to, and anticipating material risks of climate change. Drawing on a research process comprising workshops and inter-views, Simpson's empirical observations bring attention to the practical challenges of managing risk even as climate change renders actuarial models based on historical record decreasingly useful. One example is overlaying historical loss data with GIS-based modelling, in order to more precisely identify risk at property scale. In this way, the insurer can better price risk prospectively, rather than relying only on claims histories. Beyond climate risk exposure, Simpson also notes examples of innovation in practice with regard to solvency and manoeuvrability. Across all three areas, changes in technical practices in turn lead to changes in internal business processes.

Bowman and Wiseman, in 'Finance actors and climate-related disclosure regulation: Logic, limits and emerging accountability', note that climate-related corporate disclosure has become a favoured regulatory tool, aimed at leveraging financial market logics to help mitigate risks associated with climate change. Following the influential industry-led Taskforce on Climate-related Financial Disclosures, increased expectations about climate risk reporting are proliferating in legislation and regulatory guidance. Despite these developments, widespread concern remains about the limits of the disclosure paradigm, and the quantity and quality of information being disclosed. Questions of accountability and enforcement are now receiving increased attention, especially in relation to systemically important financial firms, such as banks and insurers. Bowman and Wiseman explore the logic of climate-related disclosure, emerging forms of accountability, and likely future regulatory trends in this area. They do so by using a case study of complaints to the UK Financial Conduct Authority against three listed insurance companies by civil society organisation, ClientEarth. They further discuss challenges associated with the contested legal concept of 'materiality', which underpins many financial market disclosure frameworks, and identify the need for robust assurance, accountability, and complementary regulatory design for the logic of climate-related disclosure to fulfil its aspirations.

New, Dorbor, Odoulami, and Maslo, in 'Towards attribution-based climate insurance: redefining who should pay for weather-related insurance', explore how defining attribution for climate change-related losses could be used as a basis for calculating equitable contributions to weather insurance premiums in Africa. There are several parts to the argument. Firstly, New et al. note that agricultural (and other) losses are rising, and that this is due to climate change, through climate-implicated extreme weather events such as droughts. This, in turn, leads to increased premiums for insurance covering those extreme weather events, and African countries have limited capacity to pay for increased insurance premiums. Secondly, common but shared responsibility for climate change mitigation and adaptation is already established in key international climate agreements. Thirdly, it is now technically feasible to distinguish between the quantum of 'background' risk, i.e., the risk that would be present absent climate change, and the additional risk attributable to a changed climate in order to quantify what proportion of the risk is 'natural', and what proportion is anthropogenic. New et al. propose that the cost of insurance premiums could be split accordingly between African states as policy holders on the one hand, and on the other, international climate funds to which industrialised countries contribute. Agricultural insurance for drought risk in Malawi serves as an illustrative example of how such an approach could be operationalised.

Collectively, these chapters comprise a highly diverse and thoroughly thought-provoking range of perspectives and insights, and much promise. With an eye to the potential for the private finance industry to function as a fulcrum institution – an institution whose actions can leverage the engagement of others – contributors identify multiple sites of optimism and innovation. One example is a significant African insurer in the process of amending their approaches to risk calculation in order to price climate risks more accurately, towards ensuring its financial viability in the face of changing climate harmscapes (Simpson). Insurers beginning to exclude coal from the investment portfolios (du Toit) is another example. Other contributors look to the need for new financial instruments and architecture (Gunningham) to facilitate effective action, and propose models for the fair funding and effective operation of new insurance instruments (New et al.). Others again note that continuing extension of climate modelling's potential, especially when combined with other data gathering and analysis methods such as Geographic Information Systems, is opening up new possibilities for transparency around changing climate harmscapes at local scales (Otto-Mentz and Strumpfer, Mallon, and Phelan); better data can inform better decisions-making by governments, regulators, insurers, lenders, and citizens. Also recognising the importance of climate information transparency, climate-related disclosure is becoming a favoured regulatory framework, increasingly expected by both favoured regulatory framework (Bowman and Wiseman) and regulators (Sinclair).

And yet, even as the private finance industry suggests possibilities, for many contributors, it is in fact the liminal zone between public regulators and private actors as new environmental security actors regulating climate harmscapes that suggests most promise. A recurring theme in the contributions to this volume is the call for greater robustness by public regulators in their engagement with private actors (see Sinclair). This observation is made at sectoral scale (see Gunningham, and Mallon and Phelan), and is also a call made by private actors themselves in some instances (see du Toit). Others focus on ways to make best use of newly emerging expectations (Bowman and Wiseman). Others look specifically to private-public linkages in order to amplify possibilities for finance, and insurance in particular, to play a constructive role in equitable climate adaptation (New et al.). Others still extend beyond a public-private framing to call for collaborative approaches as both desirable and necessary (Otto-Mentz and Strumpfer). However, other contributors adopt alternative perspectives, such as a call for regulators to craft regulatory frameworks that create more operating space for businesses seeking to respond to climate change (Simpson). In contrast, others (Charbonneau and Doyle) look beyond private actors towards states to drive policy collaboration at international scale.

As is perhaps now apparent, even while recognising that private actors have contributions to make towards regulating climate harmscapes, the role of public regulators has by no means diminished, much less disappeared. Rather, regulation of climate harmscapes has become more complex: there are multiple diverse actors in play, operating at multiple temporal and spatial scales, and with influence spreading beyond finance to many other sectors. Energy – old and renewable – is one key sector influenced by the finance sector: witnessing insurers beginning to step away from coal. Property is another: both insurers and lenders are key stakeholders in built environments, and property values are strongly dependent on continuing access to affordable insurance and loans. The role of public regulators is, therefore, as important as ever in governing climate harmscapes.

As a species, we continue to accelerate our fossil fuel emissions into the Earth system. As such, the prospect of mitigating climate change is receding more and more quickly, rather than drawing closer. Indeed, we are living in the Anthropocene, and driving change at planetary scale. Albrecht (2019) has responded by arguing for the need to bring the Anthropocene rapidly to a close. In his view, we should be urgently seeking to establish a new age: the Symbiocene, which would be characterised by humans living in symbiosis with the Earth and all its inhabitants. One strength of the term 'Anthropocene' is that it brings attention to humans as a driver of planetary change, and the importance of this realisation for our species cannot be underestimated. But it comes with limits: beyond the acknowledgement that humans are driving change at planetary scale, there is no sense of consciousness or purposeful direction in the term. In order to stay within Raworth's (2009) ideas of 'donut economics' and the provision of 'a safe and just operating space' on this planet, we will need to move to purposeful pursuit of sustainable alternatives. This is not a challenge solely for insurers, or the wider finance industry, but meeting this challenge will surely require their important contributions.

References

Abrahamsen, Rita and Williams, Michael. C. (2011). *Security Beyond the State: Private Security in International Politics.* Cambridge: Cambridge University Press.

Albrecht, Glenn. (2019). *Earth Emotions: New Words for a New World.* Ithaca: Cornell University Press.

Berg, Julie. (2003). The private security industry in South Africa: A review of applicable legislation. *South African Journal of Criminal Justice*, 16, pp. 178–196.

Berg, Julie and Howell, Simon. (2017). The private security complex and its regulation in Africa: Select examples from the continent. *International Journal of Comparative and Applied Criminal Justice*, 41(4), pp. 273–286.

Berg, Julie, Nakueira, Sophie and Shearing, Clifford. (2014). Global non-state auspices of security governance. In: H. Bersot and B. Ariigo, eds., *The Routledge Handbook of International Crime and Justice Studies.* New York: Routledge, pp. 77–97.

Berg, J. and Shearing, C. (2018). Governing-through-harm and public goods policing. *Annals of the American Academy of Political and Social Science*, 679(1), pp. 72–85. https://doi.org/10.1177/0002716218778540.

Bonneuil, Christophe and Fressoz, Jean-Baptiste. (2016). *The Shock of the Anthropocene: The Earth; History and Us.* London and New York: Verso.

Braithwaite, J. and Drahos, P. (2000). *Global Business Regulation.* Cambridge: Cambridge University Press.

Brauch, H. (2008). Conceptualising the environmental dimension of human security in the UN. *International Social Science Journal*, 59, pp. 19–48.

Brisman, Avi and South, Nigel. (2018). Autosarcophagy in the Anthropocene and obscenity of an epoch. In: Cameron Holley and Clifford Shearing, eds., *Criminology and The Anthropocene.* New York: Routledge, pp. 58–97 (In the Series Criminology at the Edge, B. Leclerc, R. Homel and C. Shearing, eds.).

Brisman, Avi and South, Nigel. (2020). Introduction: New horizons, ongoing and emerging issues and relationships in green criminology. In: A. Brisman and N. South, eds., *Routledge International Handbook of Green Criminology*, 2nd ed. New York: Routledge, pp. 1–36.

Brodeur, J. P. (1983). High policing and low policing: Remarks about the policing of political activities. *Social Problems*, 30(5), pp. 507–20.

Brodeur, J. P. (2006). Foreword. In: J. Wood and B. Dupont, eds., *Democracy, Society and the Governance of Security.* Cambridge: Cambridge University Press, pp. xi–x.

Brodeur, J. P. (2010). *The Policing Web.* Oxford: Oxford University Press.

Button, M. (2007). Assessing the regulation of private security across Europe. *European Journal of Criminology*, 4(1), pp. 109–128.

Carrington, D. (2019). Firms ignoring climate crisis will go bankrupt, says Mark Carney. *The Guardian*, 13 October. Available at: https://www.theguardian.com/ environment/2019/oct/13/firms-ignoring-climate-crisis-bankrupt-mark-carney-bank-england-governor [Accessed 1 June 2020].

Chalecki, E. (2013). *Environmental Security: A Guide to the Issues*. Westport, CT: Praeger Security International.

Dahlmann, Frederik, Stubbs, Wendy, De Albuquerque, Joao and Raven, Rob. (2020). The 'purpose ecosystem': Emerging private sector actors in earth system governance. *Earth System Governance*. https://doi.org/10.1016/j.esg.2020.100053.

Dalby, S. (2002). *Environmental Security*. Minneapolis, MN: University of Minneapolis Press.

De Búrca, G., Keohane, R. and Sabel, C. (2014). Global experimentalist governance. *British Journal of Political Science*, 44(3), pp. 477–486. doi: 10.1017/S0007123414000076.

Diamond, Jared. (2005). *Collapse: How Societies Choose to Fail or Succeed*. New York: Penguin Books.

Duit, Andreas and Galaz, Victor. (2008). Governance and complexity—Emerging issues for governance theory. *Governance: An International Journal of Policy, Administration, and Institutions*, 21(3), pp. 311–335. https://doi.org/10.1111/j.1468-0491.2008.00402.x.

Ericson, Richard and Carriere, Kevin. (1994). The fragmentation of criminology. In: David Nelken, ed., *The Futures of Criminology*. London: Sage, pp. 89–109.

Farber, Stephen C., Costanza, Robert and Wilson, Matthew A. (2002). Economic and ecological concepts for valuing ecosystem services. *Ecological Economics*, 41, pp. 375–392.

Gill, Victoria. (2020). Mark Carney: 'We can't self-isolate from climate change'. *BBC Science and the Environment*, 7 May. Available at: https://www.bbc.com/ news/science-environment-52582243?xtor=AL-72-%5Bpartner%5D-%5Bgnl. newsletters%5D-%5Bheadline%5D-%5Bnews%5D-%5Bbizdev%5D-%5Bisapi%5D&xtor=ES-213-%5bBBC%20News%20Newsletter%5d-2020May7-%5btop+news+stories [Accessed 1 June 2020].

Grünewald, S. (2020). Climate change as a systemic risk – are macroprudential authorities up to the task? *European Banking Institution Working Paper Series*, 62, 17 April.

Hall, Matthew and Farrall, Stephen. (2013). The criminogenic consequence of climate change: Blurring the boundaries between offenders and victims. In: Nigel South and Avi Brisman, eds., *RoutledgeInternational Handbook of Green Criminology.*, Abingdon: Routledge, pp. 120–133.

Hamann, R., Makaula, L., Ziervogel, G., Shearing, C. and Zhang, A. (2020). Strategic responses to Grand challenges: Why and how corporations build Community resilience. *Journal of Business Ethics*, 161, pp. 835–853.

Hartmann, Thom. (1999). *The Last Hours of Ancient Sunlight: Waking Up to Personal and Global Transformation*. New York: Harmony Books.

Haque, Umair. (2019). The Age of Collapse. *Resilience*, 7 August. Available at: https:// www.resilience.org/stories/2019-08-07/the-age-of-collapse/ [Accessed 1 June 2020].

Herbstein, T., Froestad, J., Shearing, C. and Nel, D. (2013). Insurance, climate risk and the barriers to change. In: T. A. Börzel and R. Hamann, eds., *Business and Climate Change Governance: South Africa in Comparative Perspective*. Houndmills: Palgrave Macmillan, pp. 156–172.

Holley, C. (2017). Environmental regulation and governance. In: P. Drahos, ed., *Regulatory Theory: Foundations and Applications*. Canberra: ANU Press, pp. 741–58.

Holley, C. and Shearing, C. (eds.). (2018). *Criminology and the Anthropocene*. Abingdon: Taylor and Francis (In the Series Criminology at the Edge, B. Leclerc, R. Homel and C. Shearing, eds.).

Hulme, K. (2009). Environmental security: Implications for international law. *Yearbook of International Environmental Law*, 19(1), pp. 3–26.

Johnston, L. and Shearing, C. (2003). *Governing Security: Explorations in Policing and Justice*. London: Routledge.

Jones, T. and Newburn, T. (1998). *Private Security and Public Policing*. London: Clarendon Press.

Kakalik, James S. and Wildhorn, S. (1977). *The Private Police: Security and Danger*. New York: Crane Russak.

Loader, I. and Walker, N. (2007). *Civilizing Security*. Cambridge: Cambridge University Press.

Loader, I. and White, A. (2017). How can we better align private security with the public interest? Towards a civilizing model of regulation. *Regulation & Governance*, 11(2), pp. 166–184.

Lundsgaarde, E., Dupuy, K. and Persson, A. (2018). Coordination Challenges in Climate Finance. *Danish Institute for International Studies Working Paper*, 3. Available at: https://pure.diis.dk/ws/files/2447789/DIIS_Working_Paper_2018_3_Coordination_challenges_in_climate_finance_FINAL.pdf [Accessed 1 June 2020].

Maitland, Frederic William. (1885). *Justice and Police*. London: Macmillan & Co.

Mancini, M. and Van Acker, D. (2020). Nudging the Financial System. A Network Analysis Approach. *FC4S*, April. Available at: https://unepinquiry.org/wp-content/uploads/2020/04/Nudging_the_Financial_System.pdf. [Accessed 1 June 2020].

Mitchell, Timothy. (2009). Carbon democracy. *Economy and Society*, 38(3), pp. 399–432. https://doi.org/10.1080/03085140903020598.

Nel, D., Shearing, C. and Reyers, B. (2011). Insurers could help address climate risks. *Nature*, 476(7358), p. 33.

Network for Greening the Financial System (NGFS). (2019). A call for action: Climate change as a source of financial risk. Paris: Network for Greening the Financial System. Available at: https://www.ngfs.net/sites/default/files/medias/documents/synthese_ngfs-2019_-_17042019_0.pdf [Accessed 1 June 2020].

Ngoc Cao, A. and Wyatt, T. (2016). The conceptual compatibility between green criminology and human security: A proposed interdisciplinary framework for examinations into green victimisation. *Critical Criminology*, 24, pp. 413–430.

O'Malley, P. (2018). Bentham and the Anthropocene. In: C. Holley and C. Shearing, eds., *Criminology and the Anthropocene*. Abingdon: Taylor and Francis. (In the Series Criminology at the Edge, B. Leclerc, R. Homel and C. Shearing, eds.).

O'Reilly, C. (2015). The pluralization of high policing: Convergence and divergence at the public-private interface. *British Journal of Criminology*, 55, pp. 688–710.

Osborne, D. and Gaebler, T. (1993). *Reinventing Government: How the Entrepreneurial Spirit Is Transforming the Public Sector*. New York: Plume.

Phelan, L., Holley, C., Shearing, C. and du Toit, L. (2020). Insurance and climate change. In: A. Brisman and N. South, eds., *Routledge International Handbook of Green Criminology*, 2nd ed. New York: Routledge, pp. 449–462.

Phelan, L., Taplin, R., Henderson-Sellers, A. and Albrecht, G. (2011). Ecological viability or liability? Insurance system responses to climate risk. *Environmental Policy and Governance*, 21(2), pp. 112–130. doi: 10.1002/eet.565.

Raworth, Kate. (2009). A safe and just space for humanity. *Nature*, 461(24), pp. 472–75.

Rhodes, R. A. W. (2007). Understanding governance: Ten years on. *Organization Studies*, 28(8), pp. 1243–1264.

Rockström, Johan, Steffen, Will, Noone, Kevin, Persson, Åsa, Chapin, F. Stuart, III, Lambin, Eric F., Lenton, Timothy M., Scheffer, Marten, Folke, Carl, Schellnhuber, Hans Joachim, Nykvist, Bjorn Björn, de Wit, Cynthia A., Hughes, Terry, van der Leeuw, Sander, Rodhe, Henning, Sörlin, Sverker, Snyder, Peter K., Costanza, Robert, et al. (2009). Planetary boundaries: Exploring the safe operating space for humanity. *Ecology and Society*. Available at: http://www.ecologyandsociety.org/vol14/iss2/art32/.

Schumacher, Ernst Friedrich. (1973). *Small Is Beautiful: A Study of Economics as If People Mattered*. London: Blond and Briggs.

Shearing, Clifford. (2015). Criminology and the Anthropocene. *Criminology and Criminal Justice*, 15(3), pp. 255–269.

Smil, Vaclav. (2002). *The Earth's Biosphere: Evolution, Dynamics and Change*. Cambridge, MA: The MIT Press.

South, N. (2015). Anticipating the Anthropocene and greening criminology. *Criminology and Criminal Justice*, 15(3), pp. 270–276.

Sparrow, M. K. (2014). Managing the boundary between public and private policing. *New Perspectives in Policing*, September, pp. 1–24. Available at: https://www.ncjrs.gov/pdffiles1/nij/247182.pdf [Accessed 1 June 2020].

Spitzer, S. and Scull, A. (1977). Privatization and capitalist development: The case of the private police. *Social Problems*, 25, pp. 18–29.

Stenning, P. and Shearing, C. (2015). Privatisation, pluralisation and the globalisation of policing. *Research Focus*, 3(1), pp. 1–8.

Thumala, A., Goold, B. and Loader I. (2011). A tainted trade? Moral ambivalence and legitimation work in the private security industry. *The British Journal of Sociology*, 62(2), pp. 283–303.

Trisos, C. H., Merow, C. and Pigot, A. L. (2020). The projected timing of abrupt ecological disruption from climate change. *Nature*. https://doi.org/10.1038/s41586-020-2189-9.

UNEP. (2015). *Aligning the financial system with Sustainable Development. The Coming Financial Climate, The Inquiry's 4th Progress Report*. Geneva: United Nations Environment Program. Available at: http://unepinquiry.org/wp-content/uploads/2015/05/Aligning_the_Financial_System_with_Sustainable_Development_4_The_Coming_Financial_Climate.pdf [Accessed 1 June 2020].

Wood, S., Eberlein, B., Meidinger, E., Schmidt, R. and Abbott, K. (2019). Transnational business governance interactions, regulatory quality and marginalized actors: An introduction. In: S. Wood, R. Schmidt, E. Meidinger, B. Eberlein and K. Abbott, eds., *Transnational Business Governance Interactions Advancing Marginalized Actors and Enhancing Regulatory Quality*. Cheltenham: Edward Elgar, pp. 1–26.

Zedner, L. (2009). *Security*. London: Routledge.

2 Co-creating sustainable risk futures

A role for insurers

Vanessa Otto-Mentz and Johan Strumpfer

Introduction

The role of short-term insurance (also called general or property and casualty insurance) is to enable society to function in the face of risk exposures. By transferring and pooling risks, insurance enables society to manage risks and potential losses. However, climate change is undermining the insurance sector's capacity to transfer and pool risk. The extent of climate change is now such that it is an existential risk to the insurance sector, with AXA's Chief Executive Officer, Thomas Buberl, stating: 'A +4°C world is not insurable' (AXA, 2017). These are challenging times. The uncertainty, the level of participation required, and the need to manage the justness of the transition to a world with net-zero carbon emissions by 2050, while simultaneously adapting for climate risks already built into the biosphere due to past carbon emissions, means climate change is indeed an emergency, as the scientists have now named it.

With the advent of the Anthropocene, the new geological epoch brought on by the industrial revolution and climate change, humans are faced with new harmscapes, including changes in probabilities and severities of climate risks. General insurance sector participants, such as the global reinsurer Munich Re, have noticed increasing loss impacts from natural catastrophes such as fire, flood, and storm events since the 1970s. Swiss Re also recently reported on a rise in natural catastrophe related primary and secondary losses (Swiss Re Institute, 2019) with extreme weather events driving insured loss experiences upwards in both quantum and frequency.

Climate change represents a shift from a stable to an unstable Earth system (Phelan, Henderson-Sellers and Taplin, 2013). This is a challenge for the insurance sector, because insurance has a statistical business model as its foundation: past experiences, e.g., of loss-causing events serve as a guide to future experiences. While statistics on historical events have until now provided a sound guide to likely future losses, this new period of fundamental instability and uncertainty means that historical records are now less helpful. Swiss Re notes that [f]or insurability not to be threatened, adaptation to a profoundly changed risk landscape is required (Gloor, 2019: 8).

Climate change requires insurers to supplement their historical models with forward-looking models.

However, we argue that the scale of the challenge is so great that the solution must be more than technical changes in approaches to modelling risks. Without collaboration within the insurance sector, with regulatory authorities, and society in general, we lose the powerful climate risk resilience role insurance can play. The public sector will need to consider how the tools of insurance can assist in protecting citizens (as per the Sendai Framework for Disaster Risk Reduction 2015–2030 (United Nations, 2015)), given the rise in the frequency of disaster risk events impacting multiple nations and regions. Business, society, and regulators need to incentivise collaboration and innovation so that we can respond to the rising risk protection gap, and protect lives and livelihoods. The emphasis will need to be on collaboration because the extent of the increasing risks is beyond the capacity of the insurance sector alone to carry risk, as it did in the past. Collaboration and co-creation of an improved future require an opening and reaching out to other actors in the same situation.

Accessible and affordable insurance solutions are a key ingredient of sustainable development in the new and yet emerging harmscapes. And so, the insurance sector, together with other stakeholders, has an important role to play in the new harmscapes in which we find ourselves. It needs to innovate and bring new risk solutions to bear. For this to take place, strategy and planning processes need to be open and participative to prepare ourselves for uncertain and unstable times. Collectively, we need to do what is necessary to protect society and the biosphere, consistent with the call for partnerships as per the UN Sustainable Development Goals (United Nations General Assembly, 2015, Goal 17). In the next sections of this chapter, we provide a practitioner's perspective on contemporary insurance practices. We then look to an earlier example of a successful co-creation initiative to propose a collaborative way forward for insurers – and others – that may secure a future in which climate risks remain manageable.

A review of contemporary insurance practices

Insurance and society's safety net

The insurance sector acts as a resilience 'safety net' for society, protecting against the risk of financial losses. In doing so, the insurance sector communicates the scope of risks to society via the risk premiums that individual insurers charge their customers, which are typically annually adjusted.

The sector also influences risk preparedness through loss mitigation advice and risk management requests to customers as prerequisites to obtaining insurance cover. A more serious risk signal occurs when insurers withdraw from risk cover previously provided or do not make insurance capacity available for new emerging risks.

However, it is important to note that in the face of a strongly competitive commercial market for insurance, individual insurers are less able to push for changes towards better risk management through purely commercial mechanisms, such as the pricing of risks or insurance contract conditions. The competitive dynamics in the market are such that insurers, acting on their own, may lose out on potential business, as another insurer with a greater appetite for risk exposures may accept the risk without conditions, or accept the risk at a lower insurance premium. Also, many customers may refrain from engaging with insurers whose risk management requirements are considered too stringent, too much effort or too costly.

These situations are only resolvable if there is some form of collaboration and decision-making at the level of the 'commons', i.e., the group of affected people. It follows then that industry-level decision-making or regulation may be desirable to ensure climate change-related risks are priced realistically and to avoid less optimal outcomes.

New regulatory focus on climate risk

The Cambridge Institute for Sustainability Leadership (2015) noted that insurance regulation plays a role in protecting 'the basic human rights of life, livelihood and shelter against natural hazards and climate risk'. It called for effective insurance regulation that 'facilitates access to insurance (both traditional and alternative) as a means to increase communities' resilience, fulfil related human rights duties of state and non-state actors and support the UN Sustainable Development Goals'.

Regulators recently began paying more attention to climate risk. For example, The Bank of England (2019) requested climate risk stress-tests from all the general insurance businesses they licence. Globally, the demands for climate action and more explicit disclosures on the financial impact of climate risk, as recommended by the Task Force on Climate-related Financial Disclosure (2019), are rising. The Task Force, which emanated from the Financial Stability Board, highlighted the need to address the financial implications as well as the governance of climate risks, inclusive of physical, transition, and liability risks.

One vocal regulator, the California Department of Insurance, has been particularly clear in its communication that action is required. On its website, the Department notes both insurer investment portfolio exposures, as well as insurance availability, as key challenges. In terms of investment portfolios, the Department urges insurers to voluntarily divest from thermal coal.

Protection gap entities

Social and economic resilience is dependent on society's ability to prepare for and recover from harms such as extreme weather events or, in insurance language, natural catastrophes. However, commercial insurance cover is, in practice, rarely sufficient for covering financial risks fully, leaving a 'protection gap'. As Jarzabkowski et al. (2018: 1) note:

> ...some 70% of global losses from natural catastrophes are not insured, equating to $1.3 trillion over the past 10 years. In 2017 alone, uninsured losses for weather-related disasters were estimated to be around $180 billion...The social and economic resilience of a country, and its political stability, are dependent on the ability to recover from disasters. In the short-term, immediate post-crisis financial response is critical... In the longer-term, reconstruction of housing, infrastructure, and businesses after a disaster is essential for recovery. Bridging the protection gap provides one way to underpin such financial recovery.

One response has been the creation of Protection Gap Entities (PGEs). PGEs are hybrid insurance schemes facilitated by bespoke public and private sector consortiums that attempt to narrow the risk protection gap. PGEs assist in building resilience against disaster risk with a focus on financial protection linked to improve pre- and post-disaster risk management.

The PGE Resilience Framework (Figure 2.1), developed by Jarzabkowski et al., illustrates how risk identification, risk reduction, preparedness, financial protection, and resilient reconstruction, taken together, enable resilience for an identified risk.

An innovative example of a PGE is the new coral reef insurance scheme in the state of Quintana Roo, on the Mexican Carribean coast, where a group of stakeholders worked together to set-up risk protection for a natural asset, the coral reef. The region is a tourist area and often suffers extreme storm events (hurricanes). Healthy coral reefs are an excellent nature-based solution to absorb wave energy before it hits the shore and therefore a useful proactive nature-based risk management 'tool'. As the Nature Conservancy (2019) notes:

> This means that should wind speeds in excess of 100 knots hit a predefined area, an insurance pay-out will be made very quickly to the trust fund, allowing swift damage assessments, debris removal and initial repairs to be carried out. Longer periods of restoration and recovery work may follow to restore the reef's value as a coastal barrier.

A more mature PGE is the Caribbean Catastrophe Risk Insurance Facility (CRIFF), which, similarly to the Mexican coral reef insurance scheme, uses a parametric trigger (PreventionWeb, n.d.). Parametric insurance cover payouts are triggered when a predefined event takes place, for example, a hurricane's windspeeds meet a given threshold in a given region. CRIFF limits the financial impact to Caribbean governments of catastrophic hurricanes

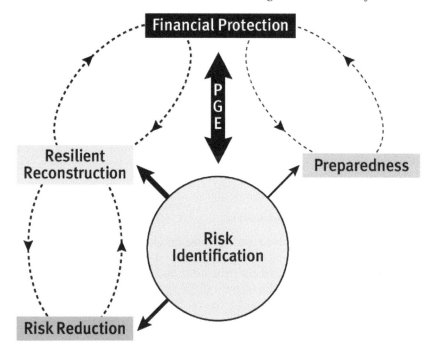

Figure 2.1 Jarzabkowski et al.'s PGE Resilience Framework.

Source: Jarzabkowski et al. (2018). Between state and market: PGEs and catastrophic risk. Cass Business School, City, University of London, 26th June 2018. Figure 5.1, p. 25. https://www.paulajarzabkowski.com/downloads/#view-file-1

(and earthquakes) by quickly providing short-term liquidity. Since its inception in 2007, CCRIF has made 40 pay-outs, totalling about $152 million, to 13 of its 21 member governments (PreventionWeb, 2019). In September 2019, CRIFF paid out $12.8 million to the government of The Bahamas following the passage of Hurricane Dorian, which caused widespread devastation in the northern part of the country.

The triple dividend of resilience

Another way to frame resilience building is to look at the benefits, or 'dividends', from investing in resilience. The dividends are: (1) avoided losses; (2) unlocking economic potential; and (3) generating benefits regardless of disasters (Tanner et al., 2015: 9–10). Taking these benefits together, societal resilience is a powerful antidote to economic and physical losses and can create a bulwark of disaster risk preparedness, which puts in place much needed financial protection against more frequent and intense natural catastrophes.

Resilience building is especially important when viewed from developing country perspectives. Developing countries did not benefit from carbon-based industrialisation. Also, insurance penetration in developing markets is generally very low when compared to the risk protection enjoyed by developed countries. This situation leaves many individuals, communities, business, and governments exposed to potential loss events, resulting in a large risk protection gap that will increase as climate risks realise. Resilience building is at the heart of the InsuResilience and Insurance Development Forum's mandates to increase access to insurance so that more people have the benefit of risk protection and financial resilience, which insurance solutions can provide.

Communicating risks through prices

Premium rate changes based on most recent loss experiences (e.g. last month, last year) do offer 'short feedback loop' risk, signalling opportunities to influence risk management behaviour and thinking in wider society. Insurance companies, particularly non-life (short-term or property and casualty) insurers in this way make the costs of different risks clear(er) to society.

There is, of course, an assumption that insurers react fast enough and have enough understanding of a changing risk environment to make reasonably accurate assessments of changing and emerging risks. However, assuming they can react and assess risk in this way, they serve as a mirror to society of the changing costs associated with risk-related behaviours, such as building in flood plains and increasing wildfire exposure. Another example is the provision for international travel, where injuries and property damages from high-altitude air turbulence are increasing and are expected to lead to exclusions to travel insurance policies in the future (Jamieson and Cereceda, 2019).

However, the ability of individual insurers to enforce this 'making costs clear to society' is limited due to commercial interests and competition discussed earlier. No one wants to be the bearer of bad news and the price of insurance is an important competitive factor in the sector, particularly non-life insurers. Hence, a different level of cooperation regarding climate change and its impacts on societal risks will be required if the insurance industry is to act as a messenger to society of emerging climate change risks.

An example of this 'message to society' is the article by Aon's head of Resilience and Sustainability (Lowe, 2018). Lowe highlights data that suggest that, for 2017, for companies on the Standard & Poor's 500 Index, quantified weather-related impact on earnings amounted to 6% of earnings. This points out that climate change-related impacts are no longer an external 'sustainability' issue, but a central strategic issue for many businesses and industries. Lowe highlights that consumer discretionary purchases, consumer staples, energy, health care, industrials, informational technology, materials, and utility industries are particularly vulnerable to catastrophic weather events.

Climate adaptation efforts to build resilience

Insurance market participants have also begun to find ways of addressing climate risk by partnering with other stakeholders. In Africa, Santam Insurance, the largest non-life insurer, has spent considerable time working with local authorities to address disaster risk, in particular, fire and flood exposures. The work stems from a study published by Santam et al. (2011), which highlighted that insurance organisations are fulcrum organisations that can exercise influence across a field.

The insight was simple yet profound: that if the *drivers* of risks could be influenced, risk exposure could reduce. Furthermore, to address the drivers of risks, the organisation would need to *influence other stakeholders*, such as local authorities, to exercise sound, proactive risk management; for example, by keeping foredunes intact on seashores to buffer against sea storm events and inland flooding, and closely watching building regulations with regard to flood and fire risk exposures, such as managing fire load.

This research fortuitously coincided with a local government initiative called Business Adopt a Municipality, which provided a practical basis for the work to continue. As a result of this work, Santam Insurance, together with its empowerment trust, is now supporting disaster risk resilience work across several district municipalities in South Africa.

Recently, the Business Adopt a Municipality project, now evolved and renamed Partnering for Risk and Resilience, was part of a study to understand how and why organisations partner with local authorities. Hamann et al. (2020: 850) found that:

> corporations commit to community resilience building when firm- and place-specific resources are at risk... but only if there is a simultaneous absence of an institutionalised response to mitigate these risks. More specifically, corporate managers explaining their strategic community resilience-building efforts explicitly pointed to the absence of the state as a reliable actor in mitigating social-ecological risks.

Their findings echo the urgent need for, and rationale of PGEs, explored above.

Climate mitigation to reduce future risk exposure

Insurers are increasingly excluding thermal coal from the underwriting and investment portfolios due to its links to climate change (see du Toit, this volume). Some insurers have made bold statements to transition their portfolios away from carbon, a trend which is picking up momentum with claims being made that coal is on its way to becoming uninsurable in the near future (Kollewe, 2019).

The Net-Zero Asset Owner Alliance brings together the world's biggest pension funds and insurers to commit to net-zero carbon emissions in their investment portfolios by 2050 (UNEP Finance Initiative, n.d.). They plan to align their investment portfolios with the 1.5°C target set out in 2015 at the Paris Climate Summit. As at 7 January 2020, the following funds and insurers have signed up: Allianz, Caisse des Dépôts, La Caisse de dépôt et placement du Québec (CDPQ), Folksam Group, PensionDanmark, SwissRe, Alecta, AMF, CalPERS, Nordea Life and Pension, Storebrand, Zurich, Aviva, AXA, CNP Assurances, and Fonds de Réserve pour les Retraites (FRR).

We also see broader field-level responses taking root, expanding and aligning around principles and guidance, such as the Task Force on Climate-related Financial Disclosures (TCFD) recommendations: ClimateWise, for example, is a member organisation established in 2007 and hosted by the Cambridge Institute for Sustainability Leadership, while another member organisation, the Principles for Sustainable Insurance (PSI) housed by the UN Environment Programme Finance Initiative was established in 2012. Both member organisations focus on improved risk responses, with principles and guidance provided to their insurance members and supporters, focused on climate risk in the case of ClimateWise and environmental, social, and governance (ESG) issues in the case of the PSI.

Recently ClimateWise updated its principles to include TCFD recommendations, whilst the PSI published guidance for ESG issues in non-life (short-term) insurance underwriting, following a global consultation process led by Allianz and supported by many other leading insurance organisations (PSI, 2019). PSI is also working on guidance to help insurers implement TCFD recommendations (UNEP Finance Initiative, 2018).

When we look more broadly, we see that The Embedding Project, an engaged scholarship initiative, is curating useful global resources, such as the Contextual Goals database to help sustainability practitioners in their work (Embedding Project, n.d.). We also see the legitimisation of non-financial performance indicators (ESG ratings) by global stock exchanges and the rising importance of the ESG ratings in credit rating agency methodologies, with the agencies incorporating climate change performance metrics, based on TCFD guidance (FTSE Russell, 2018) and the Carbon Disclosure Project, in their rating methodologies. The response from various stakeholders from across the financial system to begin to integrate ESG and specifically climate risk considerations in their day-to-day decisions indicates that market participants are starting to understand that things are indeed different with climate risk, that we have entered new harmscapes requiring new ways of work.

Co-creation as a way forward

One of the core principles of a systemic view of reality is to emphasise or 'see' the relationships. This approach is the opposite of the classical reductionist approach to complexity in practice, namely to take things apart, with the intention of generating knowledge by understanding constituent parts of a whole. However, taking things apart – even in pursuit of understanding – can come at the cost of losing sight of the essential characteristics of the whole. For example, a dissected body is no longer a living human. For too long, we have treated the 'environment' in which we live in a reductionist way.

One of the characteristics of contemporary life, compared to times past, is the much higher level of interconnectedness and interdependence of societies. This interconnectedness has affected the problems faced by various elements in societies by making these problems 'too big' to be addressed by a single player.

Despite worrying data, raised concerns, and past lessons learned, we still find that in many places in the world there are significant protection gaps. A prominent – repeated – example from recent years is property insurance and fire services that are not functional for the level of wildfire risk regions are facing. This dynamic, also feared in the South African insurance market (Charles, 2019), has been the cause of significant losses in Portugal, Spain, Greece, and Australia in 2018, 2019, and 2020.

Dealing with these types of issues requires collaboration amongst players or elements in these societies and across these societies, which go beyond the boundaries of these organisations and their traditional fields of responsibilities. It is a classic example of a 'tragedy of the commons' problem, where the problem cannot be solved at the individual level of the people or entity in the situation.

Opening up and reaching out

As noted earlier, collaboration and co-creation of an improved future require an opening and reaching out to other actors in the same situation. One way of dealing with this kind of situation is a planning approach that is open and participative (Strumpfer, 1997). This planning approach is an example of what Whittington (2019) describes as an 'Opening of Strategy' approach. In the Whittington sense, the opening of strategy has the purpose of enabling an individual entity to build alignment and consensus around a course of action that enables collaboration around a shared problematic situation. In this manner, it addresses or circumvents the tragedy of the commons situation.

The Durban Functional Region (DFR) Forum case model is instructive here. This planning forum was created in 1988, in the years before the end of the apartheid era in South Africa, in the context of the Natal-Kwa-Zulu region, which was extraordinarily fragmented in terms of governance. The lack of governance prevented common shared approaches to even the most mundane of practical problems, such as town planning and transport planning. There were several aspects to the DFR model that were key:

- It was non-political. It was enlightened and sought change, but punted no particular political agenda. The change was effected in a real sense by political players themselves in their capacities and roles within their home organisations, supported by the DFR Forum.
- Participation was largely open, and very inclusive, across a very wide range of value systems in society.
- Participation was a mixture of technical functionaries, mostly significantly influential in their own right, plus a range of more political, senior decision makers, and influencers. There was a wider group of participants that included senior officials in government from central, provincial, and local level. The press and media were also invited to selected presentation sessions.
- It was supported by an active secretariat that played an ongoing facilitative role, also employing some sponsorship funding to assist some participants. The secretariat held and supported the process space without owning it.

What the DRF approach created in the province, now called Kwa-Zulu-Natal, was a shared foundation of information, accepted by the wide spectrum of participants, a shared understanding of the inevitability of change required, as well as a vision of what should be created. Within this framework, individual parties were able to determine their course of action, to effectively work collaboratively towards a greater, shared end-goal. Taking a DRF approach to climate change for a given region, for example, South Africa, could follow the following steps:

- Agree on the current situation. Simply having a widely agreed current situation dataset around climate change and cities in this country would have a powerful influencing effect and impact on various actors. The reason for this is that it is so difficult to agree on the information. Having agreement creates its own power.
- Building scenarios of the future. This is key in creating a wider consensus on the need for action. In this case, these future scenarios would need to include other socio-political and economic dimensions in their consideration.

- Building consensus around the desired future. For the climate change group to succeed here, it would need to build appropriately scaled future regional scenarios.
- Develop a list of actions, policy proposals, general actions, and more detailed initiatives as proposals for all players that can be widely debated and that carry the support of a very wide range of participants and, thus, consequently can have a huge impact on the target 'actioning' organisations.

A less stable Earth system requires a different systemic and contextual approach to risk. It demands collaboration by stakeholders, inside and outside a given field, such as the insurance sector. Fortunately, technological advances can assist this new approach and we are witnessing the potential risk management capabilities of geographic information system mapping and the increasing role of practical scientific applications. Here initiatives such as the Green Book project by the Council for Scientific and Industrial Research in South Africa and their partners (Green Book, 2019) can assist climate risk adaptation at settlement level by sharing information and facilitating conversations in an open and participative planning approach.

Conclusion

Insurance companies can play a significant role in shifting behaviour by making the cost of risk-taking behaviour clear, provided that a framework of collaboration amongst insurers emerges that counters the competitive self-interest dynamics by taking a longer-term perspective on the impact of their investment portfolios. As Gloor (2019: 8) notes:

> Re/insurers can play a fundamental role in facilitating transition to a low-carbon economy by embedding sustainability as a core element in their business models and by reducing their own carbon footprint. Besides shifting towards an environmentally sustainable asset portfolio, re/insurers should align their underwriting policies to reduce incentives that favour further carbon-intensive energy production and consumption. Industry-wide implementation of these principles will help build the world's resilience to a changing climate.

Given the power that the insurance sector has for influencing risk management in society, it seems like an ideal mechanism to be harnessed in the wider climate change efforts. While insurance companies have a business imperative to understand and rate emerging and increasing risks due to climate change, they should also assume the role of societal educators by highlighting these risks to communities and society. They can and should work with their clients and stakeholders to ameliorate these risks as best they can through proactive and collaborative risk management programs. Similarly, or as a corollary, society, through financial and other risk regulators, needs to enable meaningful collaboration around these global and societal level risks, should not default to accusations of anti-competitive behaviours, and should work to find future-fit regulatory frameworks for enabling meaningful collaboration and climate action.

Insurance can and should play a key role in making the costs of emerging and increasing risks clear to societies by developing risk solutions and charging premiums in a manner that incentivise individuals and organisations to change their behaviour away from more climate change promoting activities and actions. The insurance sector needs climate action at societal scale if it is to be sustainable. And there is a contribution insurance can – and should – make to wider societal efforts: 'If we want to change the systems we are part of – our countries, communities, organisations, and families – we must also see and change ourselves' (Kahane, 2004: 86).

References

AXA. (2017). AXA accelerates its commitment to fight climate change. [Press release] 12 December. Available at: https://www.axa.com/en/newsroom/press-releases/axa-accelerates-its-commitment-to-fight-climate-change [Accessed 4 May 2020].

Bank of England. (2019). Insurance Stress Test 2019. [Letter sent to the largest regulated life and general insurers] 18 June. Available at: https://www.bankofengland.co.uk/prudential-regulation/letter/2019/insurance-stress-test-2019 [Accessed 4 May 2020].

California Department of Insurance. (n.d.). Climate Risk Carbon Initiative. [Website notice] Available at: http://www.insurance.ca.gov/0250-insurers/0300-insurers/0100-applications/ci/index.cfm [Accessed 4 May 2020].

Cambridge Institute for Sustainability Leadership. (2015). Insurance Regulation for Sustainable Development. Cambridge: Cambridge Institute for Sustainability Leadership. Available at: https://www.cisl.cam.ac.uk/resources/sustainable-finance-publications/insurance-regulation-for-sustainable-development [Accessed 4 May 2020].

Charles, Marvin. (2019). Cape Faces Fire Catastrophe as Experts Fear City's Worst Fire Season Lies Ahead. *Cape Argus*, 18 September. Available at: https://www.iol.co.za/capeargus/news/cape-faces-fire-catastrophe-as-experts-fear-citys-worst-fire-season-lies-ahead-33176036 [Accessed 4 May 2020].

Du Toit, L. (2021). The influence of government regulation on insurers' responses to climate change. In: Cameron Holley and Clifford Shearing, eds., *Criminology and Climate: Insurance, Finance and the Regulation of Harmscapes*. Abingdon, UK: Routledge, Criminology at the Edge series.

Embedding Project. (n.d). Contextual Goals Database. [Website resource] Available at: https://www.embeddingproject.org/goals-database [Accessed 17 May 2020].

FTSE Russell. (2018). *How the TCFD Recommendations Are Incorporated into FTSE Russell's ESG Ratings and Data Model*. London: FTSE Russell. Available at: https://content.ftserussell.com/sites/default/files/support_document/how-fr-integrates-tcfd-recommendations_0.pdf [Accessed 4 May 2020].

Gloor, M. (2019). *Insurance in a World of Climate Extremes: What Latest Science Tells Us*. Zurich: Swiss Re Institute. Available at: https://www.swissre.com/institute/research/topics-and-risk-dialogues/natcat-and-climate/insurance-world-climate-extremes.html [Accessed 4 May 2020].

Green Book. (2019). Adapting Settlements for the Future. [Website resource] Available at: https://www.greenbook.co.za/ [Accessed 17 May 2020].

Hamann, R., Makaula, L., Ziervogel, G. and Shearing, C. (2020). Strategic responses to Grand challenges: Why and how corporations build community resilience. *Journal of Business Ethics*, 161(4), pp. 835–853. doi: 10.1007/s10551-019-04345-y.

Jamieson, Alastair and Cereceda, Rafael. (2019). Researchers warn of more jet stream turbulence due to climate change. *Euronews*, 8 August. Available at: https://www.euronews.com/2019/08/08/researchers-warn-of-more-jet-stream-turbulence-due-to-climate-change [Accessed 4 May 2020].

Jarzabkowski, Paula, Chalkias, Konstantinos, Cacciatori, Eugenia and Bednarek, Rebecca. (2018). Between State and Market: Protection Gap Entities and Catastrophic Risk. London: Cass Business School, University of London. Available at: https://www.cass.city.ac.uk/__data/assets/pdf_file/0020/420257/PGE-Report-FINAL.pdf [Accessed 4 May 2020].

Kahane, A. (2004). *Solving Tough Problems: An Open Way of Talking, Listening, and Creating New Realities*. San Francisco, NC: Berrett-Koehler.

Kollewe, Julia. (2019). Coal Power Becoming 'Uninsurable' as Firms Refuse Cover. *Guardian*, 2 December. Available at: https://www.theguardian.com/environment/2019/dec/02/coal-power-becoming-uninsurable-as-firms-refuse-cover?CMP=share_btn_tw [Accessed 4 May 2020].

Lowe, G. (2018). Weather Volatility and Chronic Climate Risk: A Growing Capital Efficiency Gap. [Website article] 10 December. Available at: https://www.aon.com/reinsurance/gimo/20181210-gimo-climate [Accessed 4 May 2020].

Nature Conservancy. (2019). Insuring Nature to Ensure a Resilient Future. [Website article] 3 September. Available at: https://www.nature.org/en-us/what-we-do/our-insights/perspectives/insuring-nature-to-ensure-a-resilient-future/ [Accessed 4 May 2020].

Phelan, L., Henderson-Sellers, A. and Taplin, R. (2013). The political economy of addressing the climate crisis in the earth system: Undermining perverse resilience. *New Political Economy*, 18(2), pp. 198–226. https://doi.org/10.1080/13563467.2012.678820.

PreventionWeb. (2019). CCRIF Announces Final Payout Numbers of US$12.8 million to the Bahamas Following Hurricane Dorian. [Website News] 26 September. Available at:https://www.preventionweb.net/news/view/67877 [Accessed 4 May 2020].

PreventionWeb. (n.d.). Caribbean Catastrophe Risk Insurance Facility, the (CCRIF SPC). Available at:https://www.preventionweb.net/organizations/3924 [Accessed 4 May 2020].

Principles for Sustainable Insurance Project (PSI). (2019). *Underwriting Environmental, Social and Governance Risks in Non-Life Insurance Business*. Geneva: UNEP Finance Initiative. Available at: https://www.unepfi.org/psi/wp-content/uploads/2019/02/PSI-Guidance-for-non-life-insurance-underwriting.pdf [Accessed 4 May 2020].

Santam, WWF, UCT Centre of Criminology and Council for Scientific and Industrial Research in collaboration with UNEP FI. (2011). *Insurance in a Changing Risk Landscape: Local Lessons from the Southern Cape of South Africa*. Geneva: UNEP Financial Initiative. Available at: https://www.unepfi.org/fileadmin/documents/insurance_changing_risk_landscape.pdf [Accessed 4 May 2020].

Strumpfer, J. P. (1997). Planning as means of social change: The Durban Functional Regional Forum case. *Systems Practice*, 10(5), pp. 549–565.

Swiss Re Institute. (2019). Natural catastrophes and man-made disasters in 2018: "secondary" perils on the frontline, *Sigma*, 2 [White Paper]. Available at: https://www.swissre.com/dam/jcr:c37eb0e4-c0b9-4a9f-9954-3d0bb4339bfd/sigma2_2019_en.pdf [Accessed 17 May 2020].

Tanner, Thomas, Surminski, Swenja, Wilkinson, Emily, Reid, Robert, Rentschler, Jun and Rajput, Sumati. (2015). *The Triple Dividend of Resilience*. London and Washington DC: Overseas Development Institute and World Bank, pp. 9–10. Available at: https://www.gfdrr.org/sites/default/files/publication/The_Triple_Dividend_of_Resilience.pdf [Accessed 4 May 2020].

Task Force on Climate-related Financial Disclosures (TCFD). (2019). *2019 Status Report*. Basel: Financial Stability Board. Available at: https://www.fsb-tcfd.org/wp-content/uploads/2019/06/2019-TCFD-Status-Report-FINAL-053119.pdf [Accessed 4 May 2020].

UNEP Finance Initiative. (2018). UNEP FI Working with 16 Global Insurers to Better Understand Risk & Implement TCFD Recommendations. [News Bulletin] 13 November. Available at: https://www.unepfi.org/news/industries/insurance/unep-fi-working-with-16-global-insurers-to-better-understand-risk-implement-tcfd-recommendations/ [Accessed 4 May 2020].

UNEP Finance Initiative. (n.d). UN-convened Net-Zero Asset Owner Alliance. [Website Home]. Available at: https://www.unepfi.org/wordpress/wp-content/uploads/2019/09/AOAbrochure.pdf [Accessed 4 May 2020].

United Nations. (2015). *Sendai Framework for Disaster Risk Reduction 2015–2030*. UN Doc. A/CONF.224/CRP.1.

United Nations General Assembly. (2015). *Transforming our world: the 2030 Agenda for Sustainable Development*. UN Doc No. A/RES/70/1. Available at: https://www.un.org/ga/search/view_doc.asp?symbol=A/RES/70/1&Lang=E [Accessed 4 May 2020].

Whittington, Richard. (2019). *Opening Strategy: Professional Strategists and Practice Change, 1960 to Today*. Oxford: Oxford University Press.

3 Crime, regulation and climate finance

Neil Gunningham

The need for climate action has never been more urgent, and finance can play a powerful role in the transition to a sustainable and inclusive global economy. To achieve this transition, the world requires a significant shift in investments that make financial flows consistent with pathways toward low greenhouse gas emissions and climate-resilient development. Meeting this goal will depend on the public and private sectors coming together to support an inclusive and orderly transition from high- to low-carbon assets on a global scale – and quickly.

(Climate Finance Leadership Initiative, 2019: 3)

Introduction

Should criminologists study socially injurious behaviour or only crime, legally defined? That question goes back at least to 'The New Criminology' of the 1970s (Taylor, Walton and Young, 1973) and indeed to studies of white collar crime some decades earlier (Sutherland, 1945). This approach was controversial. Many criminologists feared that embracing anything beyond what is defined a criminal in the statute books, would threaten their objectivity and the scientific status of the discipline. Others, however, argued that so confining their focus would be to exercise a value judgment in favour of the status quo, and would conveniently ignore many of the 'crimes of the powerful' (Pearce, 1976) whose socially injurious behaviour, precisely because of their power, was never formally defined as criminal.

More recently, 'green criminology' has taken a broadly similar tack in challenging statutory definitions of what should be considered a crime (White, 2016). Brisman and South (2017), for example, argue that in the future world of the Anthropocene, both resource scarcity and climate change will be criminogenic with implications for legislation, law enforcement and the way nations regard their borders. Similarly, Holley and Shearing (2017: 14) suggest that in an age of ecological crisis, what will be needed is a criminology 'that is willing to study, define and advocate for many specific harms to the environment that are not yet defined as criminal offences', while White

(2017) argues for criminological conceptualisations of climate change as a form of ecocide.

Consistent with 'new' and 'green' criminology, this chapter argues that the most compelling question of our age is how best to mitigate climate change and takes the view that an important task for criminologists is to determine what role the criminal law, and regulation more broadly, can and should contribute to that end. Its particular focus is on finance for climate change mitigation and adaptation (hereafter 'climate finance'). While rarely recognised as such in mainstream debate, mitigating dangerous climate change and its catastrophic consequences will require vast amounts of finance – an estimated \$90 trillion over the next 15 years (Bielenberg et al., 2016) – which only the private sector has the wherewithal to supply. But scaling up climate finance – for low-carbon infrastructure, renewable energy, energy efficiency and other mitigation measures – would involve transforming a sector that has only recently begun its journey towards sustainability. Yet without such finance, a low-carbon revolution will likely be stillborn.[1]

What will be needed is nothing short of what the United Nations Environment Program (UNEP) describes as a 'quiet revolution' (UNEP, 2015). Prominent amongst those leading this revolution can and should be financial market regulators, because, as the global financial crisis made clear, financial markets left under-regulated, can cause profound economic and social harm. Against this backdrop, the chapter will argue that, in the case of climate finance, regulation can and should play crucial roles.

Accordingly, the chapter focuses on what, at least in criminology's early decades, was a largely neglected endeavour – the *development* of rules that proscribe (or require), and so criminalise certain behaviour – rather than on why some choose to break those rules. In the space available, the chapter necessarily provides an overview of the above issues rather than a detailed analysis, mapping out the core architecture of what should be involved rather than exploring the nuances of specific regulatory provisions. Self-evidently, it is normative in its orientation.

Why and how to regulate climate finance

Whether humanity manages to contain global heating will have profound implications for our species and for all others. Put briefly, humanity is on a trajectory to destroy the habitability of our planet and to precipitate the largest mass extinction of species in the last 65 million years, including our own (Intergovernmental Panel on Climate Change (IPCC), 2018). Unless climate change is rapidly contained, followed by a drawdown of carbon in the second half of the century, then climate zones will shift, extreme weather events will increase dramatically and sea levels will rise to such an extent that they will threaten the habitability of the large majority of the world's coastal cities. Some equatorial zones may become completely uninhabitable.

These and other devastating impacts of climate change will threaten either the partial or complete collapse of civilisation (Glikson, 2013).

In terms of climate finance, the compelling public policy question is: how can a rapid shift in institutional investment (i.e. of where insurance companies, banks, pension funds and other 'heavy hitters' place their money), from high-carbon to low-carbon assets, best be achieved? Such a transition will require, front and centre, regulatory mechanisms that facilitate, educate, incentivise and perhaps, mandate, institutional investors to change their investment behaviour. Such intervention in their affairs would be anathema to many financial market actors, deeply steeped as they are in free market ideology in general and Chicago School economics in particular. In their view – epitomised by the approach of the former Chair of the Federal Reserve, Alan Greenspan (Kuttner, 2018) – markets are inherently stable and self-correcting; market participants behave rationally; lending institutions have a self-interest in protecting shareholders' equity; and there is little need for government intervention. Indeed, such intervention will likely be counter-productive.

However, the real world departs radically from that which is assumed by free market ideology. For example, there is considerable asymmetry of information between market insiders and outsiders, the capacity of unregulated market actors to externalise the risks of their activities is substantial, as is the gap between the private interests of those actors and the public interest. There is also, as the Governor of the Bank of England has emphasised, the 'tragedy of the horizon', meaning that the catastrophic impacts of climate change will be felt beyond the traditional horizons of most financial actors, imposing costs on future generations that the current one has no direct incentives to fix (Carney, 2015).

Many of these pathologies of unregulated markets were manifested in the global financial crisis (GFC) of 2007–2008. Indeed, as Adam Tooze documents in his exhaustive analysis of the GFC (Tooze, 2018), it was unregulated, or under-regulated markets, that brought the world to the edge of economic collapse. Yet in the aftermath of the crisis, the financial institutions who had gambled heavily on sub-prime derivatives that ultimately proved worthless, were deemed to be too big to fail and were bailed out by governments. Thus, it was taxpayers who paid the massive price for keeping the global economy afloat: a classic example of moral hazard and of market actors externalising costs onto third parties. Greenspan subsequently stated before Congress: 'Those of us who have looked to the self-interest of lending institutions to protect shareholders' equity, are in a state of shocked disbelief' (Andrews, 2008).

Against this backdrop, it becomes apparent that regulation can and should play important roles in ensuring that financial markets operate in the public interest. In the case of climate finance, the central issue for regulators is how best to intervene in the affairs of markets and institutional investors so as to shift their investment behaviour to a low-carbon trajectory.

This involves managing three kinds of risk: physical risk (e.g. the impact of extreme weather events on the insurance industry); transition risk (e.g. the risk that fossil fuel investments will suddenly plummet in value and become 'stranded assets') and liability risk (e.g. the risk of being sued for carbon pollution). But how should these risks best be addressed? What would make for effective, efficient and equitable regulation?

Unfortunately, climate finance, as with financial markets more generally, has multiple distinctive characteristics that make 'good' regulation difficult to achieve. Crucially, such markets involve complex financial products whose intricacies – and the consequences if things go wrong – are sometimes difficult for regulators to fully grasp. One consequence is that regulators usually know far less than the banks, insurance companies and other financial institutions that they are responsible for regulating. Those markets moreover are fast-moving and products and their functions change rapidly, making it hard for regulators to keep up. The result is there is often much that regulators do not know, or do not fully understand (see Schwarcz, 2009) resulting in substantial information asymmetries between institutional investors and regulators. And pervading uncertainty and incomplete information mean that there are likely to be, in Rumsfeld's terms, not only known unknowns but also 'unknown unknowns' (Rumsfeld, 2011).

Of course, it is arguable that such problems can and should be addressed by market actors themselves, through voluntarism, self-regulation or mechanisms of informal social control. However, while there are circumstances where these approaches are worthy of consideration – most notably where the public interest and the private interest of market actors largely coincide (Gunningham, 1991) – such circumstances are relatively rare and for the most part, regulation by the state and/or third party governance will be necessary if the public interest is to be protected (Gunningham and Rees, 1997). But what kind of regulation will work best? What techniques are most likely to influence organisational behaviour, to be flexible, deliver benefits at an acceptable cost, provide practical guidance to duty holders and be easy to enforce?

Standard setting

In designing regulation and in securing compliance on the part of target groups, it is vitally important to determine what *types* of standards to adopt. Five principal, conceptually distinct, standard types are available, these being: information-based; process- and risk-based; prescriptive; principles-based and performance-based mechanisms (Bluff and Gunningham, 2004). Space precludes a full analysis. Instead, this section will focus on those which are best suited to and likely to have most traction in the case of climate finance, on identifying their strengths and weaknesses and how they could best be harnessed in the public interest.

According to the Governor of the Bank of England, Mark Carney, in a landmark speech on climate finance (Carney, 2015), the risks to financial markets posed by climate change will be minimised and their rapid transition towards low-carbon economy best facilitated if they have: (i) the right information, (ii) proper risk management and (iii) coherent, credible public policy frameworks. The first two of these factors point to the importance of (a) information-based and (b) process and risk-based standards, and these will be addressed immediately below. The third factor suggests the importance of 'New Governance' and will be addressed in the fourth section of this chapter.

Informational regulation within the environmental sphere has been defined as 'regulation which provides to affected stakeholders, information on the operations of regulated entities, usually with the expectation that such stakeholders will then exert pressure on those entities to comply with regulations in a manner which serves the interests of stakeholders' (Kleindorfer and Orts, 1998: 155). Informational regulation involves the state encouraging or requiring the provision of information about environmental or social impacts but *without* directly requiring a change in those practices. Rather, this approach relies upon economic markets and public opinion as the mechanisms to bring about improved corporate, environmental or social performance.

In the case of climate finance, information in the form of disclosure 'helps investors understand which businesses are best equipped to deal with the risks and opportunities that climate change presents. And that, in turn, creates the pressure for change that ensures the risks are managed better than they otherwise would be' (Breeden, 2018: 4).

Against this backdrop, the G20's Financial Stability Board recognised that climate change presented a 'systemic risk' to the global financial system and established a Task Force on Climate-related Financial Disclosures (TCFD) to address it. The aim was to reduce financial stability risks (a core concern of central banks) by ensuring the market has the right information to price climate risk and reward climate innovation. That information, as the TCFD recognised, needs to be standardised to allow comparability, enabling institutional investors not only to make informed decisions but to engage with companies and to bring pressure to bear to accelerate their shift to a low-carbon trajectory. In turn, companies experiencing that pressure might also be more inclined to shift their business strategy further in that direction.

The TCFD is not alone in seeking broader climate finance disclosure. The European Union (EU), through its Sustainable Finance Action Plan (European Commission, 2018), has been pre-eminent in this domain. It is not only developing a broad framework for public reporting, but a taxonomy of sustainable economic activities, standards and labels for green financial products and a green bond standard. This last, for example, is likely to enhance the effectiveness, transparency, comparability and credibility of the green bond market across the EU.

Of course, doubts can be raised about the power of informational regulation, given that it only requires disclosure (if it is mandatory) or exhorts disclosure (where it is voluntary). Governor Carney however, makes a case as to why it might nevertheless bring about far reaching changes in behaviour in the financial mainstream:

> First, companies that score well on ESG [environment, social and governance] metrics could better anticipate future climate-related risks and opportunities. This makes them more strategically resilient and therefore able to anticipate, and adapt to, the risks and opportunities on the horizon, generating true alpha[2] from ESG. Second, strong ESG scores could signal that a firm is more naturally disposed to longer-term strategic thinking and planning. Climate disclosure is increasingly seen not only as necessary in and of itself, but also as informative about the extent to which companies are focused on long-term value creation. And third, strong ESG firms may enjoy valuation premiums consistent with shifting investor preferences.
>
> (Carney, 2019: 10; own endnote)

Nevertheless, informational regulation, at least in the climate finance domain, has its own limitations. In particular, there will be a temptation for at least some financial actors to present themselves as having advanced climate risk management policies when their actual practices are far less impressive. While the scrutiny of environmental non-governmental organisations and shareholder activist groups and others may mitigate this risk to some extent, the capacity of corporate insiders to present information in ways that best suit their own interests may yet undermine the potential of informational regulation. For example, 'independent' auditors owe a greater allegiance to their clients, mindful of retaining their long-term business, than they do to the public interest or meeting the regulator's aspirations. And neither non-governmental organisations nor regulators are likely to have the resources or perhaps the skills to delve deeply into the risk management disclosure practices of large corporate entities with complex and sophisticated processes for calculating those risks and how they are purportedly being addressed. As a practical matter, it is difficult to address issues of comparability even within the same sector, let alone between sectors.[3]

There is also a further and more deep-seated problem, namely that asset and portfolio managers are short-term animals: they are often captive to the tyranny of quarterly returns, constantly fearful that if their short-term performance flags, they may have no long term to look forward to. Accordingly, their willingness to take a broader and longer-term perspective is seriously constrained. Similarly, there are problems incentivizing passive investors to demand change since they simply track the relevant stock exchange index and their fortunes rise and fall with it. As one commentator puts it: 'most pension funds heavily invest in passive index funds. In other words, they own the market, along with any mispriced risks or systemic failure' (McMahon, 2019).

Risk management and process-based regulation

Risk management is the quintessential example of what regulatory theorists refer to as process-based standards. Such standards identify a process, or series of steps, to be followed in the pursuit of a regulatory goal, as with managing hazards by incorporating the steps of hazard identification, risk assessment and risk control. At its broadest, the aim is to achieve a holistic and systematic approach for the ongoing and proactive improvement of regulatory performance across the organisation as a whole, with a comprehensive approach to risk management as its core (hereafter 'risk management').

Such an approach is often used when the regulator has difficulty specifying a goal or outcome but has confidence that the risk of adverse consequences will be reduced if particular steps (e.g. identify, assess, control) are followed. Such is the case with the financial services sector. In arguably its most sophisticated form, risk management becomes a form of 'meta-regulation': this strategy involves government 'regulating at a distance' by risk managing the risk management of individual enterprises. This implies requiring or encouraging enterprises to put in place their own systems of internal control and management (via systems, plans and risk management more generally). These are then scrutinised by regulators who take the necessary action to ensure that these mechanisms are working effectively. The goal is to induce companies themselves to acquire the specialised skills and knowledge to self-regulate, subject to external scrutiny. Accordingly, the regulator's main intervention role is to oversee and audit the plans put in place by the regulated organisation.

However, to be effective, meta-regulation requires specialist, high-quality regulators to oversee the risk management strategies of the regulated organisation, and sophisticated and motivated regulated organisations to develop and implement such strategies successfully and to regulate themselves effectively. At the very least, a receptive corporate culture is a necessary, albeit not a sufficient condition, for its success (Gunningham and Sinclair, 2009). However, in the financial services sector, these preconditions for success have rarely been met. The GFC provided a compelling case study of how meta-regulation might play out in real world circumstances, and it fell spectacularly short.

Regulators, as it turned out, often had insufficient technical skills, high turnover, limited resources, lacked the rich contextual information that is available to banks and other major financial actors and were often subject to political pressure not to over-regulate or otherwise reduce the competitive advantage of their country's financial market (Ford, 2010b). In the aftermath of the crisis it became apparent that there had been widespread and serious flaws in the risk assessment process, and that many internal firm risk assessment models were not fit for purpose (Black, 2012; Ford, 2010b). The result was that meta regulation fell far short of what it aspired to achieve. Stress tests, for example, became 'a way for banks to manage regulators, not to manage themselves' (Black, 2012: 1048). Capital adequacy requirements, which in a previous era were set according to a specific formula, had also been left to banks to determine under their own risk management processes but 'in the absence of external discipline, the bank-developed models produced extraordinarily insufficient capital reserves, unprecedentedly large leverage, and enormous systemic risk' (Ford, 2010b: 461).

In the case of climate finance, the challenges for regulators relying on meta-regulation are of a similar magnitude and in many respects of a similar nature, to those which they failed to meet in the GFC. With climate finance, the central question for prudential regulators is how to ensure that firms have developed strategic resilience such that they would be able to withstand unanticipated shocks of a disruptive transition to a low-carbon economy (i.e. transition risks), or physical shocks from extreme climate events that might impact upon them.

Two best practice mechanisms for assessing resilience to such risks are stress testing and scenario analysis. Both are based on studying the impact of unlikely but not impossible events, and both enable companies to better understand the risks they might confront under extreme conditions. Stress testing and scenario analysis would also assist regulators to assess the adequacy of the mechanisms that companies have in place to transition to a low-carbon economy and what further measures they might contemplate. However, currently there is little evidence of systematic stress testing or of credible scenario analyses being undertaken within the financial services sector.

So the challenge for regulators is how to effectively encourage, facilitate and reward (or even mandate) such measures. This will require 'linking high-level, data-driven narratives on the evolution of physical and transition risks to quantitative metrics to measure the impact on the financial system' (Carney, 2019: 7). It would, however, be premature to do so at this juncture, because neither financial market actors nor their regulators know how to do so. Meta-regulation provides no answer to this predicament, but New Governance, as the next section will explore, just might.

New Governance

New Governance involves collaboration between a diversity of private, public and non-government stakeholders who, acting together toward commonly agreed upon (or mutually negotiated) goals, hope to achieve far more collectively than they could individually (Holley, Shearing and Gunningham, 2012: 4). This form of governance relies heavily upon participatory dialogue and deliberation, flexibility (rather than uniformity), inclusiveness, knowledge generation and processes of learning, transparency and institutionalised consensus-building practices (see, generally, De Búrca and Scott, 2006).

New Governance has become increasingly popular because of the perceived capacity of these more collaborative and adaptive approaches to deliver benefits in circumstances where traditional approaches cannot

(Holley, Shearing and Gunningham, 2012: 4). For example, prescriptive legal standards, as well as some market-based instruments, depend upon a degree of centralised knowledge (e.g., to set suitable standards, prices or caps) that is often not available (Holley, Shearing and Gunningham, 2012: 4). In contrast, the sort of collaborative and participatory approaches contemplated by New Governance are said to lead to problem solving that is inclusive of context and able to capitalize on the unique knowledges and capacities of public and private actors. New Governance is also thought to cope better with the dynamism, uncertainty and complexity of problems than either traditional regulation (which can easily ossify, by freezing standards at a particular point in time or by adopting a one-size-fits-all approach). For these very reasons, New Governance is particularly apt in the context of climate finance regulation to 'allow for adaptation and adjustment given the complexity and newness of the area' (Bowman, 2015: 182).

While the terminology of New Governance does not appear to have permeated central banks and regulators, they are, albeit not under that rubric, already embracing many of its insights. The Bank of England, which has been pre-eminent in its efforts to develop best practice climate finance regulation, recognises the complexities of regulating in this area, where much is not known either by regulators or market actors, particularly when it comes to untried and complex analytical tools. As Sarah Breeden, Executive Director for International Bank Supervision at the UK Prudential Regulatory Authority, has pointed out:

> climate related financial risk disclosure -and in particular the scenario analysis ... is an evolving discipline. Learning by doing and iterating with experience is the key to success...To be meaningful we need to bring together climate scientists, macroeconomists, financial risk modellers, and business heads. And we need time to develop our analytical capabilities, to experiment across these different disciplines and to innovate.
>
> (Breeden, 2018: 4)

Similarly, Carney emphasises how,

> as companies apply the recommendations and investors increasingly differentiate between firms based on this information, adoption will continue to spread, disclosure will become more decision-useful and efficient, and its impact will grow ...As firms work to enhance their disclosures, they are being supported by various TCFD Preparers' Forums from energy to finance. The TCFD will also continue to work with market participants to refine metrics so that they are consistent, comparable and decision-useful; and it will share best practices on the disclosure of risk management and governance.
>
> (Carney, 2019: 4)

Working collaboratively with stakeholders to establish best practice examples, sharing those examples widely, developing improved scenario analysis tools, experimenting with different mechanisms to test strategic resilience to different climate outcomes, empowering investors through disclosure, allowing feedback between the market and policymaking, supporting firms as they seek to refine complex tools and methodologies, expanding the reach of these tools and amplifying their influence through networks such as the Bank of England's Climate Financial Risk Forum, allowing feedback between the market and policymaking, are all quintessential New Governance approaches. They are all to be applauded for their capacity to leverage learning and to raise the bar for all firms over time, ensuring the virtuous circle in which 'companies disclose more information, investors make better informed decisions and sustainable investment goes mainstream' (Carney, 2019: 11–12).

However, there are also essential lessons from New Governance scholarship that should not be forgotten, namely, that the state (and prudential regulators in particular) must continue to play three clear roles: definitional guidance, mandatory participation and enforcement (Gunningham, 2009).

Definitional guidance refers to the regulator describing and defining the nature of the New Governance arrangement. This, the Bank of England is already contemplating as it seeks to craft its stress testing and scenario analysis requirements, but incorporating the 'learning by doing' lessons of New Governance.

Mandating participation

While voluntarism is a sensible place to start, and encourages collaboration, over time it will, for reasons given earlier, be desirable to mandate behavioural change. The Bank of England has already hinted that this may be the case and has also flagged that 'as tools and expertise develop, we will however embed more granular requirements into our policy, to bring industry in line with our evolving expectations' (Breeden, 2018: 5). These signals must become both clearer and stronger, with a set date by which, what was previously voluntary, becomes mandatory. Without this, free riders, particularly those driven by short-termism, may gain a temporary and unfair advantage over their competitors.

Enforcement capability

Financial market regulation is littered with examples of regulatory failure with a recurrent theme being grossly inadequate compliance and enforcement. Once again, the GFC provides the most graphic examples. The UK's Financial Services Authority, for example, was abolished following an inquiry into its performance during that crisis, having been castigated by that inquiry for a

> hands off market-based regulatory approach that assumed that: markets were generally self-correcting, market discipline could be trusted to contain risk, the primary responsibility for managing risk lay with senior management not regulators because senior managers had better information, and consumers were best protected through unfettered and transparent markets.
>
> (Ford, 2010a: 293)

Accordingly, regulators must have the capability to enforce New Governance mechanisms to the extent necessary to ensure that obligations are met. However, compliance and enforcement as it relates to New Governance requires more finesse than in many other areas, because the collaborative practice through which New Governance tools are developed requires building trust, which might well be shattered if those who were partnering regulators in developing new tools one day, were subject to enforcement action for failing to comply with them the next. In practice, it should be possible to navigate this difficulty. Those who co-create new rules with the regulators are likely to be industry leaders, whereas only the laggards will be targets of enforcement action. And indeed, a failure to take such action might be perceived as giving the laggards an unfair competitive advantage. Nevertheless, it would be politic for regulators to allow sufficient lead-in time during which New Governance tools are voluntary, before making them mandatory and engaging in any action to ensure compliance.

Discussion

One might conclude from the above that regulating climate finance is fraught with difficulty; the range of available regulatory tools is limited and those tools that are available, namely informational and risk-based standards, have serious limitations.

Informational regulation only compels disclosure of information, not the proscription of behaviour deemed contrary to the public interest. Moreover, it relies on that information to be responded to in a rational way by market actors who have incentives to take a short-term view and to discount longer term risks. Such actors are also predisposed to think that they can 'make hay while the sun shines' and that they will be astute enough to bail out of the market in high-carbon assets before that market ultimately collapses in 'disorderly transition'. There is, moreover, a tension between the interests of individual asset managers and the firms for whom they work, with the former under pressure to deliver high performance in the short term, such that they are inclined to heavily discount longer term considerations.

In the case of risk-based and meta-regulation, as Ford demonstrates, regulators justified the delegation of risk assessments to firms 'on the basis that regulators did not and could not possess the knowledge those firms had about their own operational risks' (Ford, 2010b: 124). Yet regulators proved incapable of risk managing the risk management of those they regulated. They relied too heavily on the self-regulatory practices of those firms, about which they were remarkably naïve and trusting, perhaps because they simply didn't understand their complex financial products and because they themselves had insufficient resources and skills to do more.

But notwithstanding the limitations of informational and risk-based regulation, regulators have few other options. None of the other main standard types – prescriptive, principles-based or performance-based regulation (Bluff and Gunningham, 2004) – are suitable for regulating climate finance. Prescriptive regulation is not appropriate because in fluid, fast-moving markets involving complex financial products, it is simply too rigid and inflexible. Nor does it lend itself to addressing organisational pathologies such as a criminogenic corporate culture. Limited exceptions exist (e.g. capital adequacy requirements, a 'green supporting factor' (Thomä and Hilke, 2018)) but they are rare. Principles-based regulation has ostensibly been tried and found wanting (Ford, 2008). The UK Financial Services Authority, which claimed to adhere to this approach, was abolished following its perceived failure during the GFC. However, on a narrower, and arguably more accurate understanding of what principles might involve (Bluff and Gunningham, 2004) (for example, a fiduciary duty is a principles-based standard) it provides little more than a moral compass, with insufficient substance to determine whether purported principles have been adhered to or not. This leaves performance-based regulation. But this requires the regulator to be able to specify, with some precision, what outcomes it requires, and in the case of financial market regulation, it is frequently unable to do so.

Or perhaps, policymakers are simply lacking in spine and ambition and as a result are looking in the wrong place for regulatory levers to precipitate a climate finance revolution. Perhaps, if they lifted their heads above the parapet, they would find that a host of other possibilities are available. For example, as Darren Sinclair (2019) points out it would be possible to mandate restrictions on investing in (or lending to) new fossil fuel projects; to require divestment of existing fossil fuel assets or to set minimum levels of investment in clean energy projects. If these sorts of requirements were imposed then prescriptive or performance standards could readily be designed and implemented to achieve these policy ends.

However, it is one thing to require the disclosure of information or forms of risk management – both of which arguably would enable financial markets to function more efficiently – and quite another to compel them to invest their capital in particular ways. The political obstacles to enacting regulation of the latter type would be overwhelming. Such action would be anathema not only to institutional investors, but also to their political masters, not least because any such action would prompt a strong back-lash, part of which would almost inevitably involve capital flight to other jurisdictions. Put differently, while the era of laissez faire may be over – particularly given the near-catastrophic consequences of under-regulation that prompted the GFC – the grip of capitalism most certainly is not. Indeed, many would argue that we have entered an age of 'regulatory capitalism', under which markets are used as regulatory mechanisms rather than being viewed as the antithesis of regulation (Levi-Faur, 2005; Braithwaite, 2008; cited in Gunningham and Holley, 2016: 286). This is precisely what informa-tional and, to some extent, risk-based regulation, aspire to do.

However, as we have seen, there is a problem with relying exclusively on these regulatory instruments because they both have weaknesses as well as strengths. In principle, such a conclusion suggests the value of designing complementary combinations of instruments, compensating for the weak-nesses of each with the strengths of others (Gunningham, Grabosky and Sinclair, 1998). But in the case of climate finance, there are very few instru-ments that can credibly be used within the confines of regulatory capitalism: those that might be most effective are politically impractical.

The best options may lie in a broader shift from regulation to govern-ance. As Gunningham and Holley have argued: 'in the modern era, think-ing will need to go beyond a concern with regulators and states and instead situate instrument choice alongside broader contextual factors, changing patterns of law, regulation and governance and the now-increased role of non-state actors in steering and rowing more broadly' (Gunningham and Holley, 2016: 286). In the case of climate finance, network governance (Castells, 2000) may have particular potential. To date, various sustainable finance networks have been initiated, particularly by the United Nations Environmental Program, a weak and underfunded international organisa-tion, but one that has been adept at networking and thereby amplifying its influence. There are now multiple networked sustainable finance initi-atives including the Central Banks and Supervisors Network for Greening the Financial System and the UN Principles for Responsible Investment (UN PRI). This last is an international network of over 2000 investors and over $80 trillion in assets under management. Many of these networks pro-vide a rich collaborative environment that enables stakeholder to tap into the various New Governance techniques identified earlier.

Concluding comments

Designing effective climate finance regulation is a complex and challenging endeavour. There is no single or simple way of addressing it. All mecha-nisms for doing so have both strengths and weaknesses and all are vulner-able to failure. Those that might be capable of most directly intervening in the market and potentially most effective cannot be invoked within the confines of regulatory capitalism.

Against this backdrop, the best that can be done is to embrace regulation in preference to voluntarism and to design evidence-based regulatory tools, mindful of their potential limitations and in ways best able to maximise their strengths. It will be equally important to expand the policy horizon beyond regulation conventionally defined, to New Governance tools, including network governance. Of course, broader economic instruments that extend beyond the financial sector to address economic activity in general, such as imposing a price on carbon, also have a vital role to play, and climate finance instruments can never replace such over-weaning policy mechanisms.

Finally, the elephant in the room, must be named. It is an open question whether a rapid transition to a low-carbon economy is possible within the strictures of capitalism. Many of those who believe it is, argue in favour of a Green New Deal, which promises a just transition to a low-carbon economy transition for both workers and frontline communities.[4] Others, like Naomi Klein, maintain that we can have capitalism or climate but not both (Klein, 2015).

Notes

1. This chapter considers climate finance as a sub-category of sustainable finance, the latter being any form of financial service which integrates ESG criteria into business or investment decisions.
2. Alpha refers to the performance of a particular investment compared to a benchmark.
3. Note, however, increasing agitation by investors for companies to include underlying methods and metrics for risk calculation and scenario analysis in their reports to enable external review of individual firm disclosures and some comparability of disclosures between firms (personal communication, date 12 September 2019, M Bowman, Reader, Kings College London).
4. There are many versions of a Green New Deal. See for example that of the Sunrise Movement. Available at: https://www.sunrisemovement.org/green-new-deal [Accessed 28 April 2020].

References

Andrews, E. (2008). Greenspan concedes error on regulation. *New York Times*, 23 October. Available at: https://www.nytimes.com/2008/10/24/business/economy/24panel.html [Accessed 11 May 2020].

Bielenberg, A., Kerlin, M., Oppenheim, J. and Roberts, M. (2016). *The Next Generation of Infrastructure*. New York: McKinsey.

Black, J. (2012). Paradoxes and failures: 'New governance' techniques and the financial crisis. *The Modern Law Review*, 75, pp. 1037–1063.

Bluff, E. and Gunningham, N. (2004). *Principle, Performance, Process or What? New Approaches to OHS Standards Setting. OHS Regulation for a Changing World of Work*. Sydney: Federation Press.

Braithwaite, J. (2008). *Regulatory Capitalism*. London: Edward Elgar.

Bowman, M. (2015). *Banking on Climate Change: How Finance Actors and Transnational Regulatory Regimes Are Responding*. Hague: Kluwer Law International.

Breeden, S. (2018). *The Shared Response to Climate Change: Turning Momentum into Action [Speech of 19 March]*. London: Green Finance Initiative and Green Finance Committee.

Brisman, A. and South, N. (2017). Autosarcophagy in the Anthropocene and the obscenity of an epoch. In: C. Holley and C. D. Shearing, eds., *Criminology and the Anthropocene*. Criminology at the Edge Series. Abingdon, UK: Routledge/Taylor & Francis Group, pp. 25–49.

Carney, M. (2015). Breaking the Tragedy of the Horizon–climate change and financial stability. [Speech of 29 September given at Lloyd's of London].

Carney, M. (2019). A New Horizon. [Speech of 21 March given at European Commission Conference, *A global approach to sustainable finance*, Brussels].

Castells, M. (2000). Toward a sociology of the network society. *Contemporary Sociology*, 29, pp. 693–698.

Climate Finance Leadership Initiative. (2019). *Financing The Low Carbon Future: A Private Sector View on Mobilizing Climate Finance*. Oxford: Bloomberg.

De Búrca, G. and Scott, J. (2006). *Law and New Governance in the EU and the US*. London: Bloomsbury Publishing.

European Commission. (2018). *Action Plan on Financing Sustainable Growth*. COM (2018) 97. Brussels: European Commission.

Ford, C. (2008). New governance, compliance, and principles-based securities regulation. *American Business Law Journal*, 45, pp. 1–60.

Ford, C. (2010a). Principles-based securities regulation in the wake of the global financial crisis. *McGill Law Journal*, 55, pp. 257–307.

Ford, C. (2010b). New governance in the teeth of human frailty: Lessons from financial regulation. *Wisconsin Law Review*, 2010, pp. 441–487.

Glikson, A. Y. (2013). *Evolution of the Atmosphere, Fire and the Anthropocene Climate Event Horizon*. New York: Springer Science & Business Media.

Gunningham, N. (1991). Private ordering, self-regulation and futures markets: A comparative study of informal social control. *Law & Policy*, 13, pp. 297–326.

Gunningham, N. (2009). The new collaborative environmental governance: The localization of regulation. *Journal of Law and Society*, 36, pp. 145–166.

Gunningham, N., Grabosky, P. and Sinclair, D. (1998). *Smart Regulation: Designing Environmental Policy*. Oxford: Clarendon Press.

Gunningham, N. and Holley, C. (2016). Next-generation environmental regulation: Law, regulation, and governance. *Annual Review of Law and Social Science*, 12, pp. 273–293.

Gunningham, N. and Rees, J. (1997). Industry self-regulation: An institutional perspective. *Law & Policy*, 19, pp. 363–414.

Gunningham, N. and Sinclair, D. (2009). Organizational trust and the limits of management-based regulation. *Law & Society Review*, 43, pp. 865–900.

Holley, C. and Shearing, C. D. (2017). Thriving on a pale blue dot. In: C. Holley and C. D. Shearing, eds., *Criminology and the Anthropocene*. Criminology at the Edge Series. Abingdon, UK: Routledge/Taylor & Francis Group, pp. 1–24.

Holley, C., Shearing, C. D. and Gunningham, N. (2012). *The New Environmental Governance*. Abingdon, UK: Routledge.

Intergovernmental Panel on Climate Change (IPCC). (2018). Intergovernmental Panel on Climate Change Special Report on Global Warming of 1.5°C (SR15). Available at: https://www.ipcc.ch/sr15/ [Accessed on 11 May 2020].

Klein, N. (2015). *This Changes Everything: Capitalism vs. the Climate*. New York: Simon and Schuster.

Kleindorfer, P. R. and Orts, E. W. (1998). Informational regulation of environmental risks. *Risk Analysis*, 18, pp. 155–170.

Kuttner, R. (2018). The Crash That Failed. *The New York Review*, 22 November. Available at: https://www.nybooks.com/articles/2018/11/22/financial-crash-that-failed/ [Accessed 28 April 2020].

Levi-Faur, D. (2005). "Globalizing Regulatory Capitalism", Annals of the American Academy of Political and Social Science, 598, pp 6–9.

McMahon, J. (2019). Index Funds Have No Way To Manage Climate Risk. Expert Warns. *Forbes*, 16 September. Available at: https://www.forbes.com/sites/jeffmcmahon/2019/09/16/index-funds-a-favorite-in-pensions-face-greater-risk-from-climate-change/#25f218754ca6 [Accessed 29 April 2020].

Pearce, F. (1976). *Crimes of the Powerful: Marxism, Crime and Deviance*. London: Pluto Press.

Rumsfeld, D. (2011). *Known and Unknown: A Memoir*. London: Penguin.

Schwarcz, S. L. (2009). Regulating complexity in financial markets. *Washington University Law Review*, 87, pp. 211–268.

Sinclair, D. (2019). Speak loudly and carry a small stick: Prudential regulation and the climate, energy, and finance nexus. *Jurimetrics*, 59, pp. 141–166.

Sutherland, E. H. (1945). Is 'White collar crime' crime? *American Sociological Review*, 10, pp. 132–139.

Taylor, I., Walton, P. and Young, J. (1973). *The New Criminology: For a Social Theory of Deviance*. Abingdon, UK: Routledge.

Thomä, J. and Hilke, A. (2018). *The Green Supporting Factor-Quantifying the Impact on European Banks and Green Finance*. Berlin: 2° Investing Initiative. Available at: https://2degrees-investing.org/resource/the-green-supporting-factor-quantifying-the-impact-on-european-banks-and-green-finance/ [Accessed 28 April 2020].

Tooze, A. (2018). *Crashed: How a Decade of Financial Crises Changed the World*. London: Penguin.

United Nations Environment Program (UNEP) (2015). *Aligning the Financial System with Sustainable Development. The Coming Financial Climate, The Inquiry's 4th Progress Report*. Geneva: United Nations Environment Program.

White, R. (2016). Eco-justice and the moral fissures of green criminology. In: J. Jacobs and J. Jackson eds., *The Routledge Handbook of Criminal Justice Ethics*. Abingdon, UK: Routledge, pp. 96–114.

White, R. (2017). Carbon criminals, ecocide and climate justice. In: C. Holley and C. D. Shearing, eds., *Criminology and the Anthropocene*. Criminology at the Edge Series. Abingdon, UK: Routledge/Taylor & Francis Group, pp. 50–80.

4 Speak loudly and carry a small stick

Prudential regulation and the climate, energy, and finance nexus[*]

Darren Sinclair

Introduction

There is overwhelming scientific evidence that the world is facing a climate crisis. Without far reaching action to curb carbon emissions, there will be dramatic changes in weather patterns, with negative outcomes for humans, society, economies, and the natural environment (Cook et al., 2016). The latest scientific evidence not only suggests the pace of climate change is more rapid than previously thought, but also that it is accelerating (Nerem et al., 2018). Indeed, it is now thought that the planet will exceed the 1.5°C threshold—which establishes the point at which the planet will likely either avoid or suffer serious environmental harm—considerably sooner than previously expected (McKie, 2016; Henley and King, 2017: 4261). Despite this urgency, governments have yet to fully engage with the task of transitioning to a low-carbon economy (UN Environment, 2017).

Addressing climate change by reducing carbon emissions is, of course, an extremely complex, far-reaching, and challenging public policy task. In this regard, there have been some important and recent political achievements, most notably the introduction of the Paris Agreement at Conference of the Parties (COP) 21, which commits governments to action to limit global warming to 2°C (or preferably 1.5°C) (United Nations, 2015). For the first time, the Paris Agreement encompasses both developed and developing countries, including, crucially, India and China (which are responsible for a majority and growing share of total carbon emissions) (see generally Gupta, 2016).

Notwithstanding the success of the Paris Agreement, it is unclear whether countries will deliver on their pledges under it (given that it lacks the capacity to enforce individual country commitments), or indeed, even if they did,

---

[*] This article was originally published as: Sinclair, D. Speak Loudly and Carry a Small Stick: Prudential Regulation and the Climate, Energy, and Finance Nexus. (2019). *Jurimetrics Journal*, 59. Reprinted with permission of the American Bar Association. Copyright: ©2018 by the American Bar Association. All rights reserved.

whether pledges would be sufficient to avoid serious negative consequences of climate change. The consensus view is that the Paris Agreement is merely a stepping stone to a future, more ambitious and more enforceable climate change agreement, and that much stronger measures will be required to dramatically reduce carbon emissions to avoid catastrophic climate change (Raftery et al., 2017). It is far from certain, however, that the necessary political will and determination exists to drive this transformative process (McKibben, 2017).

Transitioning to a low-carbon economy will require a massive shift in investment in finance that only the private sector can provide (Maimbo and Zadek, 2017: 61–63). But the financial sector has shown little inclination to shift assets from high- to low-carbon investments. While multiple strategies are available, one of the most important is regulation because of its crucial roles in promoting financial stability, protecting investors, informing the market, reducing systemic risk, and achieving the public good. In this context, a recent, novel, and potentially significant development in climate governance is the engagement of mainstream financial regulators, in particular, prudential regulators, in addressing climate risk within the financial sector.

The entry of prudential regulators into an evolving governance landscape suggests that there is a growing momentum for policy action at the nexus of climate change, energy, and the finance sector, albeit with substantial room for improvement. As such, this chapter will examine the role of one prudential regulator, the Australian Prudential Regulation Authority (APRA), which has recently entered the climate governance space in Australia. This will include nascent steps taken by APRA to date, the likely efficacy of these steps, and opportunities for future regulatory reform by APRA. This article will also touch on relevant international developments by other prudential regulators. It will begin, however, by setting the scene for the intervention of prudential regulators given the tepid policy progress by national governments to date and the essential need for the financial sector to be involved in the transition to a low-carbon economy.

Climate policy failure and the importance of the financial sector

Traditionally, communities have turned to governments and their environmental regulators to solve environmental problems. However, the dismal history of national government interventions in tackling climate change (with global carbon emission projected to reach a record 37.1 billion tonnes in 2018) (Canadell et al., 2018), and the failure of international agreements to change this (Vandenbergh and Gilligan, 2017), do not bode well for future government-led action. Yes, there have been some encouraging commitments and developments in some quarters, namely India and China's decisions to substantially increase their investment in clean energy (Allianz Climate and Energy Monitor, 2017: 5–9) (albeit while still building coal-fired stations at a rapid pace, at least in the case of China); the European Union's (in particular Germany's and France's) ongoing support for stronger domestic and global action (Keating, 2017); and the Canadian government's renewed commitment to the Paris Agreement (after its previous government's overt hostility) (Cullen, 2016).

Arguably, however, these gains have been offset by the regressive stances of other national governments, even those of economically advanced and politically liberal nations. In particular, the US Administration is populated by climate sceptics (Viser, 2018) and has recently withdrawn from the Paris Agreement (Urpelainen, 2017); cut funds to the Environment Protection Agency (Dennis, 2018); appointed a climate sceptic, Scott Pruitt, as its head (only to have a former coal industry's Andrew Wheeler replace him as acting chief in July 2018) (Davenport, 2018; Bravender and Heikkinen, 2017); and, at the same time, is increasing investment in the coal industry (Chiacu and Volcovici, 2017; Dennis and Mooney, 2017). The new Brazilian President is also a noted climate change sceptic and has recently withdrawn a commitment to host the COP25 in 2019 (Watts, 2018), and in Australia, not only was a modest carbon tax repealed, but renewable energy targets have been wound back, and any move towards carbon emissions trading has been categorically ruled out by the federal government (BBC News, 2014; Hutchens, 2016; Murphy, 2017; Murphy, 2018). This is the same federal government that is providing political and, potentially, financial support for the building of the one of the world's largest open-cut coal mines (Jackson, 2015). These actions demonstrate not only that governments may lack the political will or inclination to reduce carbon emissions, but that they may be overtly antagonistic towards climate change action.

The net result is that there is an absence of comprehensive governance, regulatory and policy infrastructure—both internationally and domestically—to bring about the desired transition to a low-carbon economy. Internationally, emissions trading is fractured, limited, or ineffectual; nor is there an equivalent price on carbon that can be incorporated into internationally traded goods (Mori, 2017; Gan, 2018; Lloyd, 2018: 9). Domestically, in many countries, there is little political consensus on which policy tools to adopt, and little progress on integrating these into the core economic policy agendas. Indeed, the continued prevalence of many counterproductive policies (such as fossil fuel subsidies) is evidence of this (Climate Action Network Europe, 2015: 1–2; International Institute for Sustainable Development, 2017). As such, it is difficult to avoid the conclusion that governments lack either the perseverance or foresight to take serious action against climate change and the fossil fuel industry.

Even with the best political will in the world, however, governments alone may not be able to prevent climate change going beyond the proposed 2°C threshold (Vandenbergh and Gilligan, 2017). This is because of the sheer magnitude of the task confronting them in transitioning to a low-carbon economy. It has been estimated that some $90 trillion will be required,

globally, to fund this transition (Mountford, 2017). Governments are incapable of delivering on these ambitious targets without the support, commitment, engagement, and participation of the broader community, including
civil society and the business community (Steer, 2013). Further, governments
will need to leverage the necessary knowledge, expertise, and, crucially,
financial resources of the private sector to achieve comprehensive decarbonisation of their economies. In this respect, the financial sector, with its
massive collective financial assets, will be the key to achieving the transition to a low-carbon economy. Indeed, the Paris Agreement is intended to
lead to a more coordinated effort by all stakeholders, including, in particular, the finance sector, to take major strides in addressing climate change
(Robins, 2016: 11).

The finance sector is broad, varied, interlinked, and rapidly changing. As
such, there are many points at which it can and does intersect and interact
with climate change issues, either in a reactive or an enabling fashion. For
example, Mike Scott notes that while the focus of climate policy has been,
'mostly—and rightly—on heavy emitters of greenhouse gases, such as power
stations, makers of products such as steel, cement and glass, and transporta-
tion .... none of these sectors can operate without financial backing ...' (Scott,
2018). The cumulative impact of decisions by financial actors can either
exacerbate carbon emissions by continuing to invest in fossil fuel exploration, production, and utilisation, or they can support emission reductions by
investing in clean energy alternatives (UNEP, 2014: 35). Indeed, the finance
sector, and sustainable finance more generally, may prove to be more important than government action alone. Certainly, if the world is to successfully
transition to a low-carbon economy, the finance sector will necessarily have
a key role to play. The McKinsey Center for Business and Environment
notes that 'infrastructure spending required over the next 15 years, coupled
with widespread public-sector fiscal constraints, means that private finance
will be increasingly important' (Bielenberg et al., 2016: 3). Despite this, only
recently has the finance sector been thought of as part of the solution, rather
than just as part of the problem (Market Forces, 2016; Vandenbergh and
Gilligan, 2017; Wilde, 2017). Whether and how the financial sector is capable
of playing a positive role, however, is an open question.

Although the Paris Agreement is rightly 'celebrated as a [major] political milestone,' attempts to engage the financial sector in addressing climate
change, 'particularly the [fate of] many trillions of dollars managed by bankers, investors, and asset managers,' are not well formed, at least in terms of
traditional state-led governance (Miller and Swann, 2016: 70). This situation is compounded by 'a combination of behavioural biases and misaligned
professional incentives [that] may lead financial markets to be excessively
focused on short-term returns and thus not to fully price climate-related
risks' (Campiglio et al., 2018: 464). In the absence of clear policy signals and
action from governments, then, we must consider a broader conception of
climate change governance as it applies to the finance sector.

In recent years, there have been interesting, if nascent, developments in the climate finance[1] sphere that fall outside traditional state interventionist governance approaches. For example, in the case of civil society, activist non-governmental organisations (NGOs) have led the way in raising public awareness and seeking to change social norms about the undesirability of fossil fuel investment (Gunningham, 2017: 310).

A prominent example of this is the 'divestment movement' coordinated by 350.org that exerts political and social pressure on the financial investment industry (Ayling, 2017: 349–350). Despite some successes, particularly with universities and ethical investment funds, the divestment movement has its limitations; notably, it is principally focused on raising public awareness rather than effecting substantial change in investment flows within the fossil fuel sector (Gunningham, 2017: 310–311). Nevertheless, impacts are growing—a report by Arabella Advisors found that close to 1000 institutional investors (with some $6.24 trillion in assets) have now committed to fossil fuel divestment, which is an increase of 11,900% from 4 years ago (Arabella Advisors, 2018: 1). The divestment movement clearly highlights the crucial role the financial sector has to play in transitioning to a low-carbon economy, and the potential contribution of non-state actors in bringing this about through unconventional forms of governance (Ayling and Gunningham, 2017: 137–139).

Beyond the divestment movement, there is a range of other actors making their presence felt in the climate finance space. These include a variety of NGOs, some with conventional environmental grassroots support, some with a narrower, finance-related focus, and yet others with a hybrid NGO and business structure (Bäckstrand et al., 2017: 564; Taylor, 2017). While their motivations may vary, there are also elements within the financial sector itself that are moving beyond a reactive response to taking the initiative to reduce their fossil fuel exposure or increasing clean energy investments and loans (Scott, 2018). Following the Paris Agreement, for example, over 450 Chief Executive Officers from 65 countries supported integrating carbon pricing into their investment strategies.[2] In addition to mainstream financial companies, ancillary financial actors[3] (for example, ratings agencies) are beginning to engage with financial companies to address their climate performance (Cash, 2018).

Encouragingly, while national governments and politicians may be reluctant to intervene in the affairs of financial companies, there have been other interesting developments in state-led climate governance, including within Australia, the United Kingdom, and the United States. The United States, for example, has witnessed the rise of a climate 'Blue Wall', an alliance of progressive states, such as California, Oregon, and Washington to introduce more ambitious renewable energy targets and programs (Burns and Johnson, 2017). There are also plans to partner with Canada to introduce a state-based emissions trading scheme (Austen, 2017). Considering that California alone has a bigger economy than France (Respaut, 2016), this is not a trivial development. And in Australia, a similar phenomenon is occurring, with a number of state governments, namely South Australia, Victoria, the Australian Capital Territory (ACT), and Queensland introducing aggressive renewable energy targets, investing in renewable energy, and closing down (or ceasing to subsidise) old coal-fired power stations (Climate Council, 2017: iii). The Australian Climate Council recently claimed that 'States and territories continue to lead the way on renewable energy in the ongoing absence of credible national climate policy' and that Tasmania, the ACT, and South Australia are ahead of other jurisdictions (Brailsford et al., 2018: ii). Further, 'Victoria, the Northern Territory and Tasmania have set new renewable energy targets[,] … The Australian Capital Territory announced the results of its final renewable energy reverse auction, … [and] New South Wales, Tasmania, Queensland and Victoria adopted new targets to reach net zero emissions by 2050' (Brailsford et al., 2018: 15). Crucially, several of these state and territory governments plan on addressing carbon emissions with or without the support of the federal government (Brailsford et al., 2018: iii; Latimer and Wright, 2018).

But it is not just regional governments operating within federal systems that are taking up the climate policy challenge in the absence of substantive national government action. Another state governance actor, in countries such as Australia and the United Kingdom, has entered the fray. Perhaps unexpectedly, it is not a conventional environmental regulator, such as an environmental protection authority, but mainstream financial regulators, in particular, prudential regulators, that are taking the policy lead in climate finance regulation (see next section below).

Prudential regulators and the recognition of climate risk

Prudential regulators are responsible for ensuring that financial companies 'hold sufficient capital and have adequate risk controls in place' (Bank of England, n.d. a). In the United Kingdom, for example, the Bank of England has broad powers to set national interest rates and maintain financial stability, and it also oversees the regulation of financial companies through the Prudential Regulation Authority (PRA) (Bank of England, n.d. b). The PRA regulates some '1,500 banks, building societies, credit unions, insurers, and major investment firms' across the United Kingdom (Bank of England, n.d. c). And in Australia, APRA regulates 'banks, credit unions, building societies, general insurance and reinsurance companies, life insurance, private health insurance, friendly societies, and most members of the superannuation industry'.[4] Even though it is a government body, APRA is funded largely by the industries that it supervises. Other countries have equivalent domestic prudential regulators—for example, the Office of the Superintendent of Financial Institutions in Canada[5] and the Financial Markets Authority in New Zealand.[6]

Internationally, the Financial Stability Board (FSB) has taken a leading interest in carbon disclosure by the finance sector (Financial Stability Board, n.d.). The FSB monitors global financial markets and recommends minimum standards and policies.[7] Established after the G20 London Summit in 2009, it seeks to do this by coordinating national financial authorities in the development of strong regulatory, supervisory, and other financial sector policies.[8] The billionaire media owner and former New York City Mayor, Michael Bloomberg, is a United Nations climate envoy, and is heading a task force established by the FSB, aiming to improve the standard of climate reporting in the financial sector (Elliot, 2015). Bloomberg claims that major institutional investors support the task force, with action of climate viewed as a competitive advantage (Elliot, 2015).

Steve Waygood, another member of the FSB taskforce, and chief investment officer of Aviva Investors, notes that it 'is about creating a market in information that enables investors and individuals to understand where their money is invested and how it's supporting the transition to a low carbon economy' (King, 2016). The underlying rationale is that of voluntary action through enlightened self-interest—the FSB aims to shift the voluntary imperative further through providing systemic managerial tools to improve carbon disclosure standards and harness peer pressure at the same time (King, 2016).

In recent years, these pillars of economic orthodoxy have increasingly turned their attention to the financial sector, acting to address climate risks. In this respect, prudential regulators have identified several types of risks (German Federal Ministry of Finance, 2016). In late 2016, for example, a German Finance Ministry report stated that '[c]limate risks have the potential to affect financial markets. Making an orderly transition to climate-friendly investments would help to maintain the efficiency and stability of Germany's financial markets. Conversely, abrupt carbon divestment could jeopardise the stability of financial markets' (German Federal Ministry of Finance, 2016).

The German report highlighted two types of financial risks (German Federal Ministry of Finance, 2016). First, there is the risk of negative financial impacts of climate change itself, such as extreme weather events on the insurance industry, and with banks and lenders, for example, poorly performing loans due to a reduction in property values from rising seas levels (German Federal Ministry of Finance, 2016). Second, there is also the risk of financial disruption from the transition to a low-carbon economy—this includes being exposed to a future energy utility 'death spiral' (Denning, 2013: C1)[9] and 'stranded assets'(German Federal Ministry of Finance, 2016),[10] as well as missing out on new technological clean energy opportunities.

Similarly, the United Kingdom's PRA has identified three key climate-related risks confronting the insurance sector: physical risk, liability risk, and transition risk (PRA, 2015: 4). In particular, the Head of the Bank of

England, Mark Carney, has warned that investors, including insurance companies, face potentially huge losses from the creation of fossil fuel stranded assets (with rapidly declining value and little prospect of a financial recovery) (Shankleman, 2014; Carrington, 2015).

Other institutions have speculated about the collapse of a 'carbon bubble' in the valuation of companies dependent on fossil fuel-based energy production (Chu, 2018). For example, Fitch, a credit rating agency, has said that batteries could 'tip the oil market from growth to contraction "earlier than anticipated"' (Holder, 2016, citing Fitch Ratings, 2016). Further, it warns 'that if recent technology trends continue, we may see an "investor death spiral" as first the smart money—and then everyone else's—sell off oil company assets (bonds and stocks)' (Romm, 2016). As Joe Romm suggests: 'That would in turn increase the industry's costs for both debt and equity—while oil prices would be stuck at low levels as the world hits peak demand' (Randall, 2016; Romm, 2016[11]). And a recent report by Bloomberg New Energy Finance has warned investors 'to expect the "big crash" in oil by 2028—and as early as 2023', as the electric car revolution takes hold (Romm, 2016; Bloomberg NEF, 2017).

In Australia, APRA board member, Geoff Summerhayes, has explicitly rejected the notion that climate change is irrelevant to the financial sector (Yeates, 2017).[12] In particular, he claims that '[s]ome climate risks are distinctly "financial" in nature' with '[m]any of these risks [being] foreseeable, material and actionable now' and that these risks 'have potential system-wide implications that APRA and other regulators here and abroad are paying much closer attention to' (Yeates, 2017). In this respect, Summerhayes nominates the risks posed by changes in law and technology as being of particular relevance to the financial sector (Yeates, 2017).

More recently, Guy Debelle, the Deputy Governor of the Reserve Bank of Australia, has made a public speech in which he highlighted the risks that climate change poses for Australia's financial stability, including that 'insurers may face large, unanticipated payouts because of climate change-related property damage and business losses', that 'companies that generate significant pollution might face reputational damage or legal liability from their activities, and changes to regulation could cause previously valuable assets to become uneconomic', and that 'these consequences could precipitate sharp adjustments in asset prices, which would have consequences for financial stability' (Debelle, 2019).

Closely related to stranded assets is the issue of climate liability. This has emerged as a topic of discussion in Australia recently (Irvine, 2016). A leading lawyer, Noel Hutley SC, and his co-author, Sebastian Hartford-Davis, have released advice on behalf of the Centre for Policy Development and the Future Business Council, that directors of Australian companies may be personally liable for failing to adequately address the impacts of change on their business (Hutley and Hartford-Davis, 2016: 2–3). Crucially, these impacts include both the physical effects of climate change *and* the transitional costs of moving to a low-carbon economy as governments seek to meet their obligations under the Paris Agreement (Hutley and Hartford-Davis, 2016: 5).

Under the Australian Corporations Act 2001, company directors have a fiduciary duty to consider and respond to any risk that might apply to their company, and company directors that fail to meet this standard face fines of up to $200,000 and disqualification of directorships (see Chapter 1, part 1.5, sub-division 5.3 of the Act). Hutley and Hartford-Davis note that, given the high degree of scientific evidence of climate change, it will be unreasonable for company directors to consider unknown associated risks (Hutley and Hartford-Davis, 2016: 6). At a minimum, company directors are obligated to consider and disclose the potential risks and establish a business case about whether action is needed (Hutley and Hartford-Davis, 2016: 18). According to Hutley and Hartford-Davis: 'It is likely to be only a matter of time before we see litigation against a director who has failed to perceive, disclose or take steps in relation to a foreseeable climate-related risk that can be demonstrated to have caused harm to a company (including, perhaps, reputational harm)' (Hutley and Hartford-Davis, 2016: 22).

Climate liability is a potentially powerful, and uniquely personal, price signal to the financial sector. The stark implication is that directors of companies that invest in, lend to, or insure fossil fuel assets and projects could be held liable as a result of transitional climate risks. For example, if fossil fuels assets decrease in value because of government policies, then not only would the fossil fuel company directors be potentially liable, so too would those investment funds that chose to invest in them. Crucially, climate inaction by any one government may be insufficient to forestall such potential liability where the companies and directors involved have assets held in other countries where climate action may be stronger.[13]

APRA's response to climate risk in the financial sector

It is evident that there is growing concern amongst prudential regulators across the developed world that a range of climate related risks collectively present a potential existential threat to financial stability (see section, Prudential regulators and the recognition of climate risk). This might be expected to pique the interest of prudential regulators to engage in climate finance regulation. It may also be that they are concerned by the inadequacy of government action to date. And in countries such as Australia, where there is an effective government policy vacuum both in climate change generally and in climate finance in particular, prudential regulators may feel compelled to take a leadership role. This certainly appears to be the case for APRA, as over the last year or so, it has become increasingly vocal in agitating for action by the financial community (see sections, Public statements and Jawboning).

This raises an interesting dilemma. How does a non-environmental regulator, that lacks a national government imprimatur, respond to what it perceives is an imminent threat to financial order and stability? Hamstrung by a lack of government leadership, APRA, in particular, has adopted several related tactics.

Public statements

The first tactic is to raise the issue of climate finance generally and publicly to gain the attention of the financial community. As noted previously, a board director of APRA, Geoff Summerhayes, has made two very public statements about the importance of climate finance over the last year (Summerhayes, 2017a, 2017b). His statements have been widely publicised and commented on in the financial press. For example, Mr. Summerhayes stated: '[W]hile climate risks have been broadly recognised, they have often been seen as a future problem or a nonfinancial problem. The key point I want to make today, and that APRA wants to be explicit about, is that this is no longer the case' (Summerhayes, 2017a). He also noted that it is 'unsafe for entities or regulators to ignore risks just because there is uncertainty, or even controversy, about the policy outlook' (Summerhayes, 2017a).

These public statements have been strongly reinforced more recently by the public statements of the Deputy Governor, Guy Debelle, in which he stated that:

> I would very much endorse the points that Geoff [has] made. Geoff stresses the need for businesses, including those in the financial sector, to implement the recommendations of the Task Force for Climate-related Financial Disclosures. I strongly endorse this point. We have seen progress on this front in recent years, but there is more to be done. Financial stability will be better served by an orderly transition rather than an abrupt disorderly one.
>
> (Debelle, 2019)

Jawboning

The second tactic is to threaten financial companies with negative consequences if they do not act. This is commonly referred to as 'jawboning' in the financial sector.[14] A crucial aspect of jawboning is that no action is actually taken, at least at this point, apart from the issuing of the threat (Surowiecki, 2008). The expectation is that financial regulators have enough gravitas in their public statements to engender responses from the financial community. In the case of climate finance, there are two explicit threats that APRA, for example, has employed (Slezak, 2017).

The first threat is that if the financial sector does not act, it will suffer financial harm from the consequence of climate change on its investments (Summerhayes, 2017a). For example, insurers will be subject to increasing claims from more extreme weather events, and banks will be subject to losses (from their loans) of property values in coastal areas subject to sea level rises (German Federal Ministry of Finance, 2016). Ultimately, of course, as climate change disrupts major aspects of economic growth, then financial investments more generally will suffer (Summerhayes, 2017a). To this end, APRA has warned of a 'significant repricing of carbon-intensive resources and activities and reallocation of capital' (Summerhayes, 2017a).

The second threat is that if the financial sector does not act, it will be subject to new, more intrusive, regulatory policy and market interventions, either directly or indirectly (Summerhayes, 2017a). For example, corporate directors in the financial sector might be personally liable for not taking action on climate change (Summerhayes, 2017a). Indirectly, as governments eventually respond to climate change by introducing more ambitious policies that hasten the transition to a low-carbon economy, financial companies with exposure to fossil fuel assets may suffer heavy financial losses (Chu, 2018).

Further to these, even without strong government action, the rapidly increasing competitiveness of clean energy means that fossil fuel assets are likely to become progressively more unattractive investments in the near future. As APRA has noted, 'There could be either sharper, more significant policy changes and market adjustments down the track, or the physical impacts of climate change could become more severe, more likely and more unpredictable' (Chu, 2018). In this respect, the primary function of prudential regulators is to maintain financial stability. To the extent that such exhortations influence the market and, crucially, the behaviour of financial companies, they may become a self-fulfilling prophesy. That is, as investors begin to shift their asset profiles away from fossil fuels, the price of those assets are likely to decline, thus encouraging other investors to do likewise.

Stress tests

In an interesting twist on the tactic of jawboning, APRA has also announced that it will begin conducting stress tests on the financial system to assess its capability to respond to climate change shocks (Summerhayes, 2017b). Although the details of this proposed action have not been released publicly, it is clear that such action, while falling short of mandating action by financial companies, would have the clear intention of heightening awareness of both physical and transitional climate risks. To this end, APRA has already started questioning insurers, superannuation funds, and banks about their awareness of climate change risks and what action may be required (Uribe, 2017: 30).

Disclosure

A fourth tactic is to push for disclosure of carbon exposure (Summerhayes, 2017b). The financial sector is already subject to stringent financial regulations addressing their fiduciary and corporate governance responsibilities

(Iacobucci, 2015). These include corporate reporting and disclosure requirements (Iacobucci, 2015). It is here that the opportunity arises for governance in the form of climate disclosure requirements. In particular, financial companies, such as banks and insurance agencies, may be compelled to report on their activities that relate to carbon emissions. For example, the proportion of their investments or lending comprises renewable energy and other low-carbon projects and technology. Such requirements are still a form of hierarchical governance in that a state compels an entity to engage in a particular activity; the difference with direct forms of hierarchical governance described above is that informational governance does not require tangible changes in investment outcomes (see generally Karkkainen, 2001; Coglianese, 2016). Instead, the expectation is that by providing transparency, investment funds will be subject to public pressure to improve their climate performance (or risk losing investment flows and, ultimately, their social license to operate). Thus, this is, in essence, state-centred environmental governance in the form of informational regulation of the financial sector (Gunningham and Grabosky, 1998: 63–64).

In this respect, there are several non-state actors that have particular resonance in the climate finance space and align with the actions and ambitions of prudential regulators. These non-state actors focus their attention on tracking and publicising the performance of financial institutions, particularly banks, in terms of the climate change commitments and performance.[15] Market Forces, for example, is an affiliate of Friends of the Earth and a member of the international Bank Track network.[16] It profiles, publishes, and accounts for the environmental, climate change performance of banks, superannuation funds, and insurers within Australia.[17] Bank Track is the international equivalent, and has a stated mission 'to promote fundamental changes in the operations of banks so that, while conducting their business in a fully transparent and accountable manner, they contribute to the ecological wellbeing of the planet'.[18] Another example, Carbon Tracker, is a United Kingdom-based 'independent financial think tank that carries out in-depth analysis on the impact of the energy transition on capital markets'.[19]

Clearly, the activities of such non-state actors have the capacity to support the actions of prudential regulators and vice versa. As another non-state actor in this space, the Australian-based climate institute has noted, in regard to APRA's public statements, that:

> [i]t's reassuring to see that Australia's prudential supervisor understands that, regardless of controversy in the political realm, climate change is a real and rapidly evolving risk for our financial sector and broader economy … [h]is speech acknowledges many of the key financial implications of climate change which we've been researching and communicating for the past few years … [s]peeches are an important tool for APRA to communicate its concerns and priorities, so this sends a clear

signal to all Australian banks, insurers and superannuation funds that they should be considering climate risk.

(Hutchens, 2017a)

Importantly, APRA has signalled to the finance industry that it intends to conduct an industry-wide review of climate-related disclosure (Summerhayes, 2017b). In this respect, an independent Australian policy think tank, the Centre for Policy Development, has highlighted the need for genuine disclosure by stating that '[b]etter analysis and disclosure of climate risks is vital to provide the information markets need to help drive a transition to a zero carbon economy. But flawed or superficial approaches to scenario analysis will obscure more than they reveal' (Uribe, 2017: 30, quoting Travers McLeod). As such, APRA claims, that the organisation 'will expect more sophisticated answers, especially from well-resourced and complex entities' (Uribe, 2017: 30, quoting Summerhayes).

Crucially, however, APRA falls short of announcing an intention to *mandate* carbon disclosure in the finance sector, as has been contemplated in some international jurisdictions. A careful reading of APRA's public statements reveals a reliance on threats and persuasion that falls short of any legal obligation. As such, the primary appeal is to the enlightened self-interest of financial companies. This may reflect its inability to obtain political support for strong mandatory action on climate disclosure by the finance sector. In recognition of the political constraints it is operating within, APRA may be reluctant to get too far ahead of a climate sceptical national government. This policy domain, therefore, is a work in progress.

The response of other stakeholders to APRA

How have various stakeholders responded to APRA's increasing engagement on climate finance issues? In terms of government responses, perhaps surprisingly, APRA's actions have not attracted the usual hostility that might be expected from a government sceptical about climate change. Indeed, the Australian government has essentially been silent on APRA's climate finance stance.

It may be that APRA's activities and statements are flying under the political radar at present. But there may also be a more profound reason: the world of finance is being taken more seriously with political discussion and government priorities, and ipso facto, official institutions, such as the Departments of Treasury and Finance, carry a high level of policy gravitas, certainly more than environmental portfolios and their environmental regulators possess. As such, politicians are likely to be more reluctant to take on financial institutions such as APRA, at least publicly, and risk losing political capital and credibility. It may also be that as finance and economics are viewed as core areas of government business, any steps that undermine the authority of key financial institutions, such as a prudential regulator like APRA, risk undermining confidence in the national economy. For example, Australia's economic sales pitch to the world is predicated on its perceived financial stability, in particular, our high-quality financial regulation: picking at one thread of our financial regulatory tapestry could unravel other unintended threads.

Beyond the government, the Australian finance sector has been very supportive of APRA's position (and indeed this may be a further explanation for the muted response by the national government). In particular, it has started to voluntarily move in the direction of carbon disclosure and fossil fuel divestment (Market Forces, 2017b), and in this regard, it may view APRA as providing a degree of political cover for such activities. This is even more relevant given the stinging criticism banks have received from members of the government, in particular, the National Party (a conservative, rural-based political party that is a coalition member of the federal government) for refusing to fund the largely proposed Adani coal mine in Queensland, Australia: 'Some corporations unfortunately today are wimps in regard to standing up to these activists …' (Ker, 2017: 2).

But has APRA brought about any change in Australia's financial sector? Although it is not possible to attribute any advance by Australian financial companies to APRA directly, at least, APRA's actions *have* coincided with increasing commitments by Australian banks to address climate risk. In this respect, the banks have responded to climate risks in two ways: disclosure and divestment (SBS News, 2017; Williams, 2018).

During 2017, the big four Australian banks made increasingly ambitious statements about reducing their carbon exposure (Market Forces, 2017a). Interestingly, the timing of this has closely followed APRA's public statements. For example, the Australia and New Zealand Banking Group (ANZ) and the Commonwealth Bank of Australia (CBA), previously named as the largest lenders to fossil fuels, both signalled that they were actively reducing loans to some carbon-intensive sectors including the coal industry, with the CBA linking this to the Paris Climate Change Agreement in 2015 (Hutchens, 2017b). Westpac and, as noted above, the National Australia Bank (NAB) have also recently toughened their stance on lending to coal mining (as all four banks are targeted by environmental NGOs) (Market Forces, 2017b). Westpac's chief executive officer, Brian Hartzer, referred to the bank's recent policy change to rule out new lending in previously undeveloped coal basins, or for coal with low energy content, when he stated: 'Westpac recognises that climate change is an economic issue as well as an environmental issue, and banks have an important role to play in assisting the Australian economy to transition to a net zero emissions economy' (Westpac Banking Corp, 2017).

NAB announced in December 2017 that it would cease financing new thermal coal mining projects, making it 'the first major Australian bank' to reach such a decision (National Australian Bank, 2017a). Since 2016, NAB has decreased its funding for coal mining from 9 to 5%; however, the majority of the coal mining it finances (83%) is for thermal coal (National Australian

Bank, 2017a). While the bank will continue to finance coal projects already on its books, Mike Baird, Chief Customer Officer of NAB Corporate and Institutional Banking, says an orderly transition to a low-carbon Australia is critical for the economy and for continued access to energy sources (National Australian Bank, 2017b).

Arguably, the Australian banks are moving off a low base. The independent financial tracker, Market Forces, for example, has revealed that the four major Australian banks have lent nearly four times as much to the fossil fuel sector since the Paris Agreement than they have to the renewable energy—$5.6 billion versus $1.5 billion (MacDonald-Smith, 2016: 8). However, although headline lending to the coal sector has fallen away, billions of dollars are being invested through 'corporate loans, refinancing for coal ports in Queensland and NSW, and lending for gas projects' (MacDonald-Smith, 2016: 8). Of the four banks, only one–NAB–has allocated more lending to renewable energy than to fossil fuels (Zhou, 2017).

Possible future regulatory action by APRA

To date, the actions of APRA in the climate finance space may be characterised as an example of 'speaking loudly and carrying a small stick'. That is, APRA is relying on publicly issued threats to encourage voluntarism and informational regulation, with an absence of mandatory provisions and compliance and enforcement. If APRA so chose, or more desirably, was granted political support, to take stronger action, there are two obvious regulatory avenues for doing so.

First, APRA could shift from making entreaties for carbon disclosure to legally mandating carbon disclosure by the finance sector. While it is true that the Australian banks have taken significant steps in terms of carbon disclosure, mandatory provisions would add consistency, credibility, and depth to disclosure actions by the banks. Further, it would broaden the coverage of disclosure to encompass other major players in the finance sector, such as Australia's massive superannuation industry (one of the largest in the world) and the insurance sector, that are not nearly as advanced as Australian banks in going down the disclosure path.

Mandatory disclosure would open the door for APRA to take on a quasi-meta-regulation role, by assuming the role of external auditor and imposing quality control of disclosure actions, but this time with real regulatory teeth at its disposal (see generally Parker, 2007). Under this scenario, the day-to-day regulatory functions would be devolved to companies themselves, as well as capturing the contributions from a range of NGOs and independent auditors. Financial companies would be required to have in place sophisticated environmental management systems that are synchronised with their statutory regulatory obligations. In turn, government regulators would focus their efforts on informational regulation and conducting high-level reviews of company auditing processes and performance.

This might include, for example, desktop audits supplemented by a representative sample of random on-site audits over a defined period. Again, the regulator still sets the regulatory agenda in terms of any process and performance standards and remains poised to intervene more directly if such company performance fails to match their rhetoric. This is consistent with the existing and proposed future approach of APRA, where it has announced its intention to increasingly turn its attention to carbon disclosure by, and conduct climate finance stress tests on, the finance sector.

A second, and far more radical, regulatory step would be to mandate restrictions on investing in (or lending to) new fossil fuel projects, divesting from existing fossil fuel investments or minimum levels of investment in clean energy projects. In effect, this would be shifting from a process-based, to a form of performance-based, regulation. Reading between the lines, the APRA board member Geoff Summerhayes appears to hint at the likelihood of such policy action in the future:

> [W]hile climate risks have been broadly recognised, they have often been seen as a future problem or a non-financial problem. The key point I want to make today, and that APRA wants to be explicit about, is that this is no longer the case. Some climate risks are distinctly "financial" in nature. Many of these risks are foreseeable, material, and actionable now. Climate risks also have potential system-wide implications that APRA and other regulators here and abroad are paying much closer attention to.
>
> .... .
>
> [T]he days of viewing climate change within a purely ethical, environmental or long-term frame have passed.
>
> .... .
>
> What happens next isn't just a matter for rocket scientists—but also humble prudential regulators.
>
> .... .
>
> [T]here could be either sharper, more significant policy changes and market adjustments down the track, or the physical impacts of climate change could become more severe, more likely and more unpredictable.
>
> (Summerhayes, 2017a)

Obviously, taking such a profound step as mandatory divestment could not be introduced in one fell swoop, and would necessarily be phased in over time to allow the financial sector to adjust. But what is the alternative? Is it a disorderly transition with even greater risks to financial stability by having it imposed by the market or other international developments? It may well be sensible, indeed, *prudent*, to get ahead of the game, and thereby avoid the danger of the Australian finance sector being exposed to stranded fossil fuel assets, at the same time as taking opportunity of increasingly competitive clean energy projects.

There is the risk that if APRA does not take such regulatory interventions, the Australian finance sector will not reap the economic benefits of an early, gradual, and orderly transition to a low-carbon economy. Instead, they will be forced to adopt more severe and costly policies later on as they ultimately succumb to the combined pressures of technological advancements, plunging fossil fuel asset prices, and a climate crisis. It is this scenario that has led normally conservative financial regulators, directed by the Head of the Bank of England, Mark Carney, and others, to warn of the transitional climate risks confronting the financial sector—specifically, the policy, legal and technology landscape in a post-Paris 2015 world (Carney, 2018). It is their view that many financial companies (as well as governments) appear to be unaware of these very substantial transitional risks.

Whether APRA has the institutional fortitude to embark on a more robust regulatory approach to addressing climate risk in the financial sector remains on open question. However, the experience of the ongoing Commonwealth of Australia (2019) in Australia does not augur well (Chalmers et al., 2018). The Banking Royal Commissioner, Kenneth Hayne, has made a damning finding into the capacity of APRA to prevent very serious misconduct more generally in the Australian banking and financial sector:

> The law sets the bounds of permissible behaviour. If competitive pressures are absent, if there is little or no threat of enterprise failure, and if banks can and do mitigate the consequences of customers failing to meet obligations, only the regulator can mark and enforce those bounds. But neither the Australian Securities and Investments Commission (ASIC) nor APRA has done that in a way that has prevented the conduct described in this report.
>
> (Hayne, 2018: 269–270)

These findings suggest that if APRA is to be an effective climate finance regulator, it will not only need to enhance its regulatory tools, but also its regulatory culture, to overcome recalcitrant and deceptive behaviour by financial institutions.

International developments

Beyond Australia and APRA, other countries (through their respective financial and prudential regulators) are also turning their attention to climate finance regulation (Campiglio et al., 2018: 464). Initial steps have been taken, principally along the lines of climate disclosure, together with stronger regulatory intervention (Campiglio et al., 2018: 464, tbl.2). The Bank of England, for example, has been outspoken on climate risk and the financial sector (Bank of England, n.d. d). In a speech to Lloyds of London in September 2015, Governor Mark Carney stated 'that the catastrophic impacts of climate change will be felt beyond the traditional horizons of most actors—imposing a cost on future generations that the current generation has no direct incentive to fix' (Carney, 2015). Carney has warned that the financial sector should do more to disclose and address climate risks, and, to this end, has signalled that all financial institutions regulated by the Bank of England will be subjected to greater climate disclosure (Partington, 2018).

The European Systemic Risk Board report into transitioning to a low-carbon economy warned that banks exposed to fossil fuel assets could face systemic risks (European Systemic Risk Board, 2016). As such, it suggests that 'policymakers could aim for enhanced disclosure of the carbon intensity of non-financial firms', which would then allow for stress testing of the related exposure of financial firms 'under the adverse scenario of a late and sudden transition' (European Systemic Risk Board, 2016: 2).

In September 2015, the Swiss Federal Office for the Environment published the Carbon Risks for the Swiss Financial Centre report, recommending that investors and policymakers, including their investment funds, should measure climate risks, stress test their portfolios, and report climate impacts to stakeholders (Oehri et al., 2015). Further, the European Commission in Directive 2014/95/EU suggests that all large public interest entities, including banks and insurers, should disclose in their annual reporting 'relevant and useful information ... on [their] policies, outcomes and risks' relating to a number of issues, including environmental matters (European Commission, 2017). In practice, this extends to climate change and carbon risk; however, at this point, it is not a legal requirement.

In one international jurisdiction, action beyond simple disclosure, that is, actual divestment from fossil fuels, is at least being contemplated, albeit in a tentative form. In particular, the California Insurance Commissioner issued a clear statement in January 2016 to all insurers operating in California to sell their thermal coal investments (California Department of Insurance, 2016). While this is expressed as a voluntary initiative, the fact that the 'request' comes from a prominent financial regulator carries with it a degree of gravitas and an expectation that mandatory intervention may follow.

To date, however, few prudential regulators have progressed beyond jawboning to actually implementing mandatory carbon disclosure. So, for the most part, their actions are simply a public exhortation, dependent on a form of self-regulatory voluntarism on the part of the financial sector. In this way, they are effectively stepping outside their conventional hierarchical role to work alongside a network of non-state governance actors. And, importantly, the very public stance taken by these regulators has the potential to influence not only financial companies, but also embolden and strengthen the hand of others, namely non-state actors, in pressing for stronger climate action across the financial sector.

There are also interesting international developments whereby financial companies themselves are publicly urging governments to take stronger climate policy action. This is an integral part of the Institutional Investors

Group on Climate Change's core mission statement,[20] and other financial industry groups have taken a similar stance. For example, insurance companies in the United Kingdom, recently responded to a report by the PRA, entitled *The Impact of Climate Change on the UK Insurance Sector* (Prudential Regulatory Authority, 2015). In supporting the report's findings, 15 senior insurance executives published an open letter calling for much stronger action on climate change by governments (Cambridge Institute for Sustainability Leadership, 2015). Climate advocacy by the financial sector, arguably, is a reversal of traditional hierarchical governance where national governments pressure industry actors to take action on a particular issue. Instead, elements of the financial sector, in the face of government inaction, are left to assume a climate leadership role.

Financial companies may adopt three principal forms of voluntarism. First, they may commit to public disclosure of their fossil fuel and renewable energy investments and activities. This means that third parties can track their climate performance and publicly hold them accountable for any shortcomings. Second, they may publicly commit themselves to reducing their lending to and investment in fossil fuels assets and projects, and, simultaneously, commit themselves to increase lending to and investments in clean energy. Third, they may make public statements in support of stronger climate change policies and actions, particularly those that relate specifically to the financial sector itself. Further, these forms of voluntary industry leadership may be pursued through a variety of collective or collaborative efforts.

In addition to collective and collaborative activities by the financial sector, individual financial companies may commit to acting to reduce their carbon footprint (and increase renewable energy investments). According to Chris Geczy of the Wharton Wealth Management Initiative, investors worldwide are paying attention to emerging evidence that sustainable investing, such as replacing fossil fuel investments with clean energy, does not lead to lower investment returns: 'It's not a question of whether to adopt a sustainable investment strategy ... but how to adopt and how much' (Morgan Stanley, 2015). In particular, those who act decisively and early, with a deliberate analysis of their investments' exposure to climate risk, are likely to see the greatest benefit from changes in patterns of investment in sectors most exposed to climate change. Accordingly, financial companies that voluntarily reduce their carbon footprint may do so for strategic, opportunistic, or ethical/value-driven reasons.

APRA, like many of its international counterparts, is becoming more active in the climate finance space, albeit from a very low base. This is despite (or perhaps because of) a climate policy vacuum on the part of Australia's national government. The innovation here, however, is not the development of novel environmental governance approaches or regulatory instruments. On the contrary, in this regard, APRA, and its international equivalents, are taking the well-trodden path of voluntarism, informational, and process-based regulation, with an unrealised potential to adopt more robust regulatory interventions that include, in particular, enforceable performance-based standards. Instead, the innovation is the engagement of a traditional financial regulator, in this case APRA, in the climate governance of a sector of the economy that has received little or no regulatory attention in terms of its climate risk or performance. While this might be viewed as a welcome development in the wider context of transitioning to a low-carbon economy, these initial steps are very tentative indeed. Consequently, a much more comprehensive and robust regulatory response will be required by prudential regulators, such as APRA, if the financial sector is to effectively contribute to this massive and urgent task.

Notes

1. The term climate finance is used henceforth as shorthand for efforts to encourage finance sector actors to accelerate the transition to a low-carbon economy by reducing their exposures to fossil fuel assets and investing in or increasing their lending to clean energy projects and production.
2. See United Nations Climate Change Global Business Community Comes to Paris with Solutions for Taking on the Climate Challenge Across the Board [Press Release] 8 December 2015 (on file with author).
3. Ancillary financial actors, as the term is used here, refers to financial actors without a direct financial stake.
4. See http://www.gtm.apra.gov.au/AboutAPRA/Pages/Default.aspx [https://perma.cc/UD9E-ERUP].
5. See http://www.osfi-bsif.gc.ca/Eng/osfi-bsif/Pages/default.aspx [https://perma.cc/H6Q3-33CM].
6. See https://www.fma.govt.nz/about-us/ [https://perma.cc/ 8GLT-NLXK].
7. See http://www.fsb.org/about/ [https://perma.cc/J5H3-FS6J].
8. See http://www.fsb.org/history-of-the-fsb/ [https:// perma.cc/2TXH-GAFP].
9. 'The death-spiral thesis runs thusly. Subsidies and falling technology costs are making distributed solar power—panels on roofs, essentially—cost-competitive with retail electricity prices in places like the southwestern US. As more people switch to solar, utilities sell less electricity to those customers'.
10. 'Stranded assets are assets that suffer from an unexpected loss in value due to unanticipated changes in regulations, the physical environment, social norms or technology. One example of a stranded asset would be a coal-fired power plant that can no longer be operated due to stricter energy and emissions efficiency criteria'.
11. 'Using BNEF's model, we'll cross the oil-crash benchmark of 2 million barrels a few years later—in 2028'.
12. Yeates reporting comments made by Geoff Summerhayes, APRA executive board member.
13. A related area of company liability relates to utility companies, such as the electric companies, that are being held responsible for increasing wildfires sparked by equipment failures, see e.g., Penn and Eavis, 2018).
14. See 'Jawboning' in https://www.definitions.net/definition/jawboning [https://perma.cc/GDJ6-WLXY] ("'Jawboning" or "moral suasion" in economics and politics is an unofficial technique of public and private discussions and arm-twisting, which may work by the implicit threat of future government regulation').

15. See, e.g., https://www.marketforces.org.au/about-us/# [https://perma.cc/5KB3-UPZ6].
16. See https://www.marketforces.org.au/about-us/# [https://perma.cc/5KB3-UPZ6].
17. See https://www.marketforces.org.au/about-us/# [https://perma.cc/5KB3-UPZ6].
18. See https://www.banktrack.org/page/about_banktrack [https://perma.cc/BA5Y-5TFH].
19. See https://www.carbontracker.org/about/ [https://perma.cc/ JQ5Q-2CPX].
20. See http://www.iigcc.org/ about-us [https://perma.cc/G34J-VCUE].

References

Allianz Climate and Energy Monitor. (2017). Deep Dive—What Do Current Policy Developments in China, India and the US Mean for Investing in Renewables? Available at: https://newclimate.org/wp-content/uploads/2017/04/allianz-climate-and-energy-monitor-deep-dive -2017.pdf [https://perma.cc/4HVN-9UHQ].

Arabella Advisors. (2018). *The Global Fossil Fuel Divestment and Clean Energy Investment Movement*. Washington DC: Arabella Advisors. Available at: https://www.arabellaadvisors.com/wp-content/uploads/2018/09/Global-Divestment-Report-2018.pdf. [https://perma.cc/YR6M-R7DL].

Austen, Ian. (2017). Canada's Strategy on Climate Change: Work with American States. *New York Times*, 7 June. Available at: https://www.nytimes.com/2017/06/07/world/canada/canadas-strategy-on-climate-change-work-with-american-states.html [https://perma.cc/2MKC-5PCH].

Ayling, Julie. (2017). A contest for legitimacy: The divestment movement and the fossil fuel industry. *Law & Policy*, 39, pp. 349–371.

Ayling, Julie and Gunningham, Neil. (2017). Non-State governance and climate policy: The fossil fuel divestment movement, *Climate Policy*, 17, pp. 131–149.

Bäckstrand, Karin, Kuyper, Jonathan, Linnér, Björn-Ola and Lövbrand, Eva. (2017). Non-state actors in global climate governance: From Copenhagen to Paris and beyond. *Environmental Policy*, 26, pp. 561–579.

Bank of England. (n.d. a). Prudential Regulation. [Website]. Available at: https://www.bankofengland.co.uk/prudential-regulation [https://perma.cc/MCU7-5WH6].

Bank of England. (n.d. b). Governance and Funding. [Website]. Available at: https://www.bankofengland.co.uk/about/governance-and-funding [https://perma.cc/ML2Y-45QJ].

Bank of England. (n.d. c). Which Firms Does the PRA Regulate? [Website]. Available at: https://www.bankofengland.co.uk/pru dential-regulation/authorisations/which-firms-does-the-pra-regulate [https://perma.cc/FV56-YP48].

Bank of England. (n.d. d). Climate Change: Why It Matters to the Bank of England. [Website]. Available at: https://www.bankofengland.co.uk/knowledgebank/climate-change-why-it-matters-to-the-bank-of-england [https://perma.cc/H6WU-8N5K].

BBC News. (2014). Australia Votes to Repeal Carbon Tax. *BBC News*, 17 July. Available at: https://www.bbc.com/news/world-asia-28339663 [https://perma.cc/NLC5-HT2K].

Bielenberg, Aaron, Kerlin, Mike, Oppenheim, Jeremy and Roberts, Melissa. (2016). *Financing Change: How to Mobilize Private-Sector Financing for Sustainable Infrastructure*. New York: McKinsey Center for Business and Development.

Available at: http://www.indiaenvironmentportal.org.in/files/file/Financing_change_
   How_to_mobilize_private-sector_financing_for_sustainable-_infrastructure.pdf
   [https://perma.cc/JXN9-PHBX].

Bloomberg NEF. (2017). *See This Is What the Demise of Oil Looks Like.* [Web article]
   31 May. New York: Bloomberg NEF. Available at: https://about.bnef.com/blog/this-
   is-what-the-demise-of-oil-looks-like/ [https://perma.cc/GMJ8-K2RN].

Brailsford, Louis, Stock, Andrew, Bourne, Greg and Stock, Petra. (2018). *Powering
   Progress: States Renewable Energy Race.* Potts Point: Climate Council. Available at:
   https://www.climatecouncil.org.au/wp-content/uploads/2018/10/States-renewable-
   energy-report-1.pdf [Accessed 15 June 2010].

Bravender, Robin and Heikkinen, Niina. (2017). Trump Picks Coal Lobbyist to
   Help Lead EPA. *Scientific American,* 6 October. Available at: https://www.
   scientificamerican.com/article/trump-picks-coal-lobbyist-to-help-lead-epa/
   [Accessed 15 June 2010].

Burns, Alexander and Johnson, Kirk. (2017). Poised for West Coast Dominance,
   Democrats Eye Grand Agenda. *New York Times,* 4 November. Available at: https://
   www.nytimes.com/2017/11/04/us/washington-state-west-politics-democrats.html
   [https://perma.cc/NK8D-9N7G].

California Department of Insurance. (2016). *California Insurance Commissioner Dave
   Jones Calls for Insurance Industry Divestment from Coal.* [Press Release] 25 January.
   Los Angeles: California Department of Insurance. Available at: http://www.insurance.
   ca.gov/0400-news/0100-press-releases/2016/statement010-16.cfm [https://perma.cc/
   6BCD-T5M6].

Cambridge Institute for Sustainability Leadership. (2015). *ClimateWise CEOs Call
   for More Action in Building Resilience to Climate Change.* [Press Release] 1 October.
   Cambridge: Cambridge Institute for Sustainability Leadership. Available at: https://
   www.cisl.   cam.ac.uk/business-action/sustainable-finance/climatewise/news/press-
   release-climatewise-ceos-call-for-more-action-in-building-resilience-to-climate-
   change-2013-1-october-2015 [https://perma.cc/G9Y N-VY3C].

Campiglio, Emanuele, Dafermos, Yannis, Monnin, Pierre, Ryan-Collins, Josh,
   Schotten, Guido and Tanaka, Misa et al. (2018). Climate change challenges for
   Central banks and financial regulators. *Nature Climate Change,* 8, pp. 462–468.

Canadell, Pep, Le Quéré, Corrine, Peters, Glen, Andrew, Robbie and Jackson,
   Rob. (2018). Carbon Emissions Will Reach 37 Billion Tonnes in 2018, a Record
   High. *Conversation,* 5 December. Available at: http://theconversation.com/
   carbon-emissions-will-reach-37-billion-tonnes-in-2018-a-record-high-108041
   [https://perma.cc/A56R-L3VX].

Carney, Mark. (2015). Breaking the Tragedy of the Horizon—Climate Change and
   FinancialStability.[SpeechoftheGovernoroftheBankofEnglandatLloyd'sofLondon
   on 29 September]. Available at: https://www. bankofengland.co.uk/-/media/boe/files/
   speech/2015/breaking-the-tragedy-of-the-horizon-climate-change-and-financial-
   stability.pdf?la=en&hash=7C67E785651862457D99511147C7424FF5EA0C1A
   [https://perma.cc/XV3L-VXMJ].

Carney, Mark. (2018). A Transition in Thinking and Action. [Speech of the Governor
   of the Bank of England at the International Climate Risk Conference for Supervisors
   at De Nederlandsche Bank, Amsterdam on 6 April]. Available at: https://www.
   bankofengland.co.uk/-/media/boe/files/speech/2018/a-transition-in-thinking-
   and-action-speech-by-mark-carney.pdf?la=en&hash=82F57A11AD2FAF-
   D4E822C3B3F 7E19BA23E98BF67 [https://perma.cc/YR8Q-EQ3L].

Carrington, Damian. (2015). Bank of England Warns of Huge Financial Risk from Fossil Fuel Investments. *Guardian*, 3 March. Available at: https://www.theguardian.com/environment/2015/mar/03/bank-of-england-warns-of-financial-risk-from-fossil-fuel-investments [https://perma.cc/J7A4-DAKV].

Cash, Daniel. (2018). Sustainable finance ratings as the latest symptom of 'rating addiction'. *Journal for Sustainable Finance & Investment*, 8(3), pp. 242–258.

Chalmers, Stephanie, Janda, Michael, Robertson, Andrew and Jasper, Clint. (2018). Banking Royal Commission Key Findings from Kenneth Hayne's Interim Report. *Australian Broadcasting Corp. News*, 28 September. Available at: https://www.abc.net.au/news/2018-09-28/bank-royal-commission-kenneth-hayne-key-findings/10317752 [Accessed 5 November 2020].

Chiacu, Doina and Volcovici, Valerie. (2017). EPA Chief Pruitt Refuses to Link CO_2 and Global Warming. *Scientific American*, 10 March. Available at: https://www.scientificamerican.com/article/epa-chief-pruitt-refuses-to-link-co2-and-global-warming/ [https://perma.cc/B4C8-998F].

Chu, Ben. (2018). Green Technology to Burst 'Carbon Bubble' in Catastrophe for Fossil-Fuel Economies, New Research Predicts. *Independent*, 4 June. Available at: https://www.independent.co.uk/news/business/news/carbon-bubble-global-wealth-mass-unemployment-fossil-fuels-climate-change- research-a8382631.html [https://perma.cc/8FTN-4JWS].

Climate Action Network Europe. (2015). *Fossil Fuel Subsidies: Barriers to Stronger Climate Action.* [Policy Brief] December. Available at: http://www.caneurope.org/docman/fossil-fuel-subsidies-1/2814-briefing-on-fossil-fuel-subsidies-and-mitigation-potenital/file [https://perma.cc/J3VC-LHQM].

Climate Council. (2017). *Renewables Ready: States Leading the Charge.* Potts Point: Climate Council, pp. 15–17. Available at: https://www.climatecouncil.org.au/uploads/9a3734e82574546679510bdc99d57847.pdf [https://perma.cc/779F-76UH].

Coglianese, Cary, ed. (2016). *Achieving Regulatory Excellence.* Ebook.

Commonwealth of Australia (2019). Royal Commission into Misconduct in the Banking, Superannuation and Financial Services Industry (Volume 1). Available at: https://www.royalcommission.gov.au/sites/default/files/2019-02/fsrc-volume-1-final-report.pdf [Accessed 5 November 2020].

Cook, John, Oreskes, Naomi, Doran, Peter T., Anderegg, William R. L., Verheggen, Bart, Maibach, Ed W., Carlton, J. Stuart, Lewandowsky, Stephan, Skuce, Andrew G., Green, Sarah A., Nuccitelli, Dana, Jacobs, Peter, Richardson, Mark, Winkler, Bärbel, Painting, Rob and Rice, Ken. (2016). Consensus on consensus: A synthesis of consensus estimates on human-caused global warming. *Environmental Research Letters*, 11(1), pp. 1–5.

Cullen, Catherine. (2016). Justin Trudeau Signs Paris Climate Treaty at UN, Vows to Harness Renewable Energy. *CBC News*, 22 April. Available at: http://www.cbc.ca/news/politics/paris-agreement-trudeau-sign-1.3547822 [https://perma.cc/UAL8-QGML].

Davenport, Coral. (2018). How Andrew Wheeler, the New Acting E.P.A. Chief, Differs from Scott Pruitt. *New York Times*, 5 July. Available at: https://www.nytimes.com/2018/07/05/climate/wheeler-epa-pruitt.htm [https://perma.cc/HG8X-X2B9].

Debelle, Guy. (2019). Climate Change and the Economy. [Speech by the Deputy Governor of the Reserve Bank of Australia on 12 March]. Available at: https://www.rba.gov.au/speeches/2019/sp-dg-2019-03-12.html [Accessed 12 June 2020].

Denning, Liam. (2013). Utilities' Lights Flicker. *Wall Street Journal*. Available at: https://www.wsj.com/articles/lights-flicker-for-utilities-1387752421 [Accessed 5 November 2020].

Dennis, Brady. (2018). Trump Budget Seeks 23 Percent Cut at EPA, Eliminating Dozens of Programs. *New York Times*, 12 February. Available at: https://www.washingtonpost.com/news/energy-environment/wp/2018/02/12/trump-budget-seeks-23-percent-cut-at-epa-would-eliminate-dozens-of-programs/?utm_term=.9df3c8926e77 [https://perma.cc/GS8K-RBL8].

Dennis, Brady and Mooney, Chris. (2017). Trump Taps Climate Skeptic for Top White House Environmental Post. *Washington Post*, 13 October. Available at: https://www.washingtonpost.com/news/energy-environment/wp/2017/10/13/trump-taps-climate-skeptic-for-top-white-house-environmental-post/?utm_term=.6b39899c1258 [https://perma.cc/X5 RG-H29X].

Elliot, Larry. (2015). Michael Bloomberg to Head Global Taskforce on Climate Change. *Guardian,* 4 December. Available at: https://www.theguardian.com/environment/2015/dec/04/mark-carney-unveils-global-taskforce-to-educate-business-on-climate-change [https://perma.cc/DW6R-PM4H].

European Commission. (2017). *Guidelines on Disclosure of Non-Financial Information.* [ress Release] 26 June. Brussels: European Commission. Available at: http://europa.eu/rapid/press-release_MEMO-17-1703_en.htm?locale=en [https://perma.cc/HG6B-NQS9].

Financial Stability Board. (n.d.). Climate-Related Financial Disclosures. Available at: http://www.fsb.org/work-of-the-fsb/policy-development/additional-policy-areas/climate-related-financial-disclosures/ [https://perma.cc/9DTZ-S7V4].

Gan, Nector. (2018). Will China's Carbon Trading Scheme Work Without an Emissions Cap? *South China Morning Post,* 3 January. Available at: http://www.scmp.com/news/china/policies-politics/article/2125896/big-black-hole-chinas-carbon-market-ambitions [https://perma.cc/HYQ4-YAZ2].

German Federal Ministry of Finance. (2016). Climate Change and Financial Markets. [website article] 20 September. Available at: https://www.bundesfinanzministerium.de/Content/EN/Standardartikel/Topics/Financial_markets/Articles/2016-09-19-Climate-change-and-financial-markets.html [https://perma.cc/W5KU-2PDB].

Gunningham, Neil. (2017). Divestment, nonstate governance, and climate change. *Law & Policy*, 39, pp. 309–324.

Gunningham, Neil and Grabosky, Peter. (1998). *Smart Regulation: Designing Environmental Policy*. Oxford: Calderon Press.

Gupta, Joyeeta. (2016). The Paris Climate Change Agreement: China and India. *Climate-L.*, 6, pp. 171–181.

Hayne, Kenneth. (2018). *Interim Report: Royal Commission into Misconduct in the Banking, Superannuation and Financial Services Industry*. Melbourne: Commonwealth of Australia. Available at: https://financialservices.royalcommission.gov.au/Documents/interim-report/interim-report-volume-1.pdf [https://perma.cc/N2QU-LWJ7].

Henley, Benjamin J. and King, Andrew D. (2017). Trajectories toward the 1.5°C Paris target: Modulation by the interdecadal pacific oscillation. *Geophysical Research Letters*, 44, pp. 4256–4262.

Holder, Michael. (2016). Growth in Batteries and EVs 'Resoundingly Credit Negative' for Oil Sector. *Business Green*, 19 October. Available at: https://www.businessgreen.com/bg/news/2474596/growth-in-batteries-and-evs-resoundingly-credit-negative-for-oil-sector [https://perma.cc/JQ9Y-TDP2] (citing Fitch Ratings. (2016). Batteries Could Be Key Credit Disruptor; Oil Most Exposed. [Press release] 18 October. Available at: https://www.fitchratings.com/site/pr/1013282 [https://perma.cc/VP7G-KT8B]).

Hutchens, Gareth. (2016). Malcolm Turnbull Rules Out Carbon Tax or Emissions Trading. *Guardian*, 6 December. Available at: https://www.theguardian.com/environment/2016/dec/07/australia-malcolm-turnbull-rules-out-carbon-tax-or-emissions-trading [https://perma.cc/J6ZT-RV75].

Hutchens, Gareth. (2017a). APRA Says Companies Must Factor Climate Risks into Business Outlook. *Guardian*, 17 February. Available at: https://www.theguardian.com/science/2017/feb/17/apra-says-companies-must-factor-climate-risks-into-business-outlook [https://perma.cc/WH3X-M37C].

Hutchens, Gareth. (2017b). Global Banks Reduce Lending to Dirtiest Fossil Fuel Companies by Billions in 2016. *Guardian*, 21 June. Available at: https://www.theguardian.com/environment/2017/jun/21/global-banks-reduce-lending-to-dirtiest-fossil-fuel-companies-by-billions-in-2016 [https://perma. cc/NUJ4-N2WR].

Hutley, Noel and Hartford-Davis, Sebastian. (2016). Climate Change and Directors' Duties. [Memorandum to the Centre for Policy Development & Future Business Council of 7 October]. Available at: http://cpd.org.au/wp-content/uploads/2016/10/Legal-Opinion-on-Climate-Change-and-Directors-Duties.pdf [https://perma.cc/63KJ-VTN8].

Iacobucci, Edward M. (2015). Corporate fiduciary duties and prudential regulation of financial institutions. *Theoretical Inquiries in Law*, 16, pp. 183–210.

International Institute for Sustainable Development. (2017). Members Call for WTO to Play a Central Role in Ending Inefficient Fossil Fuel Subsidies. [Press Release] 11 December. Available at: http://www.iisd.org/media/members-call-wto-play-central-role-ending-inefficient-fossil-fuel-subsidies [https://perma.cc/W7WS-VF9N].

Irvine, Jessica. (2016). Company Directors to Face Penalties for Ignoring Climate Change. *Sydney Morning Herald*, 31 October. Available at: https://www.smh.com.au/business/company-directors-to-face-penalties-for-ignoring-climate-change-20161030-gsdwha.html [https://perma. cc/4GYZ-KAAZ].

Jackson, Allison. (2015). Australia Just Approved One of the Biggest Coal Mines in the World. *PRI*, 15 October. Available at: https://www.pri.org/stories/2015-10-15/australia-just-approved-one-biggest-coal-mines-world [https://perma.cc/6S3D-Q5CE].

Karkkainen, Bradley C. (2001). Information as environmental regulation: TRI and performance benchmarking—Precursor to a new paradigm? *Georgetown Law Journal*, 89, pp. 257–370.

Keating, Dave. (2017). COP23: Merkel and Macron Hail Europe's Climate Leadership, Acknowledge Shortcomings. *Deutsche Welle*, 15 November. Available at: https://www.dw.com/en/cop23-merkel-and-macron-hail-europes-climate-leadership-acknowledge-shortcomings/a-41395906 [https://perma.cc/9WEU-ZBWE].

Ker, Peter. (2017). Canavan Slams Westpac as 'Wimps' over Climate Move. *Australian Financial Review*, 28 April.

King, Ed. (2016). Bloomberg Climate Risk Initiative Targets Secret Polluters. *Climate Home News,* 2 September. Available at: http://www.climatechangenews.com/2016/02/09/bloomberg-climate-risk-initiative-targets-secret-polluters/ [https://perma.cc/2VR5-54P9].

Latimer, Cole and Wright, Shane. (2018). Federal Government Facing Energy Uproar as NSW Distances Itself from Canberra. *Age*, 19 December. Available at: https://www.theage.com. au/politics/federal/federal-government-facing-energy-uproar-as-nsw-distances-itself-from-canberra-20181219-p50n9g.html [https://perma.cc/ZU6L-QU36].

Lloyd, Graham. (2018). The Great Green Gamble. *The Weekend Australian*, 9 January. Available at: https://www.theaustralian.com.au/news/inquirer/carbon-trading-is-the-great-green-gamble/news-story/8a0b999fb59c322d4bcd0c11a28f0d81 [Accessed 12 June 2020].

MacDonald-Smith, Angela. (2016). Fossil Fuel Loans Top Renewables. *Australian Financial Review*, 4 August.

Maimbo, Samuel Munzele and Zadek, Simon (2017). United Nations Environment Programme & World Bank Roadmap for a Sustainable Financial System. Available at: http://unepinquiry.org/wp-content/uploads/2017/11/Roadmap_for_a_Sustainable_Financial_System.pdf [https://perma.cc/HH B4-8G45].

Market Forces. (2016). *Fueling the Fire 2016: How the Big Banks Are Using Our Money to Support the Dirty Fossil Fuel Industry*. Victoria: Market Forces. Available at: https://www.marketforces.org.au/info/fuelingthefire/ [https://perma.cc/D7XE-H95F].

Market Forces. (2017a). *Coal Funding Dries Up but $17Bn Funneled to Fossil Fuels by 'Big Four' Banks Since Paris Agreement*. [Press Release] 24 July. Victoria: Market Forces. Available at: https://www.marketforces.org. au/media-release-coal-funding-dries-up-but-17bn-funneled-to-fossil-fuels-by-big-four-banks-since-paris-agreement/ [https://perma.cc/7M92-9KCW].

Market Forces. (2017b). *NAB's Coal Mining Exclusion Raises the Bar for Its Competitors*. [Press Release] 14 December. Victoria: Market Forces. Available at: https://www.marketforces.org.au/media-release-nabs-coal-mining-exclusion-raises-the-bar-for-its-competitors/ [https://perma.cc/3LH3-YEP2].

McKibben, Bill. (2017). The New Battle Plan for the Planet's Climate Crisis. *Rolling Stone*, 24 January. Available at: http://www.rollingstone.com/politics/features/bill-mckibbens-bat tle-plan-for-the-planets-climate-crisis-w462680 [https://perma.cc/SF8K-J75C].

McKie, Robin. (2016). Scientists Warn World Will Miss Key Climate Target. *Guardian*, 6 August. Available at: https://www.theguardian.com/science/2016/aug/06/global-warming-target-miss-scientists-warn [https://perma.cc/U2HU-QCPU].

Miller, Alan S. and Swann, Stacey A. (2016). Climate change and the financial sector: A time of risk and opportunity. *Georgetown International Environmental Law Review*, 29, pp. 69–110.

Morgan Stanley. (2015). The Investor's Guide to Climate Change. [Website article] 11 December. Available at: http://www. morganstanley.com/articles/the-investor-s-guide-to-climate-change [https://perma.cc/9UB6-YDU7].

Mori, Simone. (2017). No ETS Deal Means It Can Still Be Strengthened. *EU Observer*, 2 November. Available at: https://euobserver .com/stakeholders/139722 [https://perma.cc/C5UV-C47S].

Mountford, Helen. (2017). 3 Steps to a Zero-Carbon Future. World Resources Institute. [Blog] 14 November. Available at: http://www.wri.org/blog/2017/11/3-steps-zero-carbon-future [https://perma.cc/6GBN-L4LF].

Murphy, Katharine. (2017). Scott Morrison Brings Coal to Question Time: What Fresh Idiocy Is This? *Guardian*, 9 February. Available at: https://www.theguardian.com/australia-news/2017/feb/09/scott-morrison-brings-coal-to-question-time-what-fresh-idiocy-is-this [perma.cc/GQN6-EF77].

Murphy, Katharine. (2018). Sorry, Matt Canavan, No One Believes Coal Magic Means Everyone Wins. *Guardian*, 30 March. Available at: https://www.theguardian.com/australia-news/2018/mar/31/sorry-matt-canavan-no-one-believes-coal-magic-means-everyone-wins [https://perma.cc/Z6X7-2FCQ].

National Australian Bank. (2017a). *Update on Financing of New Thermal Coal Mining Projects.* [Press Release] 14 December. Melbourne: National Australian Bank. Available at: http://news.nab.com.au/update-on-financing-of-new-thermal-coal-mining-projects/ [https://perma.cc/LX3P-XXCA].

National Australian Bank. (2017b). *NAB Creates a New Way to Invest in Renewable Energy.* [Press Release] 14 December. Melbourne: National Australian Bank. Available at: http://news.nab.com.au/nab-creates-a-new-way-to-invest-in-renewable-energy/ [https://perma.cc/5GX4-47SP].

Nerem, R. S., Beckley, B. D., Fasullo, J. T., Hamlington, B. D., Masters, D. and Michum, G. T. (2018). Climate-change—Driven accelerated sea-level rise detected in the altimeter era. *Proceedings of the National Academy of Sciences USA*, 115, pp. 2022–2025.

Oehri, Oliver, Horster, Maximilian, Dreher, Christoph, Fogde, Fredrik, Frank, Alexandra, Jochum, Christop and Lutz, Viola. (2015). *Carbon Risks for the Swiss Financial Centre: Summary.* Vaduz, Lichtenstein: Centre for Social & Sustainable Products. Available at: https://yoursri.com/media-new/down load/en_ zusammenfassung_schlussbericht_final_29092015-eng_spg.pdf [https://perma. cc/7EAK-96PS].

Parker, Christine. (2007). Meta-regulation: Legal accountability for corporate social responsibility. In: Doreen McBarnet, Aurora Vioculescu and Tom Campbell, eds., *The New Corporate Accountability: Corporate Social Responsibility and the Law.* Cambridge: Cambridge University Press, pp. 207–240.

Partington, Richard. (2018). Mark Carney Warns of Climate Change Threat to Financial System. *Guardian*, 6 April. Available at: https://www.theguardian.com/business/2018/apr/06/ mark-carney-warns-climate-change-threat-financial-system [https://perma.cc/AL8N-ZY3T].

Penn, Ivan and Eavis, Peter. (2018). California Utility Customers May Be on Hook for Billions in Wildfire Damage. *New York Times*, 14 November. Available at: https://www.nytimes.com/2018/11/14/business/energy-environment/california-fire-utilities.html [https://perma.cc/BKP4-T83L].

Prudential Regulatory Authority. (2015). *The Impact of Climate Change on the UK Insurance Sector: A Climate Change Adaptation Report.* London: Prudential Regulation Authority. Available at: https://www.bankofengland.co.uk/-/media/boe/files/prudential-regulation/publication/impact-of-climate-change-on-the-uk-insurance-sector.pdf?la=en&hash=EF9F E0FF9AEC940A2BA722324902FFBA49A5A29A [https://perma.cc/QJC5-XUY6].

Raftery, Adrian E., Zimmer, A., Frierson, Dargan M. W., Startz, R. and Liu, P. (2017). Less than 2 °C warming by 2100 unlikely. *Nature Climate Change*, 7, pp. 637–641.

Randall, Tom. (2016). *Here's How Electric Cars Will Cause the Next Oil Crisis.* [Web article] 25 February. New York: Bloomberg. Available at: https://www.bloomberg.com/features/2016-ev-oil-crisis/ [https://perma.cc/6WFK-MASN].

Respaut, Robin. (2016). California Surpasses France as World's Sixth-Largest Economy. *Reuters*, 7 June. Available at: https://www.reuters.com/article/us-california-economy-idUSKCN0Z32 K2 [https://perma.cc/P9LW-WDWH].

Robins, Nick. (2016). How Paris Became the Capital of Climate Finance. *UN Environmental Programme, Working Paper No. 16/06.* Available at: http://unepinquiry.org/wp-content/uploads/2016/04/ How_Paris_Became_the_Capital_of_Climate_Finance.pdf [https://perma.cc/8A4E-SEGB].

Romm, Joe. (2016). Electric Car Revolution May Drive Oil 'Investor Death Spiral'. *ThinkProgress*, 21 October. Available at: https://thinkprogress.org/oil-investor-death-spiral-35773e131250/ [https://perma.cc/VD96-PPLB] (citing Fitch as the source of the information).

SBS News. (2017). NAB Will No Longer Back New Coal Projects. *SBS News*, 14 December. Available at: https://www.sbs.com.au/news/nab-will-no-longer-back-new-coal-projects [https://perma.cc/3AC5-5REC].

Scott, Mike. (2018). The Financial Sector Can Do More to Tackle Climate Change. It's Time to Step Up. *Forbes*, 12 September. Available at: https://www.forbes.com/sites/mikescott/2018/09/12/the-financial-sector-can-do-more-to-tackle-climate-change-its-time-to-step-up/#40c642893934 [https://perma.cc/W85L-UVU6].

Shankleman, Jessica. (2014). Mark Carney: Most Fossil Fuel Reserves Can't Be Burned. *Guardian*, 13 October. Available at: https://www.theguardian.com/environment/2014/oct/13/mark-carney-fossil-fuel-reserves-burned-carbon-bubble [https://perma.cc/MC7T-WGRD].

Slezak, Michael. (2017). Banks Warned of 'Regulatory Action' as Climate Change Bites Global Economy. *Guardian*, 29 November. Available at: https://www.theguardian.com/australia-news/2017/nov/29/ banks-warned-of-regulatory-action-as-climate-change-bites-global-economy [https://perma.cc/MV W9-AHAC].

Steer, Andrew. (2013). Business and Government Must Come Together for Strong Climate Action. *World Resources Institute*. [Blog] 20 November. Available at: http://www.wri.org/blog/2013/11/business-and-government-must-come-together-strong-climate-action [https://perma.cc/FGZ8-4G5Z].

Summerhayes, Geoff. (2017a). Australia's New Horizon: Climate Change Challenges and Prudential Risk. [Speech of an Executive Member of the Australian Prudential Regulation Authority at the Insurance Council of Australia Annual Forum] 17 February. Available at: https://www.apra.gov.au/media-centre/speeches/australias-new-horizon-climate-change-challenges-and-prudential-risk [https://perma.cc/R99X-Q9AS].

Summerhayes, Geoff. (2017b). The Weight of Money: A Business Case for Climate Risk Resilience. [Speech of an Executive Member of the Australian Prudential Regulation Authority at the Centre for Policy Development] 29 November. Available at https://www.apra.gov.au/media-centre/speeches/weight-money-business-case-climate-risk-resilience [https://perma.cc/DEE8-EFVH].

Surowiecki, James. (2008). Stop the Jawboning—It's Not Working. *New Yorker*, 27 October. Available at: https://www.newyorker.com/business/james-surowiecki/stop-the-jawboningits-not-working [https://perma.cc/VQK2-PQ8M].

Taylor, Jonathan. (2017). Increasing and Improving Climate Finance: The Role of Non-state Actors. [Speech by the Vice-President of the European Investment Bank at a European Parliament Side Event at COP23 on 15 November]. Available at: https://www.eib.org/attachments/press/cop23_increasing_and_improving_climate_finance_vptaylor_15112017.pdf [Accessed 20 June 2020].

United Nations (2015). Available at: https://unfccc.int/files/essential_background/convention/application/pdf/english_paris_agreement.pdf [Accessed 5 November 2020].

Uribe, Alice. (2017). APRA Doubles Down on Climate Change. *Australian Financial Review*, 1 December.

Urpelainen, Johannes. (2017). Trump's Withdrawal from the Paris Agreement Means Other Countries Will Spend Less to Fight Climate Change. *Washington Post*, 21 November. Available at: https://www.washingtonpost.com/news/monkey-cage/

wp/2017/11/21/trumps-noncooperation-threate ns-climate-finance-under-the-paris-agreement/?noredirect=on&utm_term=.106cc2d761d2 [https://perma.cc/G2BP-HTHY].

Vandenbergh, Michael and Gilligan, Jonathan M. (2017). Government Action Isn't Enough for Climate Change: The Private Sector Can Cut Billions of Tons of Carbon. *Conversation*, 21 June. Available at: https://theconversation.com/government-action-isnt-enough-for-climate-change-the-private-sector-can-cut-billions-of-tons-of-carbon-79728 [https://perma.cc/42BD-XKTZ].

Viser, Matt. (2018). 'Just a Lot of Alarmism': Trump's Skepticisim of Climate Science Is Echoed Across GOP. *Washington Post*, 2 December. Available at: https://www.washingtonpost.com/politics/just-a-lot-of-alarmism-trumps-skepticism-of-climate-science-is-echoed-across-gop/2018/12/02/f6ee9ca6-f4de-11e 8-bc79-68604ed88993_story.html?utm_term=.f6534d488c25 [https://perma.cc/6YL7-MZUA].

Watts, Jonathan. (2018). Brazil Reneges on Hosting UN Climate Talks Under Bolsonaro Presidency. *Guardian*, 27 November. Available at: https://www.theguardian.com/world/2018/nov/28/brazil-reneges-on-hosting-un-climate-talks-under-bolsonaro-presidency [https://perma.cc/46T3-7XXC].

Westpac Banking Corp. (2017). *Westpac Launches Updated Climate Change Action Plan*. [Press Release] 28 April. Sydney: Westpac Banking Corp. Available at: https://www.westpac.com.au/about-westpac/media/media-releases/ 2017/28-april/ [https://perma.cc/X597-ZVPD].

Wilde, Simon. (2017). Green Finance? Why Global Banks Are Pledging Billions to Fight Climate Change. *Conversation*, 10 November. Available at: https://theconversation.com/green-finance-why-global-banks-are-pledging-billions-to-fight-climate-change-87273 [https://perma.cc/GZ 6M-DPG3].

Williams, Ruth. (2018). 'There's Nowhere to Hide': Companies Warned on Climate Risks. *Sydney Morning Herald*, 20 January. Available at: https://www.smh.com.au/business/markets/theres-nowhere-to-hide-companies-warned-on-climate-risks-20180112-h0hljq.html [https://perma.cc/PJ44-ZHN2].

Yeates, Clancy. (2017). Climate Change A 'Material' Risk for the Financial System: APRA. *Sydney Morning Herald*, 17 February. Available at: https://www.smh.com.au/business/banking-and-finance/climate-change-a-material-risk-for-the-financial-system-apra-20170217-guffhm.html [https://perma.cc/Y23H-LGDE] (reporting comments made by Geoff Summerhayes, APRA executive board member).

Zhou, Naaman. (2017). Big Australian Banks Invest $7bn More in Fossil Fuels than Renewables, Says Report. *Guardian*, 5 March. Available at: https://www.theguardian.com/australia-news/2017/mar/06/ big-australian-banks-invest-7bn-more-in-fossil-fuels-than-renewables-says-report [https://perma.cc/UL8S-TRS9].

5 The contradictory roles of the insurance industry in the era of climate change

*Mathieu Charbonneau and Aaron Doyle**

Introduction

The insurance industry is a central institution in knowing and attempting to govern risk (Ericson, Doyle and Barry, 2003; Ericson and Doyle, 2004). Private insurers manage and distribute risks, and in doing so, also shape and distribute responsibilities for those risks (Abraham, 1986; Baker, 2002). Private insurers work in concert with the state in dividing and sharing responsibility for various risks. Far from being directed by neutral calculations of risk, the operations of insurers are inherently moral and political. Insurance arrangements are often themselves imbued with 'moral risk' (Ericson and Doyle, 2006) – that is, they may paradoxically encourage and facilitate risky behaviour, not only by insured parties, but also by insurers themselves.

Climate change is a key threat faced by the insurance industry. The increasing risks created by climate change, driven by emissions of carbon dioxide as the primary greenhouse gas and the implications of those risks for insurers, are huge and extremely complex. The insurance industry has been planning for, and dealing with, climate change risks for many years (Mills, 2005): indeed, long before global warming was a public issue, literature from Munich Reinsurance first warned about growing flood damage as a result of climate change. A Munich Re brochure on flood inundation noted way back in 1973:

> Investigations into the overall trend of claims experience are indispensable, and here climatic variations become most significant. Such investigations involve a study of thermodynamic processes such as, for example, the rising temperature of the earth's atmosphere (as a result of which glaciers and the polar caps recede ...). We wish to enlarge on this complex of problems in greater detail, especially as ... its

---

* The authors wish to thank Turo-Kimmo Lehtonen for past discussions, having greatly contributed to some of the ideas presented in this chapter.

conceivable impact on the long-range risk trend has hardly been examined to date.

(Munich Re 1973, quoted from Stahel, 2009: 321)

Fast-forward to 2020. As Forbes magazine noted in early 2020, 'Recently, global risk advisory Willis Towers Watson and the Society of Actuaries both named climate change the biggest risk to the industry' (Stone, 2020), although climate change's place as pre-eminent insurance risk has been temporarily superseded by the COVID-19 pandemic.

Climate change is, of course, generating or contributing to a wide range of increasingly severe insurance events, such as hurricanes, wildfires, hail, wind and ice storms, and floods, depending on geographical location (Lamond and Penning-Rowsell, 2014; CCIR, 2016). Climate change is also leading to new health issues, such as the spread of diseases (Wu et al., 2016), as, for example, malaria-carrying mosquitoes move into newly warmed regions.

This chapter presents an overview of how the insurance industry is responding to climate change based on a review of academic literature, industry reports and documents, trade publications, and media accounts. While our focus is global, we pay particular attention to examples from North America and Europe, where the insurance industry is concentrated. Insurance and other private and state risk management infrastructures are already facing gargantuan pressures due to increasing climate-related uncertainties. At the same time, these new climate uncertainties constitute the raw materials that private insurers capitalise on and climate risks also mean possible openings for profit. We outline the industry's roles in relation to climate change as compensator, resistor and mitigator, facilitator, and investor. The insurance industry always has an ambivalent relation to any risk – it thrives on providing insurance coverage of the risk, as long as the risk is manageable and relatively foreseeable, and insurers are not disastrously over-run by claims. As we will show, the insurance industry also contributes to, promotes, and profits from fossil fuel industries and anthropogenic climate change in a broad variety of ways, even as it provides coverage against the very same climate risks it is helping to create. We conclude by briefly exploring what members of the public and policy makers might do in promoting action on global warming, given the insurance industry's contradictory roles.

Financing climate change insurance risks

We begin with some necessary background about how the insurance industry may cope with the challenge of the growing scale of climate risks, as a context for understanding the industry's various roles in relation to climate change. The influential late German social theorist Ulrich Beck (1999) argued that we live in a 'world risk society', defined by new human-made risks, which are defining elements of what he called the current situation of a new phase of modern life, 'second modernity'. These risks, such as climate change, are driven by and are effects of advancing science and technology, and can only be apprehended and dealt with by science. For Beck, a defining property of these new risks was that they are of such complexity as to be 'incalculable' and 'uninsurable'. However, Beck did not empirically investigate the insurance industry in any detail, and underestimated the capacities and resourcefulness of private insurers in competitive marketplaces. Insurers will find ways to cover just about anything (Ericson and Doyle, 2004).

In contrast to Beck's vision, billionaire investor Warren Buffett stated in 2016, that '[as] a citizen, you may understandably find climate change keeping you up at nights. As a homeowner in a low-lying area, you may wish to consider moving. But when you are thinking only as a shareholder of a major insurer, climate change should not be on your list of worries', as Razmig Keucheyan (2018: 484) notes. Buffett's comments represent an alternative, optimistic perspective for the insurance industry in terms of the impact of climate change on the insurance business – that the industry can manage them and will find a way to turn a profit. This assumes, of course, that the industry will be able to finance rising claims from increasingly frequent and severe weather events (Keucheyan, 2018: 485).

The most basic type of market-based response, which private insurers have long used in managing major catastrophic events and situations, is reinsurance, whereby front-line insurers take on risks and, in turn, buy insurance themselves from larger back-up companies so that risks do not swamp the front-line insurers. The reinsurance industry, a vast, often behind-the-scenes international financial realm, backs up frontline primary insurers, who prepare for disasters that might overwhelm their financial capacity by transferring their risk exposure to reinsurance markets. One reason reinsurance is necessary is that climate change-induced catastrophes generate potential 'risk aggregation' or 'hyper-correlation' issues for insurers: that is, catastrophic risks that, because of their engulfing multidimensional nature, threaten to swamp front-line insurers who may be providing multiple types of insurance in affected geographical areas. In traditional insurance, insured risks must be independent in space and across different insurance markets to be manageably underwritten by insurers in order to avoid insurers being overwhelmed by a causally-related wave of claims in different types of insurance (see Freeman and Scott, 2005). Weather-related catastrophes, for example, a major hurricane like Katrina in 2005, can trigger massive claims over large geographical areas and across many insurance lines (e.g. life insurance, home insurance, car insurance, business insurance, etc.). Another example of a mammoth event demonstrating risk aggregation was 9/11: 'Claims from 9/11 on policies spanning property, aviation, liability, life assurance, business interruption and many more lines of cover totalled $40 bn, according to leading reinsurance group Munich Re'

(Jenkins, 2019). Veteran insurance journalist Patrick Jenkins wrote in 2019 in *The Financial Times* that 'climate change is the new 9/11 for insurance companies' (Jenkins, 2019). This is why reinsurance is crucial for climate risk coverage, since, in backing primary insurers exposed to disasters, it can cushion against the impact of risk aggregation on insurers' portfolios. Reinsurance increases the capacity of front-line insurance companies to cover very large-scale events and reduces the size of financial reserves they need to maintain.

Leigh Johnson (2015) has argued that reinsurers are not necessarily threatened by climate change: that, indeed, increasingly catastrophic losses due to climate change may represent helpful 'cyclical devaluations' for reinsurers, who face regular capital over-accumulation in soft market periods. Johnson argues that major catastrophes result in:

> revision of catastrophe models and re-estimation of exposed values, processes which absorb additional (re)insurance capital and provide technoscientific legitimacy for raising rates. Reframing climate change risk in terms of ecologically-sourced devaluation suggests that, rather than posing an immediate existential threat, in the short to medium term the uncertain impacts of global climate change might constitute a recurrent "catastrophic fix" for particular segments of financial capital. This highlights both the productivity of uncertainty about climate change impacts and the limits of presuming that the operations of the private insurance market can produce a built environment more adapted to climate change.
>
> (Johnson, 2015: 2503)

As Johnson's example suggests, insurance and reinsurance can have the paradoxical effect of supporting the status quo when the absence of insurance might force various forms of adaptation, including fighting climate change or mitigating its effects (see also O'Hare, White and Connelly, 2016). This is an example of 'moral risk', simply put, insurance encouraging risky behaviour by different parties in the insurance relationship (Ericson and Doyle, 2006).

In addition to reinsurance, another market-based response to climate risks at the disposal of the insurance industry is the financial transfer of catastrophic risks through insurance-linked securities (ILS). ILS, such as catastrophe bonds or 'cat bonds', are financial instruments allowing the securitisation of packaged catastrophic risks (see Keucheyan, 2018: 489–492). In recent years, the ILS market has become the main alternative to the reinsurance industry in the financial transfer of climate risks. Catastrophe bonds deliver a substantial investment return for the purchaser. However, if a catastrophe of a certain magnitude occurs, the bondholder forfeits some or all of the amount of the bond to the insured. Catastrophe bonds may be structured using parametric insurance, whereby an environmental index value, established by an independent scientific organisation, is used to trigger and determine insurance payouts. This can make the insurance simpler and cheaper to use and simplify and speed up the claims process as it avoids questions of causality and quantification of loss. One instance of parametric insurance was put in place in 2016 through the government of Mexico's 'sovereign cat bonds' program (see Keucheyan, 2018). The Mexican state issued catastrophic securities in order to attract private investors as a means to fund its environmental disaster policy. In 2016, Hurricane Patricia triggered the Mexican bond as it 'hit the west coast of the country. [...] if the hurricane exceeded a certain central pressure (measured in millibars), the investors would lose 50 per cent of the principal; if it exceeded a higher central pressure, they would lose 100 per cent.' (Keucheyan, 2018: 493).

More recently, however, major credit rating agency, Fitch Ratings, stated that it 'believes that, as well as the impacts of catastrophe losses, payment of those losses and some redemptions from investors as a result, the ILS market is also suffering from investor reluctance to allocate more funds as there is increasing nervousness regarding climate risks' (Evans, 2019). According to Etzion, Kypraios and Forgues (2019: 530), 'modeling which underlies catastrophe bonds is not demonstrably better than guesswork at predicting the financial consequences of extreme events. [...] market actors are under no illusions about the level of precision and accuracy provided by the models.' With the development of financial risk transfer mechanisms, (re)insurers might not feel directly incentivised to promote and contribute to the adaptation of buildings, infrastructures and the environment to climate change (Johnson, 2015). Financial market responses to climate risks could even 'put adaptation policies at the mercy of erratic behavior of financial markets' (Keucheyan, 2018: 497).

When environmental or other catastrophes potentially threaten insurers' solvency and outstrip available reinsurance, and for those many people who are uninsured, state institutions often act as insurers of last resort (see Ericson and Doyle, 2004). 'For every dollar of insured losses borne by insurers in Canada, three to four dollars are borne by governments and home and business owners' (Moudrak et al., 2018: 9). As the 'ultimate risk manager' (Moss, 2002), the state provides the paramount institutional mode of catastrophic risk management, offering public reinsurance, a public backstop, and/or public disaster assistance and recovery funds for those without insurance. Public institutions also act as regulators of insurers' financial solvency, in setting capital reserve standards. Through policy- and law-making, the state can make private coverage mandatory, partially underwrite risks, and even publicly cover risks for an entire population. Insurance market regimes for various risks, fuelled by climate change, are negotiated in complex ways between the state and private insurers from jurisdiction to jurisdiction.

Insurance as compensator

We now move into a discussion of the various roles of insurers in relation to climate change. Firstly, the conventionally understood role of insurers is, of course, that of compensator, that is financial protector through paying compensation for losses. It is important to note, however, that how this role plays out in particular insurance contexts is negotiated in tandem with state institutions, and also that insurers' protector role may be constrained by the bottom line, given that, unlike the state, private insurers have no mandate to protect all citizens. Private insurance can operate as a profound mechanism of social solidarity, socialising risk among the insured, but the extent to which it does so varies from insurance pool to insurance pool, depending on decisions of the insurer about who is included and at what premium. Indeed, especially in the neoliberal era, private insurance has been marked by the unpooling of risk, segmentation and inequality among populations, and the exclusion of less desirable insured from risk pools (Ericson, Barry and Doyle, 2003). Insurers increase premiums for the more risky, and, if it is not commercially viable to protect particular insured because of the effects of climate change or for other reasons, insurers may simply exclude the bad risks in certain risk pools or decide to step out of some whole markets, partially or altogether. For example, facing $24 billion in losses due to unprecedented climate change-driven wildfires in California in 2017 and 2018, insurers refused to renew tens of thousands of home insurance policies, dropping so many in fact that the state government had to introduce a moratorium on cancelling home insurance policies (CDI, 2019; Stone, 2020). Many other California homes saw massive premium increases stemming from the increased fire danger from climate change.

> In 2016 the average annual home insurance premium in the state was around $1000, making California one of the cheapest places to insure a home. Recently, however, some annual policies in fire-prone areas have recently risen to $19,000 on the open insurance market, while even California's backstop wildfire insurance program, the FAIR Plan, quotes a fire-specific policy on a similar home at $6000 per year.
>
> (Stone, 2020)

Non-renewals and coverage denials are leading to growing numbers of residents, especially those most at risk, being uninsured, and with no other option but to pay for property damages out-of-pocket or with governmental disaster assistance. The limits of private insurance as protector against climate change are also made clearer when we examine the variety of flood risk management regimes in different countries. Increased flooding risk is, of course, a major consequence of climate change. Other researchers have warned that, as climate change continues to unfold, and resultant flooding worsens, private flood insurance coverage could increasingly be limited to 'high reward areas where insurance is available to those with the ability to pay rising premiums' (Johnson, 2015: 2503), 'leaving only the high risks to the state' (Elliott, 2017: 434). As Keucheyan (2018: 485–486) explains:

> a possible scenario is that increases in premiums will have 'exclusionary effects', meaning that climate risk insurance will become too expensive for the lower-income segments of the population. These segments would thus remain unprotected from climate risk, or protected only by state intervention and humanitarian aid. This would increase premiums even further, since the level of premiums depends *ceteris paribus* on the number of insured.

Around the world, in various jurisdictions or regions, flood and especially 'overland' flood damages (as opposed to sewer backup) are not necessarily covered independently by private insurance (Sandink et al., 2010). Private insurability relies on diverse flood risk regimes in different countries, each sharing responsibility in different configurations between the insurance industry and the state. For example, flood coverage is privately offered as optional in the UK, with the government's Flood Re program working together with insurers to make sure there is coverage. France offers public, compulsory coverage, with private insurers administering policies (Thistlethwaite and Feltmate, 2013: 49). Another variation is the US National Flood Insurance Program (NFIP), a hybrid public-private insurance regime. In the US, the federal government publicly underwrites flood risks in the most vulnerable areas, and government-backed flood coverage is administered and sold by private insurers through conditional coverage. The NFIP passes on some of the price of flood risk to those who choose to live in flood-prone areas. As Collier (2014) and Elliott (2017) detail, the NFIP operates in a realm in between risk socialisation and individualisation. This regime has been shaped by repeated political and moral debates over individual 'deservingness' and collective protection in facing flood exposure, and resulting reforms (Elliott, 2017). Through pricing incentives, insurers' role as compensator blurs with the role of protector against climate changes, as high insurance prices or lack of insurance coverage may deter people from building in or moving to flood-prone areas.

Meanwhile, private insurance coverage for flood risks remains very limited in Canada (Lamond and Penning-Rowsell, 2014), even as flood risks worsen due to climate change. As reported by the Insurance Bureau of Canada (IBC), 'for the first time [in 2015], a few Canadian insurers began offering overland flood insurance to homeowners in specific areas. But at the moment, flood insurance is likely unaffordable for the 10% of homeowners who need it the most: those living on floodplains and in other areas at high risk of flooding...Canada is the only G7 country that doesn't have a national flood program in place' (IBC, 2016: 45). The Canadian flood risk management regime is thus largely non-insurantial, based on a government assistance policy patchwork of federal disaster management measures. Due to the rise in frequency and severity of weather-related events, government liabilities have significantly increased. In a 2016 report, the Office of the Parliamentary Budget Officer of Canada estimated annual costs of CAD673 million for floods over the next five years (OPBO, 2016).

In short, then, flood insurance is negotiated between private insurers and governments, and the availability of flood insurance is uneven across and within different nations, even as flood risks worsen. Risk skimming, that is the exclusion of 'bad risks' from insurance pools, might be one of the major responses of the insurance industry in the era of climate change. As Elliott notes, 'as other risks, currently privately underwritten, intensify under climate change (e.g. wind, wildfire), increasing insurance premiums may mean that more and more people cannot afford to buy their way into private networks of risk sharing. They too may be left to the state to handle, and a 'splintering protectionism' generated, in which increasing burdens are unequally felt by different citizens' (Elliott, 2017: 431).

More marginalised people who experience various dimensions of inequality – for example, the poor or racialised – tend to be more impacted by climate change to start with due to a range of intersecting factors (Oppenheimer et al., 2014). Inequalities in the availability of insurance compound these harms.

Insurance as resistor of and mitigator of climate change

Insurers still have some incentives not simply to cover risks, but to intervene actively in the risk environment and try to reduce the effects of climate change on claims, as they do with other risks and lines of insurance. Insurance functions in many ways as a form of governance beyond the state (Ericson, Doyle and Barry, 2003; Ericson and Doyle, 2004; Baker, 2010), sharing and dividing responsibility for risks with the state, and this is apparent in the governance of climate change.

There are a range of possible motivations for these efforts: firstly, insurers have all the same reasons as ordinary citizens to resist climate change, although their expert knowledge may make them even more aware of its effects. Beyond that, insurance claims operations are, of course, more profitable if claims in general and climate change-related claims in particular are minimised. Fighting climate change also helps promote positive public perceptions of the industry.

Reinsurers in particular have the motivation, resources, expertise, and international reach to play a significant role in fighting climate change. As Lehtonen (2017: 16) notes, 'reinsurance companies are leading global actors in enlightening governments, investors and stakeholders about the horrors of climate change'.

Insurers and reinsurers have extensive expertise, and, are publicly recognized as 'objective' risk experts. Thus people wanting to demonstrate that climate change is real will point out that it must be real because the insurance industry treats it as real. Climate scientists, frustrated by a lack of international policy movement on climate change, have tried to use the insurance industry to help promote recognition of the seriousness of climate change risk (Weinkle, 2020). The relationship between the insurance industry and climate science is complex and politicised. As Jessica Weinkle (2020: 1 and 8) argues:

> The extent to which the insurance industry directs, funds, and validates the production and use of science for estimating risk is itself a full blown political enterprise that functions to prioritize industry interests in views of hurricane risk and potentially narrow the broader discussion of disaster losses to the single solution of insurance pricing.... the science of hurricane behavior is uncertain and vast enough that scientists can create modeled risk estimates to suit the needs of insurers depending on what they wish to accomplish as they compete against one another in the market and interact with regulators.

Weinkle traces, for example, the implication of the insurance industry in the controversial Near Term 'event catalogs' following Hurricane Katrina, 'catalogs' that modelled high risks leading to costly premiums.

In order to mitigate losses stemming from climate change, insurers are also pushing to foster 'climate resilience' (see IBC, 2018). Private insurers advocate for collaborations with governments in promoting climate adaptation measures. For example, in its 2018 *Fact Book*, the Canadian property and casualty insurance industry trade association proposed a 'call to action', in terms of collaborations with governments in flood risk reduction and climate change adaptation, including six steps: 'Educate and empower consumers to mitigate'; 'Improve land-use planning'; 'Make targeted infrastructure investments'; 'Improve building codes'; 'Share data'; and 'Preserve and restore wetlands'. (IBC, 2018: 49). Through its involvement in the Munich Climate Insurance Initiative, for example, the industry works with research institutes and non-governmental organisations (NGOs) and attempts to help adaptation to climate change globally, including in developing countries with little insurance coverage (Munich Climate Insurance Initiative, n.d.).

Insurers also use insurance arrangements to responsibilise insureds to take further preventive measures. For example, the NFIP-subsidised flood insurance coverage discussed earlier is only offered in communities implementing flood management measures, such as floodplain management and building standards, set by the Federal Emergency Management Agency (OECD, 2016).

Insurer loss prevention efforts can, however, sometimes be selective. To return to the example of California wildfires, insurers have even employed their own private fire crews to try to reduce damage and cut claims.

These crews mostly focus on fire mitigation strategies, like installing sprinkler systems and creating firebreaks (Varian, 2019). Private fire crews travel into evacuation zones in trucks equipped with water tanks and hoses and retardant, looking nearly identical to their government counterparts – though their sole task is to protect specific insured homes. David Torgerson, president of Wildfire Defense Systems, noted that while his teams are capable of fighting fires, 'that's not our mission in this case'. 'Our task with the insurance industry is more so to prepare the homes and secure them, prior to and after the fire, and contribute to the survivability', he said (Cagle and Ho, 2019). Such private fire crews employed by the insurer, AIG, to fight California wild fires came under criticism for being selective in whom they rescued, only protecting the homes of wealthy insured (Funk, 2009).

Insurance as facilitator of climate change

While insurers work to deal with, mitigate, and compensate for the damaging effects of climate change, another very different type of role is that they are also major facilitators of climate change they are guarding against. To give a simple example, car insurance is a product that indirectly but centrally fuels climate change. In Canada, for example, car insurance represents property insurers' largest market, ahead of personal property insurance (IBC, 2018), and one of the very largest markets for private insurance in general. The availability of various insurance coverage is also one of the key financial conditions enabling the development of fossil fuel extraction projects, such as offshore oil rigs or oil sands extraction and pipeline projects in Canada. Despite pressure from activists and lobby groups, major insurance companies Chubb and Zurich recently increased their coverage of Canada's controversial Trans Mountain oil pipeline. 'Any company that claims to care about the climate and human rights cannot insure Trans Mountain while it presses ahead with plans to enable a huge expansion of some of the world's dirtiest oil', said Elana Sulakshana, Energy Finance Campaigner at Rainforest Action Network (Cohn, Jessop and Hussain, 2020).

Another of the roles of insurance in promoting climate change is that insurers also provide liability insurance coverage that may protect corporations as well as their directors and officers who may be sued for contributing to climate change. Massive law suits against companies or groups of companies for knowingly contributing to climate change have become increasingly common:

> Recent estimates suggest that there have been close to 1,000 climate change related class action lawsuits filed in 25 countries. Rhode Island, for example, filed a suit that alleges 21 companies knowingly contributed to climate change and failed to adequately warn citizens about the risks posed by their products.
>
> (KPMG, 2019)

Indeed, such lawsuits are seen by some commentators as one way in which governments may finance the costs of dealing with climate change, although others argue that it may be difficult to legally demonstrate liability (Horton, 2018). There are also further unresolved legal questions about whether, if corporations and their officers are held liable for climate change, this would be covered by their liability insurance, and the cost of lawsuits passed on as claims to their insurers. The industry journal *Canadian Underwriter* reports:

> This coverage will likely be tested in the courts, however, particularly by the major energy producers that are likely to be subject to repeated legal action. Insurers may be challenged when they refuse to defend policyholders....it remains to be seen whether climate risk will represent the next asbestos or tobacco liability risk for the property and casualty insurance industry.
>
> (Gambrill, 2020)

Whether or not the insurance industry is ultimately found responsible for coverage of liability claims for climate change, clearly many forms of insurance facilitate the continued production and use of fossil fuels.

Insurance as investor in climate change

A fourth type of role is that of insurers as investors in climate change. A less publicly well-known aspect of the insurance industry is that it controls vast seas of capital resulting from premiums collected, and, crucially, generates profits through investing this capital, so much so that the claims process may be operated at a loss, as long it generates enough capital in premiums for insurers to invest profitably (Ericson et al., 2003). Private insurers are among the largest institutional investors globally, along with banks, pension funds, and other investment funds (Chesnais, 2004). Insurance companies hold colossal portfolios of investments in other spheres of business, including, among others, fossil fuels. These vast financial holdings mean that private insurers potentially exert considerable power, as shareholders, over the governance of other commercial and industrial sectors by virtue of their collective capital investments in these other sectors. A report from the Asset Owners Disclosure Project (AODP) analysed, with its annual Global Climate 500 Index, a total of 116 insurers managing an overall investment portfolio of $15.3 trillion (AODP, 2016). The report argued that the insurance industry was slow off the mark compared to other massive institutional investors in reacting to the financial risks of fossil fuel investments for shareholders. For example, while 13% of pension funds were actively measuring their total investment portfolio's carbon emission, only 5% of insurers did so (AODP, 2016). The report further argued that fossil fuel investments are becoming increasingly financially risky. Trillions of dollars in carbon reserves will have to remain unused in order to limit climate change and this creates financial risks for those, including insurers, who put money into fossil fuel investments that may not have a future. The AODP report concluded that the insurance industry does not seriously consider risks of 'stranded assets', related to fossil fuels and other heavy carbon-emitting industries, that is investments that could become worthless with a move away from fossil fuels (AODP, 2016). In other words, fossil fuels might prove a risky investment for insurers. These financial risks are one of multiple reasons that insurers might consider divesting from fossil fuels.

Conclusion

These contradictory roles are perhaps not surprising, given the size and complexity of the insurance industry, and the ways in which it is intertwined with so many aspects of contemporary societies. One could easily argue that governments also both fight and facilitate climate change. At the same time, there are specific aspects of the insurance industry that also come into play, including the fact that insurers' risk management efforts may be constrained by the profit motive that insurers are not publicly accountable unlike governments, and that private insurance is marked by iatrogenic tendencies that create moral risks even as it guards against other risks. These tendencies undermine the insurance industry's potential role as climate protector.

Given these different roles, private insurers could easily apply a range of pressures to contribute to the transition to a low-carbon economy. As environmentalist and author Bill McKibben (2019) states:

> In some ways, the insurance industry resembles the banks and the asset managers: it controls a huge pool of money and routinely invests enormous sums in the fossil fuel industry. Consider, though, two interesting traits that set insurance apart. The first is, it knows better. Insurance companies are the part of our economy that we ask to understand risk, the ones with the data to really see what is happening as the climate changes, and for decades they've been churning out high-quality research establishing just how bad the crisis really is. [...]. The second thing that makes insurance companies unique is that they don't just provide money; they provide insurance. If you want to build a tar-sands pipeline or a coal-fired power plant or a liquefied-natural-gas export terminal, you need to get an insurance company to underwrite the plan. Otherwise, no one in his right mind would invest in it.

McKibben begins to highlight some of the leverage points insurers could apply to fossil fuel operations. And, if the insurance industry has leverage points to create pressure for the 'great transition' away from fossil fuels, members of the public with environmental concerns can in turn look for other leverage points to create pressure on the insurance industry itself to fight climate change.

As already noted, some key ways insurers could exert pressure for change are: (1) divestment from fossil fuels and (2) denying insurance coverage to fossil fuel-related projects. For various business and ethical reasons, insurers are already pursuing both kinds of pressure to some degree. Yet, nearly 50 years after the insurance industry called attention to problems with global warming (Stahel, 2009) and more than 20 years after the first report from the United Nations Framework Convention on Climate Change's Intergovernmental Panel on Climate Change, insurers are still slow to restrict underwriting and divest from fossil fuels and move to a low-carbon economy. As of October 2019, '17 insurers have adopted policies restricting coal insurance over the last two years, while four have announced policies on tar sands coverage' (Seekings, 2019). As a report from the NGO, Unfriend Coal, points out, '[t]he combined assets covered by [coal] divestment policies increased from $4 trillion to more than $6 trillion [from 2017 to 2018], or from 13% to 20% of the insurance industry's global assets' (Bosshard, 2018: 4). On 1 July 2019, major insurer, Chubb Ltd, became 'the first U.S. insurer to phase out its coal investments and insurance policies [by 2022], saying [...] it will no longer sell insurance to or invest in companies that make more than 30% of their revenue from coal mining' (Volcovici and Nair, 2019). And close to half of the global reinsurance industry now limits coal coverage (Seekings, 2019).

Decisions from insurers and reinsurers to phase out coal and tar sands have not been the result purely of corporate wisdom on the part of the insurance industry. Instead, these steps by insurers have followed major divestment campaigns on insurers from environmental NGOs and social movements, for instance from Unfriend Coal (Bosshard, 2018) and Insure our Future (Insure Our Future, n.d.) campaigns, both partnerships with other NGOs, such as Greenpeace and the Sierra Club.

While such business decisions represent a clear step in the right direction and are expected to contribute to a growth of private investments in renewable energy infrastructures (Renew.biz, 2019), (re)insurers still lags behind other institutional investors, especially pensions funds, in reducing their portfolio risks of stranded assets from investments in heavy carbon emitting industries (AODP, 2016). Climate-related risks constitute a source of financial instability, 'affecting the value of financial assets worldwide'. (Awazu Pereira da Silva, 2019). During a 2015 speech at Lloyd's of London, former Bank of England Governor, Mark Carney, suggested that the insurance industry might be underestimating climate change risk in terms of global financial stability (Hamilton, 2015).

One way forward would be for governments to regulate fossil fuel investments from private corporations like insurers. Given the global scale of climate change and the dangers it poses to the economy, to the environment, and to society, it may be that nation-states might be the only actors able to establish cost-benefit analyses on such a long-term basis as to acknowledge the policy and fiscal advantages of diversifying the energy mix (see Lazarus and van Asselt, 2018). For instance, in 2018, Ireland became the first country to pass a bill requiring to phase out its fossil fuel investments (Carrington, 2018). Civil society initiatives, public policy, international collaborations, and political will, not private insurance business strategies, might be the best ways to ensure the livelihood and well-being of future generations by transitioning to a low-carbon economy.

References

Abraham, K. S. (1986). *Distributing Risk. Insurance, Legal Theory, and Public Policy*. New Haven, CT: Yale University Press.

Asset Owners Disclosure Project (AODP). (2016). *Global Climate 500 Index 2016. Insurance Sector Analysis*. London: Asset Owners Disclosure Project. Available at: https://aodproject.net/wp-content/uploads/2016/07/AODP-GCI-2016_INSURANCE-SECTOR-ANALYSIS_FINAL_VIEW.pdf/ [Accessed 25 May 2020].

Baker, T. (2002). Risk, insurance, and the social construction of responsibility. In: T. Baker and J. Simon, eds., *Embracing Risk* (Vol. 1). Chicago: The University of Chicago Press, pp. 33–51.

Baker, T. (2010). Insurance in sociolegal research. *Annual Review of Law and Social Science*, 6, pp. 433–447.

Beck, U. (1999). *World Risk Society*. Cambridge: Polity Press.

Bosshard, P. (2018). *Insuring coal no more. The 2018 scorecard on insurance, coal, and climate change*. Unfriend Coal. Available at: https://waterkeeper.org/wp-content/uploads/2018/11/Scorecard-2018-report-US-print-version.pdf/ [Accessed 25 May 2020].

Cagle, S. and Ho, V. (2019). 'Not our mission': Private fire crews protect insured, not the public. *The Guardian*, 3 November.

California Department of Insurance (CDI). (2019). *New Data Shows Insurance Is Becoming Harder to Find as a Result of Wildfires*. Los Angeles, CA: California Department of Insurance. Available at: http://www.insurance.ca.gov/0400-news/0100-press-releases/2019/release063-2019.cfm [Accessed 25 May 2020].

Canadian Council of Insurance Regulators (CCIR). (2016). *Natural Catastrophes and Personal Property Insurance*. [Issues Paper]. Toronto: Canadian Council of Insurance Regulators. Available at: https://www.ccir-ccrra.org/Documents/View/2839 [Accessed 25 May 2020].

Charpentier, A. (2008). Insurability of climate risks. *The Geneva Papers on Risk and Insurance - Issues and Practice*, 33(1), pp. 91–109. https://doi.org/10.1057/palgrave.gpp.2510155.

Chesnais, F. (2004). Le capital de placement: Accumulation, internationalisation, effets économiques et politiques. In: F. Chesnais, ed., *La Finance Mondialisée. Racines Sociales Et Politiques, Configuration, Conséquences*. Paris: La Découverte, pp. 15–50.

Cohn, C., Jessop, S. and Hussain, N. (2020). Major insurers increase cover for Trans-Mountain oil pipeline - filings. *Reuters*, 12 May. Available at: https://www.reuters.com/article/canada-pipeline-climate-insurance/major-insurers-increase-cover-for-trans-mountain-oil-pipeline-filings-idUSL8N2CP83Q [Accessed 25 May 2020].

Collier, S. J. (2014). Neoliberalism and natural disaster: Insurance as political technology of catastrophe. *Journal of Cultural Economy*, 7(3), pp. 273–290.

Elliott, R. (2017). Who pays for the next wave? The American welfare state and responsibility for flood risk. *Politics & Society*, 45(3), pp. 415–440. https://doi.org/10.1177/0032329217714785.

Ericson, R. V. and Doyle, A. (2004). *Uncertain Business. Risk, Insurance, and the Limits of Knowledge*. Toronto: University of Toronto Press.

Ericson, R. V. and Doyle, A. (2006). The institutionalization of deceptive sales in life insurance: Five sources of moral risk. *British Journal of Criminology*, 46(6), pp. 993–1010.

Ericson, R. V., Doyle, A. and Barry, D. (2003). *Insurance as Governance*. Toronto: Toronto University Press.

Etzion, D., Kypraios, E. and Forgues, B. (2019). Employing finance in pursuit of the sustainable development goals: The promise and perils of catastrophe bonds. *Academy of Management Discoveries*, 5(4), 530–554. https://doi.org/10.5465/amd.2018.0137.

Evans, S. (2019). Climate change risk perception contributes to ILS slowdown: Fitch. *Artemis*, 3 September. Available at: https://www.artemis.bm/news/climate-change-risk-perception-contributes-to-ils-slowdown-fitch/ [Accessed 25 May 2020].

Freeman, P. K. and Scott, K. (2005). Catastrophic risks and insurance. In: F. A. Messy and OECD, eds., *Comparative Analysis of Large Scale Catastrophe Compensation Schemes*. Paris: Organisation for Economic Co-operation and Development, pp. 187–234.

Funk, M. (2009). Too Big to Burn: AIG plays God in a man-made firestorm. *Harper's Magazine*, October. Available at: https://harpers.org/archive/2009/10/too-big-to-burn/ [Accessed 25 May 2020].

Gambrill, D. (2020). How climate change may heat up your liability lines. *Canadian Underwriter*, 7 February. Available at: https://www.canadianunderwriter.ca/climate-change/how-climate-change-may-heat-up-your-liability-lines-1004173608/ [Accessed 25 May 2020].

Horton, J. B. (2018). Parametric insurance as an alternative to liability for compensating climate harms. *Carbon & Climate Law Review*, 12(4), pp. 285–296. https://doi.org/10.21552/cclr/2018/4/4.

Insurance Bureau of Canada (IBC). (2016). *Facts of the Property and Casualty Insurance Industry in Canada 2016*. Toronto: Insurance Bureau of Canada. Available at: http://assets.ibc.ca/Documents/Facts%20Book/Facts_Book/2016/Facts-Book-2016.pdf [Accessed 25 May 2020].

Insurance Bureau of Canada (IBC). (2018). *2018 Facts of the Property and Casualty Insurance Industry in Canada*. Toronto: Insurance Bureau of Canada. Available at: http://assets.ibc.ca/Documents/Facts%20Book/Facts_Book/2018/IBC-Fact-Book-2018.pdf [Accessed 25 May 2020].

Insure Our Future, "About us," Available at: https://www.insureourfuture.us/about [accessed November 4 2020].

Jenkins, P. (2019). Why climate change in the new 9/11 for insurance companies, *Financial Times*, 9 September. Available at: https://www.ft.com/content/63c80228-cfee-11e9-99a4-b5ded7a7fe3f [Accessed 25 May 2020].

Johnson, L. (2015). Catastrophic fixes: Cyclical devaluation and accumulation through climate change impacts. *Environment and Planning A*, 47(12), pp. 2503–2521. https://doi.org/10.1177/0308518X15594800.

Keucheyan, R. (2018). Insuring climate change: New risks and the financialization of nature: Debate: Insuring climate change. *Development and Change*, 49(2), pp. 484–501. https://doi.org/10.1111/dech.12367.

KPMG. (2019). *Combating Climate Risks: The Future of Insurance.* [Webpage Insights]. Available at: https://home.kpmg/xx/en/home/insights/2019/03/combating-climate-risks-the-future-of-insurance-fs.html [Accessed 25 May 2020].

Lamond, J. and Penning-Rowsell, E. (2014). The robustness of flood insurance regimes given changing risk resulting from climate change. *Climate Risk Management,* 2, pp. 1–10. https://doi.org/10.1016/j.crm.2014.03.001.

Lazarus, M. and van Asselt, H. (2018). Fossil fuel supply and climate policy: Exploring the road less taken. *Climatic Change,* 150(1–2), pp. 1–13. https://doi.org/10.1007/s10584-018-2266-3.

Lehtonen, T. -K. (2017). Objectifying climate change: Weather-related catastrophes as risks and opportunities for reinsurance. *Political Theory,* 45(1), pp. 32–51. https://doi.org/10.1177/0090591716680684.

McKibben, B. (2019). Money is the oxygen on which the fire of global warming burns. *The New Yorker,* 17 September. Available at: https://www.newyorker.com/news/daily-comment/money-is-the-oxygen-on-which-the-fire-of-global-warming-burns [Accessed 25 May 2020].

Mills, E. (2005). Insurance in a climate of change. *Science,* 309 (5737), pp. 1040–1044. https://doi.org/10.1126/science.1112121.

Moss, D. A. (2002). *When All Else Fails. Government as the Ultimate Risk Manager.* Cambridge, MA: Harvard University Press.

Moudrak, N., Feltmate, B., Venema, H. and Osman, H. (2018). *Combating Canada's Rising Flood Costs: Natural Infrastructure Is an Underutilized Option.* Waterloo, Ontario: Prepared for Insurance Bureau of Canada, Waterloo, Canada. Intact Centre on Climate Adaptation, University of Waterloo. Available at: http://assets.ibc.ca/Documents/Resources/IBC-Natural-Infrastructure-Report-2018.pdf. [accessed 5 November 2020].

Munich Climate Insurance Initiative. "Who we are," Available at: https://climate-insurance.org/about/ [accessed November 4 2020].

Munich Re. (1973). *Flood Inundation.* [Brochure]. Munich: Munich Reinsurance.

O'Hare, P. A., White, I. and Connelly, A. (2016). Insurance as maladaptation: Resilience and the 'business as usual' paradox. *Environment and Planning C: Government and Policy,* 34(6), pp. 1175–1193.

OECD, 2016. Financial Management of Flood Risk. Paris: OECD Publishing.

Office of the Parliamentary Budget Officer (OPBO). (2016). *Estimate of the Average Annual Cost for Disaster Financial Assistance Due to Weather Events.* Ottawa: Office of the Parliamentary Budget Officer. Available at: http://www.pbo-dpb.gc.ca/web/default/files/Documents/Reports/2016/DFAA/DFAA_EN.pdf [Accessed 25 May 2020].

Oppenheimer, M., Campos, M., Warren, R., Birkmann, J., Luber, G., O'Neill, B. and Takahashi, K. (2014). Emergent risks and key vulnerabilities. In: C. B. Field, V. R. Barros, D. J. Dokken, K. J. Mach, M. D. Mastrandrea, T. E. Bilir, M. Chatterjee, K. L. Ebi, Y. O. Estrada, R. C. Genova, B. Girma, E. S. Kissel, A. N. Levy, S. MacCracken, P. R. Mastrandrea, and L. L. White, eds., *Climate Change 2014: Impacts, Adaptation, and Vulnerability. Part A: Global and Sectoral Aspects. Contribution of Working Group II to the Fifth Assessment Report of the Intergovernmental Panel of Climate Change.* New York (NY): Cambridge University Press, pp. 1039–1099.

Renew.biz. (2019). Fossil fuel divestment to "benefit renewables." *Renew.Biz.,* 14 October. Available at: https://renews.biz/55809/fossil-fuel-divestment-to-benefit-renewables/ [Accessed 25 May 2020].

Sandink, D., Kovacs, P., Oulahen, G. and McGillivray, G. (2010). *Making Flood Insurable for Canadian Homeowners*. [Discussion Paper, November]. Zurich: ICLR and Swiss Re. Available at: https://www.iclr.org/images/Making_Flood_Insurable_for_Canada.pdf [Accessed 25 May 2020].

Seekings, C. (2019). Almost half of global reinsurance market restricts cover for coal. *The Actuary*, 17 October. Available at: https://www.theactuary.com/news/2019/10/almost-half-of-global-reinsurance-market-restricts-cover-for-coal/ [Accessed 25 May 2020].

Stahel, W. (2009). In favour of a proactive insurance approach to climate change. *Geneva Papers on Risk and Insurance – Issues Practice*, 34, pp. 319–322. https://doi.org/10.1057/gpp.2009.17.

Stone, A. (2020). Insurers struggle to address climate risk. *Forbes*, 30 January. Available at: https://www.forbes.com/sites/andystone/2020/01/30/climate-change-will-make-more-of-the-world-uninsurable/#61ba207655a5 [Accessed 25 May 2020].

Thistlethwaite, J. and Feltmate, B. (2013). *Assessing the Viability of Overland Flood Insurance: The Canadian Residential Property Market*. Waterloo, Ontario: University of Waterloo & The Co-operators. Available at: https://www.cooperators.ca/~/media/Cooperators%20Media/Section%20Media/AboutUs/Sustainability/Assessing%20the%20Viability%20of%20Flood%20Insurance%20in%20Canada%20-%20Eng.pdf [Accessed 25 May 2020].

Varian, E. (2019). While California Fires Rage, The Rich Hire Private Firefighters. *New York Times*, 26 October. Available at: https://www.nytimes.com/2019/10/26/style/private-firefighters-california.html [Accessed 25 May 2020].

Volcovici, V. and Nair, S. S. (2019). U.S. insurer Chubb pulls back from coal. *Reuters*. Available at: https://www.reuters.com/article/us-chubb-ltd-ch-coal-policy-idUSKCN1TW3I2 [Accessed 25 May 2020].

Weinkle, J. (2020). Experts, regulatory capture, and the "governor's dilemma": The politics of hurricane risk science and insurance. *Regulation and Governance*, 14(4), pp. 637–652.

Wu, X., Lu, Y., Zhou, S., Chen, L. and Xu, B. (2016). Impact of climate change on human infectious diseases: Empirical evidence and human adaptation. *Environment International*, 86, pp.14–23. doi: 10.1016/j.envint.2015.09.007.

6 Quantifying changing climate risks and built environments in Australia

Implications for lenders, insurers and regulators

Karl Mallon and Liam Phelan

Introduction

In this chapter we focus on the governance of changing climate risks for built environments in Australia: our particular interest is the implications of changing climate risks for three key stakeholders in Australia's built environments: insurers, lenders and regulators. We do so through discussion of Cross Dependency Initiative's (hereafter XDI) 2019 analysis, entitled *Climate Change Risk to Australia's Built Environment: A Second Pass National Assessment* (hereafter the *Assessment*), to review present and future climate risks to Australia's built environment (Mallon et al., 2019). XDI is a risk analysis company that provides infrastructure risk analysis and quantification for governments and utilities in Australia and internationally.

The implications of changing climate risks are perhaps most apparent for insurers underwriting properties for climate-implicated weather risks: a changing climate means that past experience of climate risk is, over time, less useful as a guide to future risk. However, perhaps counter-intuitively, the financial risks sit much more heavily with lenders for two reasons. Whereas insurers typically renew contracts annually, lenders' contractual exposure to climate risks is typically for longer periods – terms up to 30 years are common. Further, as the *Assessment* shows, climate risks will increase markedly for many properties through to 2100. Both insurers and lenders are heavily regulated, and so the role of regulators also warrants careful consideration. Regulators in Australia and internationally have in recent years made some acknowledgement of the financial dimensions of climate risks: the need for adequate disclosure is one area where regulators have been vocal. Nevertheless, in light of the high-resolution analysis provided by the *Assessment*, i.e., quantification of climate risk at local scale, we join others in arguing that regulators could require much more of insurers and lenders.

The *Assessment* extends on an earlier Federal Government report with a similar focus published ten years previously (Department of Climate Change, 2009). That earlier report made the observation that '[c]limate change involves taking our heavily populated urban and peri-urban coastal society outside the established comfort zone of the recent past. A new national agenda must be prepared now to ready Australia for the hard decisions that will be required to reduce risk' (Bruce Thom in Department of Climate Change, 2009: 169). However, a decade later this is yet to occur, and the scale of the exposure has worsened.

The *Assessment* makes notable contributions in several respects to effective governance of climate risks in Australia. First, the *Assessment* is comprehensive in scope, covering around 15 million addresses in all 544 local government areas (LGAs) across Australia. Second, the *Assessment* focuses on five key climate-implicated, loss-causing hazards in Australia: riverine flooding, coastal inundation, forest fires (bushfires), wind gusts and drought-driven subsidence of clay soils. Third, drawing on a carefully considered methodology, the *Assessment* provides a set of four key metrics for translating climate risk into financial risk that are helpful for understanding changes in climate risks over time. In sum, the *Assessment* begins to quantify climate risk to built environments at local scale, provides useful guidance towards understanding climate risks to built environments in Australia, and offers guidance for informing effecting adaptation responses to climate change.

Karl Braganza, Head of Climate Monitoring at the Australian Bureau of Meteorology, once pointed out that the impact of greenhouse gas emissions on the climate is like hitting a glass vase with a hammer: we have a high degree of confidence that the vase will break, but there is considerable uncertainty on where the pieces of the vase will land (Mallon et al., 2019: 72). The *Assessment* brings together vast amounts of data and computing power to make an informed attempt at understanding where some of these shards will land and how much damage they might cause. Translating from climate risk to financial risk with reference to built environments is both challenging and essential. One part of the challenge is working across scales – from climate change as a globally coherent phenomenon to risks manifest at local scale. Another part of the challenge is working across disciplines – from climate and weather science through engineering to financial analysis. And yet meeting the challenge is essential if there is to be effective and just governance of changing climate risks. The discussion of the *Assessment*'s implications for three key players in Australia's built environment – insurers, lenders and regulators – are sobering and timely: climate change is a profound source of risk to built environments and one that calls for effective adaptation: and we are already late in that regard.

The chapter proceeds as follows. In the following section we introduce earlier work on some of the likely financial ramifications of increasing climate risk for insurers – the first key stakeholder in built environments and previous work to quantify climate risks to Australia's built environments. In section Climate change risk and Australia's built environment, we describe the key indicators used in the *Assessment* and their utility in understanding climate risks to building stock, and draw on metrics and maps to briefly describe the scale of climate risk. This section also discusses the careful methodology employed for the *Assessment*. We ask readers to bear with us as we then step through the technical dimensions of the analysis because transparency around methodology, particularly the bounds of the analysis in the *Assessment* is important for grappling effectively with the *Assessment*'s implications for stakeholders. In sections (The scale of the risk, and LGAs most at risk: 2020 and 2100), we discuss the scale of the risk. In section Implications for risk governance, we return our focus from the technical back to the implications of changing climate risks for three key stakeholders in built environments: beginning with insurers, we also cast our gaze towards lenders and then regulators. The conclusion presents some final observations.

Climate change risk and Australia's built environment

A changing climate harmscape with financial implications

In the absence of effective mitigation, climate change will push the Earth system into a radically different state – one that is both unstable and unfamiliar to human societies (Phelan et al., 2013). A changed climate means significant increases in climate change-exacerbated weather risks. Changes in climate risks to property, in turn, create challenges for insurers, lenders and regulators. Previous attention to climate risks and insurance has demonstrated that climate change will, in the first instance, lead generally to increases in climate-implicated weather risks, and necessarily lead to increased insurance costs (Phelan, 2011; Phelan, Henderson-Sellers and Taplin, 2011). In short: as we continue to change the climate, insurance premiums will move from affordable to expensive. Premiums can in fact become so expensive that they are unaffordable, leading to properties becoming uninsurable in practice. This has started to play out already for some climate-implicated risks in some parts of Australia (Ting et al., 2020). In Australia key risks to property include riverine flooding, coastal inundation, forest fires (bushfires), wind storms and drought-driven subsidence of clay soils.

Unmitigated, climate change will both escalate risks and lead to a shift in climate risks from relative predictability to relative unpredictability. Under such circumstances, insurance premiums would move from affordable to unaffordable and then from unaffordable to incalculable (Phelan, 2011; Phelan et al., 2011). At that point, where properties are uninsurable in principle, insurers will no longer be able to sell insurance at any price.

In the meantime, however, understanding how changes in climate risks will play out is useful for informing adaptive responses to climate change. To that end, high resolution analysis, i.e., an understanding of how climate impacts will manifest at the scale of LGAs, can inform effective context-specific adaptation.

Context for this analysis

In 2009 the Australian Government Office of Climate Change and Energy Efficiency released the report *Climate Change Risks to Australia's Coast – A First Pass National Risk Assessment*. The analysis was one of the key outcomes of the National Climate Change Adaptation Framework endorsed two years earlier by the Council of Australian Governments (COAG – comprising the Federal, State and Territory governments). The 2009 assessment focused on risks to settlements, infrastructure, industries and natural ecosystems in the coastal zone where Australia's population is centred, and provided an analysis of residential property at risk from erosion and inundation around the Australian coastline at the end of this century using a 1.1 m sea level rise projection. The analysis did not include the effects of storm surge in many areas. Inundation risk was quantified using Geoscience Australia's National Exposure Information System infrastructure database for each state, the Northern Territory and for key LGAs. The assessment suggested the replacement value (in 2008) of existing residential buildings at risk from inundation ranges from AUD41 billion to AUD63 billion. To illustrate: the assessment suggested that for New South Wales, Australia's most populous state, around 40–60,000 residences were at risk, in LGAs in Sydney (Rockdale) and to Sydney's north (Lake Macquarie, Wyong and Gosford) and south (Wollongong, Shoalhaven).

Measuring climate harm to built environments

In the ten years since the *First Pass National Risk Assessment* there have been improvements in the sophistication and detail of climate models as well as substantial increases in raw computing power. The earlier assessment's suggestion that residential buildings at risk of coastal inundation were valued in the range $41–63 billion is a useful first indicator, but it does not accommodate the resilience of built structures, nor allow for adaptation. Nor does it include the amount of maladaptation that has occurred with a growing population in the intervening decade. The *Second Pass National Assessment* builds on the earlier work and provides a more comprehensive assessment, covering all of Australia, a greater number of assets and more hazards. As indicated above, the *Assessment* covers more than 15 million addresses in all of Australia's 544 LGAs for five key hazards.

The *Assessment* provides four key indicators to convey the risks of extreme weather and climate change to the built environment. Described below, the indicators are all informed by estimates of vulnerability as well as exposure and event probabilities. Each indicator tells a different story about the acceleration, spatial distribution, financial intensity and scale of climate risks. Taken together, they can be used to indicate the way forward for prudent, orderly and targeted adaptations.

TTIP (total technical insurance premium)

The technical insurance premium (TIP) is the annual average loss per address for all hazard impacts. The TIP is based on the cost of damage to an asset, expressed in 2020 AUD with no discounting or adjustments for other transaction costs. The total TIP (TTIP) is the sum of all TIPs for a group of addresses, such as all addresses in a LGA. As such, the TTIP is useful in drawing attention to those geographical areas that have the largest financial risk associated with climate change hazards. TTIP can display bias towards areas with a larger number of properties, such as high-density city suburbs. However, as the same replacement value is used for each address, regardless of location, it is not biased by differences in property values. When assessing higher density areas, the modelling includes a density modification to adjust for the lower percentage of total addresses being subject to flooding/inundation risk (i.e., in multi-storey buildings, flood risk may be limited to ground floor addresses).

VAR% (percentage of value at risk)

The percentage of value at risk (VAR%) is the TIP expressed as a percentage of a single asset's replacement cost, specified for one-year period with no discounting of the TIP or the asset replacement cost. Another way to express this is as follows: VAR% = TIP/asset replacement cost. The VAR% can also be applied to a portfolio of properties, in which case Average VAR% is the TTIP divided by the total replacement value of all assets, making it a non-dimensional average for TIP.

The VAR% is an excellent way of overcoming the bias of the TTIP toward larger, more populous areas, allowing the risks to two quite different areas to be compared on an equal measure. Thus, the percentage impact to the homes in a small population, low-density rural LGA can be compared to a high-density inner city LGA. However, the VAR% can tend to draw attention to small communities where many or all of the addresses share the same risk, for example, a large proportion of buildings are in a flood zone or low lying near the coast or exposed to clay soils.

Even though the VAR% for a given community may be very large when benchmarked against state peers, the actual financial quantum of risk may still be quite small – and the TTIP will help inform that. However, even though this total may be small, it still indicates a major financial risk for that community and perhaps an affordability challenge in insurance and adaptation.

HRP# (high-riskproperties)

An asset is classed as becoming high risk if its VAR% for a given year exceeds 1 per cent of its asset replacement value (i.e., the cost of replacing the building, but not the land). This is based on the United States' Federal Emergency Management Agency (FEMA) thresholds for government insurance schemes, which highlight properties in an (historic) 1-in-100 flood zone, also known as 'Rating A Zones' – however the analysis takes the extra step of accommodating the vulnerability and resilience of the property. The number of HRP is the sum of all addresses in an LGA where the VAR% is above 1% in a given year.

In principle, any HRP can be insured, however the annual premium may be unaffordable for many. For example, a VAR% of 1 per cent for a house that costs $500,000 to construct would be $5,000 per year or around 8 per cent of the median salary in Australia in 2020.

HRP% (high-risk properties as a percentage)

The number of HRP can also be expressed as a percentage of all properties in a given area. HRP are usually those with substantial exposure to severely damaging hazards, such as flooding or coastal inundation as opposed to soil contraction – which may only cause minor damage or forest fire where the probabilities of loss remain small. This indicator is therefore useful to highlight areas that have a concentration of acute risk to individual buildings.

Methods for generating analysis

A brief review of the methods used for generating the indicators above is useful for understanding how the analysis used in the *Assessment* is able to begin to span both scales and disciplines. The analysis spans scales from climate change at global scale to likely changes in frequency and intensity of hazards at local scale and the analysis spans disciplines from climate science through engineering to financial analysis.

The method comprises four steps. Firstly, the analysis assumes a standard, modern dwelling at each address. This can be customised, but for the analysis, the 'standard asset' is described as constructed in 2000, with concrete foundations, a floor height above ground of 0.45 m and a V500 standard wind rating (designed for a 1-in-500-year return frequency wind storm event).

Secondly, both damage and failure thresholds are identified for various key components of the standard asset if exposed to each of the five key hazards. Damage thresholds are breached when an asset is broken or excessively weakened – an example would be a windstorm blowing the roof off a house. Failure thresholds are breached when an element of the asset prevents the asset from performing its function and can occur without damage. For example, a heat wave that exceeds an electrical control system's operating temperature may temporarily prevent the asset functioning, but there will be no damage and as the heat wave passes and the temperature drops the electrical control system will begin functioning again.

Thirdly, annual probabilities of damage caused by each of the five hazards are determined with reference to a range of data on forests, soils, floods, topology, elevations, tides and waves. This hazard-specific data is coupled with long-term data from local meteorological stations.

Lastly, future probabilities of damage are calculated by extracting from global climate change models the changes in the statistical distribution of key parameters such as heat, precipitation, wind and humidity. The analysis uses a 'business-as-usual' greenhouse gas emissions scenario (RCP8.5, from the Intergovernmental Panel on Climate Change) augmented with climate modelling from leading research institutes to indicate the impacts of climate change on weather events and sea levels. Models come from a short list of those that are known to perform well (i.e., replicate historical climate characteristics) in Australia. Specific models are selected to 'stress test' for each hazard – thus a model which tends to predict a drier future is used for stress testing against drought, and a model that predicts a wetter future is used for stress testing against flood risk. This selection process avoids masking risks or diluting impacts through averaging an ensemble of models. However, while the *Assessment* draws on a multi-model test it is not an ensemble test and results should be interpreted as a stress-test, not a mean projection.

The analysis does not cover hazards other than riverine flooding, coastal inundation, forest fires, wind gusts and drought. That is, the analysis makes no comment on other hazards such as flash flooding (pluvial flooding), coastal erosion, grass fires, land slip, cyclones, hail or heat impacts.

The scale of the risk

The *Assessment* is detailed. Here we provide an overview only of the *Assessment*'s projections for climate-driven changes from 2019 through to the year 2100 for the five key hazards for Australia's built environment. It is important to note at the outset that the impacts are not shared evenly across Australia. Some risks, such as from subsidence and bushfire, are broadly distributed. Other risks, such as riverine flooding and coastal inundation are highly concentrated, thus presenting an acute social and economic risk for affected LGAs.

The current scale of extreme weather and climate change related risk is already significant. The *Assessment* finds that in 2020 there are already 383,300 addresses across Australia that would be classified as HRP. This includes around 30 years of climate change impacts from the baseline year of 1990. Looking forward, this number is projected to increase to 735,654 in 2100, an increase of 92 per cent. The 2100 figure is for existing development only, meaning that it does not account for population growth driving new development in high-hazard areas, nor for continued use of inadequate building standards, both of which unabated, will substantially increase this number. Shifting attention from the number of properties to the cost of losses per property, the national TTIP is projected to increase by 55 per cent between 2020 and 2100.

Riverine flooding is already a problem. The *Assessment* suggests that flood risk is already a major problem in a substantial number of LGAs. In many areas the TTIP is dominated by a small number of properties that have very high annual average losses. In general, the results suggest that flood risk is currently material for about 5 per cent of addresses. The degree of risk then depends on the vulnerability of the property at that address. Riverine flooding is a major driver of both TTIP and HRP#. Though flooding effects a smaller number of properties than hazards such as subsidence, flooding generally causes more severe financial impacts. Between 2020 and 2100, the TTIP from flooding is projected to increase by 29 per cent. One in five LGAs will have TTIP double due to flood. This projection does not include pluvial flooding (flash flooding).

Coastal inundation can be localised but with high impact when it occurs. The total proportion of addresses at risk is starting at a low level but is projected to increase exponentially through the century. As with riverine flooding, whilst coastal inundation affects only a small proportion of all addresses, the financial impacts can be severe. The TTIP from coastal inundation is projected to increase by 111 per cent between 2020 and 2100.This projection does not include coastal erosion.

Forest fire has a relatively low probability of causing damage to any individual property in a given year, but has broad-scale implications due to its disruptive impact. As recent years have shown, the increases in severity and duration of forest fire events is leading to longer fire seasons and loss of life and property. Looking forward, the *Assessment* suggests that fire conditions will intensify in many areas. More worrying still, forest fire conditions will extend into areas not normally associated with forest fire, and areas that are not generally considered at risk from bushfires may become vulnerable in the future. The TTIP for forest fire is projected to increase by 54 per cent between 2020 and 2100. This projection does not include grass fires, or coincidence with drought conditions.

Subsidence is a problem for any construction on reactive soils (clay-type soils that swell on wetting and shrink on drying), which are widely distributed across the country. While the amount of damage from subsidence is often modest and non-catastrophic for a single building, the probability of droughts combined with the large numbers of exposed properties makes this a potentially large source of damage and loss. In individual cases, subsidence can be severe enough to cause structural damage. Between 2020 and 2100, the TTIP from subsidence risk is projected to increase by 36 per cent.

Wind remains an area of analysis characterised by uncertainty because Global Circulation Models do not yet capture well small-scale storm systems or cyclone behaviour. The *Assessment* looks at changes in the frequency of wind speeds capable of damaging buildings based on their design thresholds (but does not include cyclone risk). Changes are found to be generally modest, and even decrease in some areas, but there remains considerable uncertainty in the model outputs. The climate change trends identified are relatively small compared to uncertainties, so major conclusions are not made. However, the uncertainty in results should not lead to complacency about wind and storm damage as the poleward warming of ocean waters implies that the cyclone belt will also extend southward bringing wind speeds beyond current design specifications in southern building code zones.

LGAs most at risk: 2020 and 2100

The following tables list the ten LGAs most at risk for all five key hazards (coastal inundation, riverine flooding, forest fire, subsidence and wind) in 2020 (Table 6.1) and in 2100 (Table 6.2). Each table lists LGAs with reference to the four indicators used in the *Assessment*: TTIP, VAR%, number of high-risk properties (HRP#) and HRP as a percentage of all properties in the LGA (HRP%).

Note that the different metrics for risk draw out very different rankings and insights.

As might be expected, many LGAs that are currently most at risk in 2020 (see Table 6.1) continue to be most at risk as the climate continues to change (see Table 6.2). Figure 6.1 provides a visual representation of LGAs most at risk for all hazards in 2100.

Table 6.1 The ten LGAs most at risk in 2020 for all hazards (coastal inundation, riverine flooding, forest fire, subsidence and wind). The listed LGAs are spread across four Australian states: Queensland (Qld), Victoria (Vic), New South Wales (NSW), Western Australia (WA) and South Australia (SA).

Rank	TTIP	VAR%	HRP#	HRP%
1	Gold Coast, Qld	Greater Shepparton, Vic	Gold Coast, Qld	Greater Shepparton, Vic
2	Brisbane, Qld	Wangaratta, Vic	Brisbane, Qld	Wangaratta, Vic
3	Sunshine Coast, Qld	Mid Murray, SA	Greater Shepparton, Vic	Murray, WA
4	Greater Shepparton, Vic	Murray, WA	Sunshine Coast, Qld	Maranoa, Qld
5	Central Coast, NSW	Gold Coast, Qld	Fraser Coast, Qld	Mid Murray, SA
6	Fraser Coast, Qld	Fraser Coast, Qld	Wangaratta, Vic	Federation, NSW
7	Moreton Bay, Qld	Tweed, NSW	Mandurah, WA	Horsham, Vic
8	Wangaratta, Vic	Maranoa, Qld	Bundaberg, Qld	Mandurah, WA
9	Tweed, NSW	Noosa, Qld	Tweed, NSW	Fraser Coast, Qld
10	Mackay, Qld	Douglas, Qld	Moreton Bay, Qld	Hinchinbrook, Qld

Source: Mallon et al. (2019)

Table 6.2 The ten LGAs most at risk in 2100 for all hazards (coastal inundation, riverine flooding, forest fire, subsidence and wind).

Rank	TTIP	VAR%	HRP#	HRP%
1	Gold Coast, Qld	Greater Shepparton, Vic	Gold Coast, Qld	Greater Shepparton, Vic
2	Brisbane, Qld	Wangaratta, Vic	Brisbane, Qld	Murray, WA
3	Sunshine Coast, Qld	Mid Murray, SA	Sunshine Coast, Qld	Adelaide Hills, SA
4	Greater Shepparton, Vic	Murray, WA	Central Coast, NSW	Wangaratta, Vic
5	Central Coast, NSW	Gold Coast, Qld	Newcastle, NSW	Mundaring, WA
6	Moreton Bay, Qld	Tweed, NSW	Greater Shepparton, Vic	Mid Murray, SA
7	Fraser Coast, Qld	Fraser Coast, Qld	Fraser Coast, Qld	Maranoa, Qld
8	Tweed, NSW	Mandurah, WA	Moreton Bay, Qld	Noosa, Qld
9	Mackay, Qld	Douglas, Qld	Mandurah, WA	Narrabri, NSW
10	Mandurah, WA	Noosa, Qld	Tweed, NSW	Western Downs, Qld

Source: Mallon et al. (2019)

Recommendations

The *Assessment* provides the following five public policy recommendations.

1 *Establish legal requirements for risk disclosure:* Establish unambiguous legal requirements for purchasers, investors and tenants of built property and infrastructure to be advised of the full range of extreme weather and climate change risks that may affect the property over its full lifetime.

2 *Require fit-for-purpose construction in high hazard areas:* Ensure design standards and planning requirements for infrastructure and development match location-specific hazards. All tiers of government seek to achieve full insurability by ensuring projected VARs of less than 1 per cent of the replacement cost of the property over its design lifetime under worst-case climate change projections.

3 *Plan for infrastructure system resilience:* Federal and state governments require that all critical infrastructure – including water, power, transport and telecommunications – be assessed both at an asset level and at an interdependent system level. Establish an overarching standard risk tolerance (for example, 1-in-500-year event tolerance) such that extreme weather event failures do not cause cascading failures across sectors.

4 *Develop risk based insurance pricing:* Financial regulators require that insurance industry products fairly reflect both site-specific hazard probabilities and asset-specific vulnerability, thus providing lower premiums for more resilient designs and materials and a clear market signal that investment in resilience will be fairly rewarded by lower premiums.

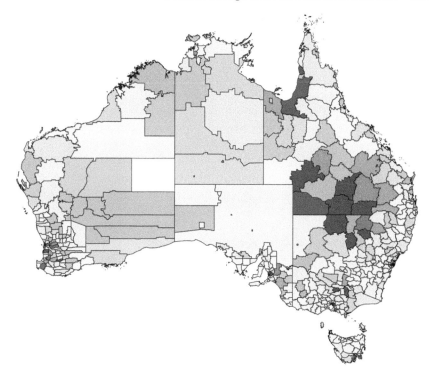

Figure 6.1 High risk properties as a percentage of all addresses (HRP%) by local government area in 2100. Yellow colouring though orange to red indicates a percentage range from 0 per cent through to 50 per cent of addresses, and is largely centred on the populated Eastern seaboard and other capital cities (Adelaide and Perth). Blue and green colouring indicates negligible change or a change in the absolute number of properties that is too small to be statistically significant – hence the large areas in remote areas.

5 *Adaptation for highly exposed areas:* State and Federal governments implement support schemes to finance adaptation in areas at high risk. This can finance resilient construction, municipal works or relocation.

Implications for climate risk governance

Insurers

The long-established role of insurance in facilitating economic activity dates back to antiquity (Trennery, 1926; Pfeffer and Klock, 1974: 27) and an accessible and reliable insurance system remains essential for economic stability. It is unsurprising, therefore, that states are wary of letting insurers fail. Australia has had an insurer collapse in recent decades: HIH insurance collapsed in early 2001, inspiring headlines such as 'HIH collapse threatens economy' (McIlveen, 2001), and the collapse triggered a Royal Commission (Commonwealth of Australia [HIH Royal Commission] and Owen, 2003).

The implications of changes in climate risks are perhaps most apparent for insurers and the first important observation with regard to insurance for climate-implicated risks is that premium calculations are already out of date. For the most part actuarial data based on long-term losses will be slanted towards the past, be absent of knowledge of the future and will therefore always be a poor representation of the present.

The problem is mirrored in physical approaches to loss modelling. For example, flood models are often based on long-term weather station data for precipitation probabilities – weather stations that may have been collecting data for 100 years. As was found in ground truthing the data set in the *Assessment* for certain locations, the probabilities of these events have already moved away markedly from a baseline that may be 30 or more years old.

The faster climate change occurs, the worse the mismatch between current risk levels and historical data. This means that insurance loss to premium ratios will generally be miscalculated, which will likely lead to persistent loss of profitability in a highly competitive industry with small margins. The repeated lowering of profitability expectations by insurers in Australia in recent years may be indicative of a system challenged by premium calculations failing to capture climate change already present in weather risks. The results of the analysis would suggest that recent bullish comments by Warren Buffett (2016) regarding the ability of the insurers to ride out climate change, are inconsistent with the insurance system lagging behind the science.

As such, insurers need to have a climate-informed underwriting system in order to stay profitable and competitive. This will tend to favour bigger, better resourced insurers. Smaller insurers will have to exit extreme weather-exposed locations and markets, limiting their exposure –and business – to those in which there is little or no exposure to riverine floods, coastal inundation, forest fire, subsidence and wind.

One short-term commercial positive in the *Assessment* for insurers' business models is the demonstration that the need for insurance will increase – more areas will effectively become flood zones, coastal inundation is a new type of cover that will be required, and subsidence, land slip and erosion hazard cover will be needed in new areas.

Lastly, the 2019/20 bushfires clearly showed that the ability to provide affordable cover in locations exposed to forest fire will be constrained if the local and regional fire-fighting capacity is not adequate to contain increasingly intense, extended and widespread fire seasons. Recent examples from the United States are illustrative: costs of insurance cover are increasing in the aftermath of forest fire events in California and some insurers are withdrawing from providing cover to forest fire-exposed addresses (CDI, 2019). Fire brigades were an invention of early insurers, as a means of minimising property losses. Similarly, it is now incumbent upon governments to demonstrate the capacity to manage effective fire services if insurers are expected to provide affordable cover in forest fire-exposed locations.

Mortgage and commercial lenders

While climate risks are perhaps more easily apparent for insurers, counterintuitively perhaps, the financial risks of climate change sit much more heavily on the shoulders of banks than insurers for two reasons. Firstly, banks' contractual exposure to climate risks is typically for longer periods: mortgages can be issued for terms of up to 30 years, where insurers only ever assume risk in annual increments. Secondly, as demonstrated in the *Assessment*, climate risks will increase markedly for many properties in the next decades through to 2100.

What might concern mortgage lenders and property financiers most is their dependency on the insurance industry. The challenge for most lenders is that while they depend on the insurance industry to ensure their properties are protected from financial loss, lenders are unable to secure commitments from insurers for long-term price paths or estimates for future premiums, let alone long-term insurance for the term of their exposure.

Beyond insurers, lenders are also dependent on planning schemes and building codes – none of which appear to be getting ahead of climate change. An example illustrates: in Northern Australia, one insurer, Suncorp, facilitates lending to people to retrofit adjustments to their properties *beyond that required by the building code* in order to provide better protection from cyclones (Suncorp, 2020). In return insurance premiums are lowered. An insurer's initiative such as this can be welcomed as a prudent move, but it also underscores that the building code and planning system is poorly matched to climate-implicated risk, in this case, cyclones.

A few years ago, lenders may have been able to claim that the future impacts were not foreseeable, and that it was reasonable to assume that insurance would continue to be available and affordable in all areas. But the XDI national risk maps in the *Assessment* demonstrate this is an incorrect assumption. Currently about one in 20 properties are probably already in a situation where adequate cover will become either unavailable or unaffordable. Within the 80-year range of current climate models' projections through to 2100 – consistent with the expected lifetime of new buildings – the number of affected properties can be expected to double and increase further assuming increases in population.

In addition, it's not inconceivable that homeowners may seek to hold lenders legally accountable for financial harms. Banks have an implied fiduciary responsibility to ensure that borrowers can afford to service the loan they are being given. Banks do this by checking a borrower's income and their expenses, including food, car costs, school fees, and amongst other things, insurance. Lenders compliance or otherwise with responsible lending laws – designed in part to ensure that borrowers can afford to repay loans without substantial hardship – have come into focus through the recent Royal Commission into Misconduct in the Banking, Superannuation and Financial Services Industry in Australia (Commonwealth of Australia, 2019) and associated legal action (ASIC, 2020; Maurice Blackburn Lawyers, 2020). While it is probably not reasonable for a borrower to be expected to predict the future costs of insurance during the term of their mortgage, it is reasonable for a bank to have a forward quantification (the XDI national risk maps draw on those calculations). As such, it has been suggested that banks could be held responsible for the financial duress of a home owner who cannot service their mortgage and/or maintain effective insurance cover where the serviceability test did not include climate change impacts to forward-looking insurance premiums.

Considering that annual insurance premiums equivalent to 5 per cent of the value of the property being insured (as high as \$30,000 per year) are now emerging (Ting, 2020), one could conceive of future actions brought about by home owners claiming their inability to service a mortgage is due to excessive insurance costs or unavailable cover – which the bank could reasonably have been able to foresee. A similar argument might be run on the loss of wealth caused by climate-driven decreases in property value – there is increasing evidence from around the world of 'climate gentrification' – changes in the value of property due to changes in climate change risk (Nathan, 2019).

Looking ahead, banks will likely increasingly need to implement property screening at point of mortgage sale if they are going to avoid both legal liabilities and accumulating increasing levels of climate-threatened assets. This presents banks a time-sensitive version of the prisoner's dilemma. There is an early disincentive for a bank to reject mortgages due to climate change because the income is lost today while the risk of losses is smallest at the beginning – and businesses, shareholders and employees are rewarded for their performance today, rather than the risks they prevented in future years. However, later a bank chooses to enact screening relative to its peers, the bigger the share of the toxic assets in the property sector the bank is assuming. At the point when other competitors are screening out climate-threatened mortgages, banks without screening will be increasingly identified as the lending institutions of choice for HRP – and with each high-risk mortgage, higher risk is 'baked into' the bank's loan book for up to 30 years.

Regulators

Both insurance and lending are regulated financial sectors, and therefore the role of regulators in enabling or preventing climate harms through insurance and lending also bears some attention. Regulators internationally have made some acknowledgement of the concept of certain types of harm caused by climate change. France's Energy Transition Law (Article 173) enacted in 2015 is an example of mandatory intervention: it employs a 'comply or explain' approach, requiring listed companies to disclose risks, or explain why they're choosing not to. Also in 2015, the Financial Stability Board (FSB, constituted of nation states' central banks and others) established the Taskforce for Climate-related Financial Disclosures (TCFD) at the behest Mark Carney – then Governor of the Bank of England. Carney effectively warned that undisclosed climate change risks – such as too much fossil fuel exposure or too little resilience to worsening extreme weather risks – represented a new form of risk that could trigger a repeat of the 2008 global financial crisis.

Since the launch of the TCFD's first report in 2016 (TCFD, 2016), more than 1,000 companies have expressed support for the TCFD and its recommendations to report climate-related risks to markets and regulators (TCFD, 2020). In the United Kingdom, United States, Australia and elsewhere, regulators have also expressed support for the TCFD's recommendations that companies should voluntarily assess and disclose climate-related risks (see, for example, APRA, 2019).

There is of course a clear short-term motivation for insurers and lenders to not disclose climate risk: there is little financial incentive to parade one's dirty underwear for all – and especially the share market – to see. It is perhaps unsurprising; therefore, that compliance and disclosures have been lacklustre. As noted by Reserve Bank of Australia (RBA, 2019), a review by ASIC (2018) found that most Australian listed companies consider climate risks to some extent, but that 'climate risk disclosure was often too fragmented, general, or not comprehensive enough to be useful for investors' (RBA, 2019).

Regulators have not been silent on the issue of inadequate disclosure. The Bank of England, for example, has issued much more specific guidance on the disclosure they expect: specific mention of counterparty (or default) risk in equities, i.e., assessing the transition and physical risks carried by the companies in which financial institutions are investors, as well as the requirement to achieve asset-level granularity across physically exposed business lines like residential mortgages (Bank of England, 2019). Thus, we might conclude that the regulators are closing in on insurers', lenders' and investors' financial exposures to climate risk. Nevertheless, given the inherent motivation for not disclosing, institutions will – in the absence of other mechanisms – likely demonstrate minimum compliance. Regulators could require much more of both insurers and lenders.

The focus of the FSB and regulators is clearly defined by their experience of the 2008 global financial crisis – the FSB was established at the 2009 meeting of the G20 (a group consisting of the 19 largest state economies and the European Union). The FSB was attuned to the risk that the chain reaction of toxic financial assets had carried up through the financial system, leading ultimately to urgent and expensive government responses.

However, toxic financial assets, such as mortgages vulnerable to climate change, also carry risk downwards, to harm property owners and others who live in those properties.

In 2018, the Queensland Government ran a hypothetical scenario session focussed on discovering the mechanisms by which the property industry could iterate towards adaptation for climate risk-exposed dwellings (Green Cross, 2018). The scenario centred on a hypothetical owner of an apartment who learns the apartment's location is increasingly vulnerable to flooding. The session explored the scenario as it evolved over a 20-year period, during which the apartment owner was joined by their mortgage provider, their insurer, the local council and a property manager – who all strove to help the owner to respond to the growing flood risk, while abiding by the commercial requirements of their organisations. As the scenario evolved the property became damaged by an extreme event, the insurance costs increased to eventually become unaffordable. As the insurer departed, the property began to decrease in value, causing the mortgage provider to seek to higher and higher levels of equity from the owner. The owner was then unable to sell the property as it had become un-mortgageable. Nor could the owner convince council to build flood defences because of negative impacts the works would have on the wider local amenity. Over time, the apartment owner found themselves increasingly abandoned by institutions that were obliged to defend their own interests first.

When the apartment owner sought legal redress for losses suffered through no fault of their own, they found that each of the other parties had acted lawfully. The conclusion of the exercise – which included professionals from all of these sectors at the table – was that the property market, as currently configured, is unable to provide basic physical, financial and legal consumer protections for the single largest purchase most people will ever make. In pithier terms: climate change breaks the property market.

There is an evidently key role for regulators in property markets, given that regulators oversee two key players in built environments – insurers and lenders. And yet regulators are seeking disclosure of climate-related financial risks to financial markets, but they are not seeking disclosure of climate change risks to the very customers upon which the whole market rests. One possible conclusion, in light of how the hypothetical Queensland scenario played out, is that regulators are unwittingly enabling climate harm to property owners, to the short-term financial advantage of insurers, lenders and public sector agencies collecting rates.

Conclusion

There is assumed consumer protection in the property sector, which is in fact absent, i.e., financial risk to built environments are assumed to be managed, but a changing climate means this is increasingly not so. The *Second National Assessment* provides helpful insight into the scale of extreme weather risks for built environments in Australia and the general impact climate change may have on these risks. The analysis is provided at high resolution, i.e., at the scale of LGAs, and this can be used to plan for climate resilience and adaptation – with property-specific information about climate change and extreme hazards. Working across scales and disciplines, as is achieved with this analysis, is necessarily challenging, and, as with any scientific analysis, uncertainty is an ever-present element.

Nevertheless, with this information now at hand, it is incumbent upon decision makers in business and government to enact systems that make visible now the future impacts of climate change on Australia's built environment and to continue to instigate plans and actions to build social, economic, infrastructure and environmental resilience. Responding to these challenges will bring benefit beyond local scales and for all stakeholders. For example, publicly-listed companies are now required to disclose their material climate risks in shareholder statements, while ratings agencies are accounting for climate change impacts at municipal scale when calculating sovereign debt risk. Awareness of climate risks to investors' property portfolios will allow more reliable financial ratings and, coupled with action to address climate impacts, will ensure improved financial outcomes for businesses in these areas.

Greenhouse gas emissions have increased in the ten years since the first *Assessment* report (Global Carbon Project, 2019). We are, in fact, continuing to accelerate rather than rein in greenhouse gas emissions, thus, the likelihood of resolving the climate crisis is receding rather than drawing nearer. As such, climate change mitigation – a rapid reduction to zero net greenhouse gas emissions – is increasingly urgent. In the meantime, however, climate impacts are already manifesting and a clear-eyed assessment of changes in climate risk is essential so that Australia can assure the safety of its people and economy with an orderly, prudent and timely investment in national resilience. The *Assessment* sign posts the way.

References

Australian Prudential Regulation Authority (APRA). (2019). *Climate Change: Awareness to Action*. Sydney: Australian Prudential Regulation Authority. Available at: https://www.apra.gov.au/sites/default/files/climate_change_awareness_to_action_march_2019.pdf [Accessed 12 May 2020].

Australian Securities and Investments Commission (ASIC). (2020). ASIC to Appeal Westpac Responsible Lending Federal Court Decision. [Media Release]. Available at: https://asic.gov.au/about-asic/news-centre/find-a-media-release/2019-releases/19-246mr-asic-to-appeal-westpac-responsible-lending-federal-court-decision/ [Accessed 12 May 2020].

Australian Securities and Investments Commission (ASIC). (2018). Climate Risk Disclosure by Australia's Listed Companies. Available at: https://download.asic.gov.au/media/4871341/rep593-published-20-september-2018.pdf [Accessed 12 May 2020].

Bank of England. (2019). *The 2021 Biennial Exploratory Scenario on the Financial Risks from Climate Change*. London: Bank of England. Available at: https://www.bankofengland.co.uk/paper/2019/biennial-exploratory-scenario-climate-change-discussion-paper [Accessed 12 May 2020].

Buffett, W. E. (2016). *To the Shareholders of Berkshire Hathaway Inc.* [Letter] 27 February. Omaha: Berkshire Hathaway Inc. Available at: http://www.berkshirehathaway.com/letters/2015ltr.pdf [Accessed 28 May 2018].

California Department of Insurance. (2019). New Data Shows Insurance Is Becoming Harder to Find as a Result of Wildfires. [Press release] 20 August. Available at: http://www.insurance.ca.gov/0400-news/0100-press-releases/2019/release063-2019.cfm [Accessed 3 May 2020].

Commonwealth of Australia [HIH Royal Commission] and Owen, N. J. (2003). *The Failure of HIH Insurance*. Canberra: Commonwealth of Australia.

Commonwealth of Australia [Royal Commission into Misconduct in the Banking, Superannuation and Financial Services Industry] and Hayne, K. M. (2019). *Final Report of the Royal Commission into Misconduct in the Banking, Superannuation and Financial Services Industry*. Canberra: Commonwealth of Australia. Available at: https://treasury.gov.au/publication/p2019-fsrc-final-report [Accessed 12 May 2020].

Department of Climate Change. (2009). *Climate Change Risks to Australia's Coast: A First Pass National Assessment*. Canberra: Department of Climate Change.

Global Carbon Project. (2019). Carbon Budget and Trends 2019. Available at: www.globalcarbonproject.org/carbonbudget [Accessed 14 April 2020].

Green Cross. (2018). *Home Ownership Exposure to Climate Risk: Developing an Understanding of the Implications of Climate Change to Long-Term Home Ownership*. Brisbane: Green Cross. Available at: https://www.greencrossaustralia.org/media/9997813/0001grc_hypothetical%20report%20p6_final.pdf [Accessed 11 May 2020].

Mallon, K., McKinlay, M., Haughton, N., Hamden, R., Tedder, R. and Lamb, J. (2019). *Climate Change Risk to Australia's Built Environment: A Second Pass National Assessment*. Sydney: XDI Cross Dependency Initiative. Available at: https://xdi.systems/wp-content/uploads/2019/10/Climate-Change-Risk-to-Australia%E2%80%99s-Built-Environment-V4-final-reduced-2.pdf [Accessed 14 April 2020].

Maurice Blackburn Lawyers. (2020). Westpac Loans Class Action. [Website Class Action Update]. Available at: https://www.mauriceblackburn.com.au/class-actions/current-class-actions/westpac-loans-class-action/ [Accessed 12 May 2020].

McIlveen, L. (2001). HIH collapse threatens economy. *The Australian*, p. 2.

Nathan, A. (2019). Climate is the Newest Gentrifying Force, and Its Effects Are Already Re-Shaping Cities. [Blog]. *Science in the News*. Available at: http://sitn.hms.harvard.edu/flash/2019/climate-newest-gentrifying-force-effects-already-re-shaping-cities/ [Accessed 9 May 2020].

Pfeffer, I. and Klock, D. R. (1974). *Perspectives on Insurance*. Englewood Cliffs: Prentice-Hall.

Phelan, L. (2011). Managing climate risk: Extreme weather events and the future of insurance in a climate-changed world. *Australasian Journal of Environmental Management*,18(4), pp. 223–232. https://doi.org/10.1080/14486563.2011.611486.

Phelan, L., Henderson-Sellers, A., and Taplin, R. (2013). The Political Economy of Addressing the Climate Crisis in the Earth System: Undermining Perverse Resilience. *New Political Economy*, 18(2), pp. 198–226. https://doi.org/10.1080/13563467.2012.678820.

Phelan, L., Henderson-Sellers, A., Taplin, R. and Albrecht, G. (2011). Ecological viability or liability? Insurance system responses to climate risk. *Environmental Policy and Governance*, 21(2), pp. 112–130. https://doi.org/10.1002/eet.565.

Reserve Bank of Australia (RBA). (2019). *Financial Stability Review*. [October Review]. Sydney: Reserve Bank of Australia. Available at: https://www.rba.gov.au/publications/fsr/2019/oct/pdf/financial-stability-review-2019-10.pdf [Accessed 11 May 2020].

Suncorp. (2020). What is the Cyclone Resilience Benefit? [Web FAQs]. Available at: https://www.suncorp.com.au/insurance/home/home-building.html#faq-accordion-ky1uc5 [Accessed 3 May 2020].

Task Force on Climate-related Financial Disclosures (TCFD). (2020). More than 1,000 Global Organizations Declare Support for the Task Force on Climate-Related Financial Disclosures and its Recommendations. [Media Release] 12 February. Available at: https://www.fsb-tcfd.org/wp-content/uploads/2020/02/PR-TCFD-1000-Supporters_FINAL.pdf [Accessed 9 May 2020].

Task Force on Climate-related Financial Disclosures (TCFD). (2016). *Phase I Report of the Task Force on Climate-Related Financial Disclosures*. Basel: TCFD. Available at: https://www.fsb-tcfd.org/wp-content/uploads/2016/03/Phase_I_Report_v15.pdf [Accessed 9 May 2020].

Ting, I., Scott, N., Palmer, A. and Slezak, M. (2020). The Rise of Red Zones of Risk. *Australian Broadcasting Corporation*, 3 January. Available at: https://www.abc.net.au/news/2019-10-23/the-suburbs-facing-rising-insurance-costs-from-climate-risk/11624108 [Accessed 21 April 2020].

Trennery, C. F. (1926). *Origin and Early History of Insurance*. London: P.S. King & Son.

7 The influence of government regulation on insurers' responses to climate change

*Louise du Toit**

Introduction

Climate change presents an unprecedented challenge to the insurance industry[1] (Hecht, 2008: 1559; Botzen, van den Bergh and Bouwer, 2010: 578; De la Mare, 2013: 190): for example, climate change makes climate-related extreme weather events less easy to predict, thereby increasing uncertainty, which makes it difficult to price risk; and also increases the magnitude of losses, which will potentially affect insurers' solvency (Hecht, 2008: 1561 and 1565). Following Hurricane Andrew, which struck Florida and the Bahamas in 1992, several small insurers in Florida declared bankruptcy (Leggett, 1993: 21 and 23; Paterson, 2001: 21). More recently, US insurers' payouts for wildfires increased from \$4.2 billion in 2016 to \$16 billion in 2017 (AM Best, 2018), and Camp Fire in 2018 resulted in the liquidation of at least one small insurer (Morris, 2018). De la Mare (2013: 196) argues that '[t]he importance of insurance in the global economy can hardly be overstated', and Haufler (2006: 7) notes that the solvency of insurers 'is crucial to the economic health of the nation'.

Due to the vulnerability of insurers to extreme weather events and other climate-related risks (Leggett, 1993; International Association of Insurance Supervisors and Sustainable Insurance Forum, 2018), it was thought that they would be early to take substantive action on climate change (Jones and Phillips, 2016: 132). However, insurers have been slow to act, and their responses have primarily been limited to trying to reduce their exposure to financial losses due to climate change and managing exposure to risk (Newell and Paterson, 2010: 62–63), rather than trying to actively implement measures that could contribute to deep reductions in global greenhouse gas emissions (Paterson, 2001: 21 and 27).[2] Indeed, Phelan et al. classify most actions of insurers as 'adaptive' or 'weakly mitigative' (Phelan et al.).

* I would like to thank Prof. Cameron Holley, Prof. Clifford Shearing and Dr. Liam Phelan for their valuable inputs into and comments on earlier drafts of this chapter. The responsibility for any errors in this final version remains my own.

This research has benefited from funding received while a Postdoctoral Research Fellow at the African Climate and Development Initiative, the University of Cape Town Law Faculty, and the Griffith Criminology Institute (Griffith University).

There have been increasing calls for stronger action on the part of insurers, with many focusing on their investment policies and arguing specifically that insurers must shift investment away from fossil fuels in order to contribute to climate change mitigation, which will be essential, *inter alia*, to ensuring the ongoing viability of the insurance industry (see Leggett, 1993: 3; Phelan et al., 2011: 126, 2020). The year 2013 saw the start of a gradual but increasing trend for insurers to undertake to divest from coal-based businesses and cease to provide insurance cover to new coal-fired power plants or coal mines (referred to collectively herein as 'coal exclusion policies'). A 2018 report on the approach of the world's 80 largest insurers to climate-related risks and opportunities suggests that such decisions are 'becoming a barometer of commitment to climate action' (Belsom et al., 2018: 18).

This chapter considers government regulation[3] as one amongst several key influences shaping insurers' responses to climate change, with a focus on the coal exclusion policies that have been introduced by a handful of insurers. The next section provides an overview of the responses of the insurance industry to climate change, with particular reference to insurers' coal exclusion policies. The section following discusses climate change-related government regulation of the insurance industry and reviews practices in a selection of countries. Thereafter, the impact of climate change-related government regulation as well as other key influences on insurers is considered. The following section briefly explores further measures that could be implemented by governments and regulators to encourage stronger insurer responses to climate change. The final section concludes.

Insurers and climate change

The response of the insurance industry to climate change

The insurance industry is among society's 'most pervasive and powerful institutions' and is a core institution in the 'risk society' within which we live (Ericson, Doyle and Barry, 2003: 3 and 7–8). There have been various debates about the potential of the insurance industry to play a leading role in addressing climate change (Leggett, 1993; Hecht, 2008: 1619–1620; Phelan et al., 2011; Herbstein et al., 2013), or, in the words of Froestad et al. (2011), to act as a 'fulcrum institution'—a term coined to describe those 'institutions that occupy influential positions in nodal assemblages and networks, and which are threatened by the erosion of ecological systems upon which they depend, in one way or another' (Shearing, 2015: 262). Such arguments are based on the power and resources held by the insurance industry as well as its vulnerability to climate change as a result of increasing claims and payouts arising from more frequent and increasingly intense climate change-related weather events (Paterson, 1999: 26; Paterson, 2001: 21–22; Hecht, 2008: 1613–1614; Mills, 2009: 334; Herbstein et al., 2013). De Castries (2015) also points out that as the insurance industry is concerned with 'protection—of people, goods, and physical assets—on the one side and investments, to enable this protection, on the other', it is one of the only industries that is capable of contributing to both adaptation and mitigation efforts.

While the responses of the insurance industry to climate change have been numerous and varied—as documented comprehensively by Mills (2009, 2012)—it is important to note that the industry has generally responded defensively by trying to decrease its exposure to large-scale climate-related financial risks, including through trying to improve its actuarial analysis, withdrawing insurance cover from certain areas and shifting the burden, for example, by increasing insureds' premiums as well as creating financial instruments such as catastrophe bonds (Paterson, 1999: 26–27, 2001: 21–27; Herbstein, 2015: 93–94). Further, more proactive, responses include the introduction of pay-as-you drive insurance, reduced premiums for climate-resilient buildings, more stringent building requirements, reduced premiums for drivers of hybrid cars, the offering of carbon offsets, carbon disclosure and commitments to attain carbon neutrality (Paterson, 2001: 27; Hecht, 2008: 1593–1604; Mills, 2009: 338–346).

However, it has been argued that these responses are not sufficient to avoid dangerous climate change (Leggett, 1993; Mills, 2005; Hecht, 2008; Phelan et al., 2011) in that they are 'adaptive' or 'weakly mitigative' rather than 'strongly mitigative' (Phelan et al., 2011: 114; Phelan et al., 2020). Furthermore, the potential of the insurance industry to act as a fulcrum institution has not been realised. A theme that has emerged in this regard relates to the extent, and nature, of government regulation (see for example, Hecht, 2008; De la Mare, 2013; Herbstein et al., 2013). This is discussed in the section Government regulation of the insurance industry.

There are numerous and complex reasons for the failure of the insurance industry to meet early expectations that it would play a central role in responding to, and mitigating, climate change. While these cannot be discussed fully here, it has been highlighted that insurers are not motivated to mitigate greenhouse gas emissions (a 'collective good'), as individual insurers do not stand to benefit financially from such actions (Hecht, 2008: 1610). There is also a concern that individual insurers' climate change risk reduction efforts (in this case, climate change mitigation) may enable competitors to 'free ride' off any resultant risk reduction (Herbstein et al., 2013). Furthermore, any risk reduction may result in reduced premiums (Herbstein et al., 2013). Herbstein (2015: 136) argues that the insurance industry simply has not viewed climate change 'as posing a threat big enough to warrant a fundamental shift away from its traditional risk management responses'. This is echoed by Thistlethwaite and Wood (2018: 289) who highlight that while insurers acknowledge the risk posed by climate change, they believe that 'climate change risk ranks very low compared to other risk drivers'.

In regard to arguments—including by Leggett (1993)—that insurers should shift their investments away from fossil fuels, there are various barriers inherent to the insurance industry that hinder such action, such as the internal organisational division between risk managers and investment managers (Paterson, 2001: 31). More generally, publicly owned corporations have a duty to their shareholders and must ensure that their insurance and investment operations are profitable, which may result in them investing 'conservatively' (UNEP-FI, 2012: 11; Golnaraghi, 2018: 14 and 39) and being more concerned with profits in the short term, rather than with risks that may transpire in the longer term (Hecht, 2008: 1589).

Wright and Nyberg (2017: 1635) argue that corporations generally are 'ill-suited' to addressing climate change, *inter alia*, because they have short-term objectives. Warren Buffett spoke to this when he argued that shareholders of the insurance operation of Berkshire Hathaway did not need to be concerned about climate change as it did not pose a threat to profitability in the short term. Specifically, he reasoned:

> The sponsor [of the proxy proposal regarding climate change] may worry that property losses will skyrocket because of weather changes. And such worries might, in fact, be warranted if we wrote ten- or twenty-year policies at fixed prices. But insurance policies are customarily written for one year and repriced annually to reflect changing exposures. Increased possibilities of loss translate promptly into increased premiums.
>
> (Buffett, 2016: 25–26)

However, 'short-termism is not sustainable' (Bansal and DesJardine, 2014: 76). On the contrary, the ongoing viability of the insurance industry requires a longer-term view and a transition to a zero-carbon economy (Phelan et al., 2011: 126; Campiglio et al., 2018: 462). Broadening the perspective beyond the industry to wider societal considerations, Hecht (2008: 1561) argues that '[i]f insurers do not rise to the challenge of climate change, there could be a serious financial and social crisis on a global scale'.

Exclusion policies for investment in and underwriting of coal

An area that has been receiving increased attention in recent years is the investment activities of the insurance industry (and, indeed, institutional investors in general) (see Ayling and Gunningham, 2017; Bosshard, 2018). Storebrand, a Norwegian pension fund and insurance company, was the first insurer to divest from coal in 2013 (Storebrand, 2013). The first major global insurer to divest from coal was AXA, which in 2015 announced it would divest from those businesses most exposed to coal-related activities (De Castries, 2015). Other major insurers and reinsurers have followed these examples, as reflected in Table 7.1 below (arranged chronologically, according to the date of the initial divestment). A number of policies were introduced in the lead-up to the 21st Conference of the Parties (COP 21) under the

Table 7.1 Insurers' coal exclusion policies

Insurer	Country of domicile	Initial divestment date	Threshold[a]	Date of withdrawal of insurance	Position on Forbes Global 2000 list—2019
Storebrand	Norway	Jul, 2013	30%	–	1258
KLP	Norway	Nov, 2014	5%	–	–
Oslo pension & insurance	Norway	Mar, 2015	TBC	–	–
AXA	France	May, 2015	30%	Apr, 2017	85
Aviva	United Kingdom	Jul, 2015	30%	–	232
Natixis assurances	France	Oct, 2015	50%	–	–
Allianz	Germany	Nov, 2015	30%	May, 2018	23
CNP assurances	France	Nov, 2015	15%/25%	–	285
SCOR	France	Nov, 2015	30%	Sep, 2017	942
Munich Re	Germany	2016	30%	Aug, 2018	147
Swiss Re	Switzerland	2016	30%	Jul, 2018	474
Aegon	Netherlands	May, 2016	30%	–	460
HCF	Australia	Dec, 2016	TBC	–	–
Zurich insurance group	Switzerland	Nov, 2017	30%	Nov, 2017	117
Generali	Italy	Feb, 2018	30%	Nov, 2018	144
Lloyd's of London	United Kingdom	Apr, 2018	30%	–	–
Hannover Re	Germany	Jun, 2018	25%	Apr, 2019	—
Uniqa	Austria	Jan, 2019	30%	Jan, 2019	1607
Mapfre	Spain	Mar, 2019	30%	Mar, 2019	646
QBE insurance group	Australia	Mar, 2019	30%	Jul 2019	800
Talanx	Germany	Apr, 2019	25%	Apr, 2019	484
Vienna insurance group	Austria	May, 2019	30%	May, 2019	1192
Chubb	United States of America	Jul, 2019	30%	Jul, 2019	137
Nationale Nederlanden	Netherlands	Jul, 2019	30%	Jul, 2019	–
Suncorp	Australia	Jul, 2019	0%	Jul, 2019	701

[a]The threshold for exclusion essentially establishes a minimum threshold for companies that generate revenues from coal mining or electricity generation from coal. Insurers that have implemented coal exclusion policies undertake to withdraw investment from companies whose coal-related revenues exceed the established threshold. Such an exclusion may be expressed in terms such as the following: 'Swiss Re has decided to stop investing in companies that generate at least 30 per cent of their revenue from thermal coal mining or generate at least 30 per cent of their power from thermal coal'.

Source: (Swiss Re, 2017: 27)

United Nations Framework Convention on Climate Change (UNFCCC), held in Paris in late-2015, where the landmark Paris Agreement was agreed to. To date, 25 major insurers and reinsurers—including Allianz, Aviva, Generali, Lloyd's of London, Munich Re, Natixis, SCOR, Swiss Re and Zurich Insurance Group—have announced decisions to divest from coal. Furthermore, 16 of these—including AXA, SCOR, Zurich Insurance Group, Allianz, Swiss Re and Munich Re—have also decided to withdraw insurance cover for coal companies or coal projects.

Table 7.1 shows that insurers that have implemented coal exclusion policies are generally amongst the world's largest publicly owned corporations. Furthermore, these insurers are located overwhelmingly in Europe. Indeed, Haufler (2006: 4) notes the 'significant variation between European and American insurance cultures' in regard to their insurance industries' responses to climate change. Within Europe, there are also regional distinctions with a larger number of coal exclusion policies having been implemented by insurers domiciled in France, Germany and Norway. This points to the potential influence of government regulation on insurers' climate change responses. Government regulation of the insurance industry, in relation to climate change and climate-related risks, is now considered.

Government regulation of the insurance industry

Regulation and climate risk

Insurers are typically regulated by governments legislatively and via regulatory authorities, and, though regulation of insurers differs by jurisdiction, regional similarities and differences can also be evident. Generally, regulators are concerned with ensuring that insurance is available and affordable (market regulation) and that insurers remain solvent (solvency regulation) (Klein, 1995: 368; Mills, 2008: 64). In order to ensure the affordability of rates, regulators may prevent insurers from increasing their rates. For instance, following the hurricane season in Florida in 2005, regulators prevented insurers from raising their premiums in order to reflect increasing risk, which led to several insurers withdrawing from high-risk coastal areas (Hecht, 2008: 1608).

A marked difference has been observed in the approaches of regulators in the US as opposed to those in Europe. The approach of regulators in the US has been described as being more prescriptive, rules-based and focused on accounting principles, while the approach of regulators in Europe has been described as more progressive, prudential and concerned with assessing insurers' overall financial risk (Grace and Klein, 2009). The Solvency II regime came into effect in the European Union in 2016 (replacing the Solvency I regime), introducing a harmonised prudential framework for insurers that, amongst other things, is intended to facilitate a more accurate assessment of each insurer's risks (European Commission, 2015).

It has been argued that, globally, insurance regulation appears to be more concerned with consumer protection than with addressing climate risk, and furthermore that the objectives of insurance regulation are not necessarily aligned with tackling climate change in the short term (Hecht, 2008: 1607; Herbstein et al., 2013). However, 'regulators should be deeply concerned about how to regulate more effectively to deal with this long-term risk' (Hecht, 2008: 1610).

With regard to investment, government regulation may constrain insurers' investment activities in relation to climate change (Paterson, 1999: 28–29; Herbstein, 2015: 153). In the European context, it has been noted that the capital requirements of the Solvency II regulations do not 'incentivise investments in long-term opportunities aligned with a low-carbon transition' (Uhlenbruch, 2019: 40). Former Chairman and CEO of AXA, Henri de Castries, specifically noted:

> As long as the 'systemic risk' of carbon is not correctly embedded into regulatory frameworks, through efficient 'carbon pricing' mechanisms and more broadly favorable treatment for longer-term investments that are necessary to limit climate risks, it will always be a story of a few responsible actors doing their best within a broader financial system that is not designed for sustainability.
>
> (De Castries, 2015)

However, promisingly, regulators are giving increased attention to the risks posed by climate change and are increasingly recognising that climate change must be addressed by insurers in order to ensure the viability of the insurance industry as well as the stability and resilience of financial systems.

In the UK, Mark Carney—former Governor of the Bank of England—has highlighted the Bank of England's efforts to 'consider whether insurers and banks have adequate governance arrangements to develop strategies for identifying and mitigating climate risk across their entire businesses, both their liabilities and assets and over sufficiently long time horizons' (Carney, 2018). In the US context, a review conducted by Deloitte—regarding the preparedness of insurers in relation to climate-related risks and regulators' view thereof—found that 'US state regulators and lawmakers thus are watching the implications of climate-related risks very carefully and are becoming increasingly concerned about how well insurers are managing them' (Bachir, Gokhale and Ashani, 2019: 8).

National regulatory examples

In France—where four of the insurers and reinsurers that have implemented coal exclusion policies are domiciled (as indicated in Table 7.1)—the national government adopted the Energy Transition Law[4] in August 2015, in the lead-up to COP 21. In addition to ambitious climate change and energy-related targets, significantly, article 173 places disclosure obligations on listed companies, banks and credit institutions and institutional investors. Of particular relevance, article 173-VI requires that institutional investors (including insurance companies) disclose: how environmental, social and governance criteria are integrated in their investment decision-making processes, the exposure of their activities to climate-related risks, the emissions associated with the investment portfolio and the alignment of the investment portfolios with international and French climate change objectives (2° Investing Initiative, 2015: 7–8).

In explaining its decision to implement a coal exclusion policy, Swiss Re stated the following:

> Given ongoing developments (eg, from France's Energy Transition Law), we expect more regulation with regard to disclosure on risks related to climate change. Carbon-intense companies might also be confronted with higher taxes or tighter regulation on carbon emissions.
>
> (Swiss Re, 2017: 27)

It is also significant that Aviva stated that its *Strategic Response to Climate Change*, which includes divesting where necessary, 'encapsulate[s] our approach to addressing the requirements of article 173 [of the French Energy Transition Law]' (Aviva, 2017: 32).

While article 173 is not prescriptive, Brånå highlights that investors feel obliged to comply with this law 'for reputational reasons' and argues that 'the signalling effect from the state backing such a policy should not be underestimated' (2017: 102).

While not legally binding, the City Council of Paris in 2018 took the unprecedented step of passing a motion (titled '*Voeu relatif à la responsabilité du secteur de l'assurance dans la pollution de l'air*') calling on insurers to withdraw investments and support from the coal industry. Allianz, SCOR and Generali were specifically mentioned in the motion due to their provision of underwriting services to coal projects and coal companies in Poland (Pinson, 2018).

In Norway—where three insurers that have implemented coal exclusion policies are domiciled—the Norwegian Parliament has set guidelines regarding the observation and exclusion of companies from the portfolio of the Government Pension Fund Global (Norwegian Ministry of Finance, 2016). Section 2(2) of the guidelines, entitled 'Guidelines for observation and exclusion from the Government Pension Fund Global', provide that mining companies and power producers may be subject to observation or exclusion if they derive at least 30 per cent of their revenue from thermal coal or if at least 30 per cent of their operations are based on thermal coal (Norwegian Ministry of Finance, 2016). Kommunal Landspensjonskasse (KLP), a public pension and insurance provider, initially divested from coal in November 2014 with a threshold of 50 per cent. It subsequently decreased its threshold to 30 per cent and stated that this decision was 'based on the Norwegian parliament's new guidelines for the GPFG [Government Pension Fund Global]' (KLP, 2015: 1).

In the United Kingdom—where two insurers have implemented coal exclusion policies—the UK's insurance regulator, the Bank of England Prudential Regulation Authority (PRA), has been prominent in highlighting the risks that climate change poses to financial stability. In 2015, the PRA published a report dealing specifically with the insurance industry—*The Impact of Climate Change on the UK Insurance Sector*—which identified three oft-cited risks posed by climate change to financial stability, namely physical risks, liability risks and transition risks (PRA, 2015). In 2019, the PRA issued a supervisory statement regarding enhancing banks' and insurers' approaches to managing the financial impacts of climate change (PRA, 2019a). In 2019, the PRA also issued life and general insurance stress tests, both of which were, *inter alia*, intended to assess how insurers are managing climate change-related risks (PRA, 2019b). The former Governor of the Bank of England, Mark Carney, in particular has played a prominent role in highlighting the risks posed by climate change (Carney, 2015, 2016). The Financial Conduct Authority is also responsible for regulation of the insurance industry. In 2017, it commissioned a report on how climate change could impact the financial system (Robins, 2017).

In the Netherlands—where two insurers have implemented coal exclusion policies—the insurance regulator, De Nederlandsche Bank, has climate change firmly on its agenda and has started to assess the impacts of climate change on Dutch insurers (DNB, 2016, 2017), has requested major Dutch financial institutions to submit data on their exposure to carbon-intensive sectors, and is developing a climate stress test to demonstrate the resilience of Dutch financial institutions to energy transition-related risks (DNB, 2018: 99). In this regard, Aegon announced that 'applying a coal exclusion … addresses concerns by the American and Dutch regulators' (Aegon, 2016).

In the United States—where insurance regulators are state-based, and where Chubb recently became the first major American insurer to divest from coal—former California Insurance Commissioner Dave Jones has made climate-related disclosure mandatory for insurance companies that are licensed in California and that write at least $100 million in direct premiums (California Department of Insurance, n.d.). Jones also called for such insurers to voluntarily divest from their investments in thermal coal (California Department of Insurance, 2016). Following this call, Munich Re America stated:

> The California Insurance Commissioner has asked all insurance companies doing business in California to voluntarily divest from their investments in thermal coal. … In response, we are determining the exposure to coal in our portfolios on a regional basis.
>
> (Munich Re America Corporation, 2016: 4)

In 2018, the California Department of Insurance commissioned a comprehensive report on the risks posed by climate change to the Californian insurance industry (Mills et al., 2018). As noted above, Aegon linked its decision to apply a coal exclusion policy to 'concerns by the American and Dutch regulators' (Aegon, 2016).

In Australia—where three insurers have implemented coal exclusion policies—Executive Board Member of the Australian Prudential Regulation Authority (APRA), Geoff Summerhayes, has specifically drawn attention to the issue of climate change and its relevance for insurers and emphasised that while climate risks had perhaps previously been viewed as a distant or 'non-financial' problem, that this is no longer the case and that '[s]ome climate risks are distinctly "financial" in nature' (Summerhayes, 2017a). He has also pointed out that 'raising awareness about climate risk, and the need for resilience, is entirely within APRA's regulatory mandate of promoting financial system stability' (Summerhayes, 2017b). APRA is working to increase its understanding of climate risks and is also assessing the awareness of regulated entities and, over time, 'will expect more sophisticated answers, especially from well-resourced and complex entities' (Summerhayes, 2017b). In the future, the APRA will consider conducting stress tests related to climate risk and has encouraged entities to conduct their own stress tests in the meantime (Summerhayes, 2017b).

The influence of government regulation on insurers' climate change responses

The preceding section has outlined national laws and regulatory actions that are concerned specifically with insurers' management of climate-related risks and climate-related investment. However, the presence of strong national laws on climate change is also important. Indeed, in a survey regarding business responses to climate change, the majority of the companies surveyed ranked national climate policies 'as most important in shaping their climate strategies' (Ernst & Young, 2010: 10). While not specifically discussed in detail, in the majority of the domicile countries included in Table 7.1, strong national policies on climate change and/or energy are present. For example, all of the European countries listed in Table 7.1 have established greenhouse gas emission reduction targets, and many have supporting instruments, such as a carbon tax (for example, Norway) or support for renewable energy (for example, Germany).

It is notable that insurers generally have identified 'regulations' as the primary factor influencing underwriting (UNEP-FI, 2012: 14), and have, over the last decade, consistently named 'regulation' as one of the top risks facing the insurance industry (CSFI, n.d.). In a study on the impact of regulatory pressure and competitive dynamics on energy-intensive companies, Okereke and Russel (2010: 107) found that '[c]urrent regulation as well as awareness of future international and domestic policy developments appeared to be the most important external drivers of climate strategy building'. Furthermore, compliance with carbon-related regulation was motivated by fears of becoming uncompetitive as well as the prospect of financial benefits (Okereke and Russel, 2010: 109).

As noted in the section directly above, insurers that have implemented coal exclusion policies have referred to regulation in relation to such decisions, with several insurers specifically referring to the French Energy Transition Law and the Norwegian parliamentary guidelines. Furthermore, Natixis announced: 'Ending financing for the thermal coal-based economy ... is underpinned by: ... [t]he vital recognition of the multiple risks associated with the coal industry, these being not just environmental, but economic and regulatory as well' (Natixis, 2015). Other insurers have referred to regulatory pressures too, such as Aegon, which stated that 'applying a coal exclusion ... addresses concerns by the American and Dutch regulators' (Aegon, 2016). Allianz announced: 'With this step [divesting equity stakes in coal-based business models] we contribute to ... preparing for imminent developments in climate regulation across the globe' (Allianz, 2015). Storebrand also stated: 'Companies that specialize in carbon-intense projects are vulnerable to climate policy and shifting regulations' (Morales, 2014). AXA has also acknowledged that 'regulatory initiatives, including at French, European Union and international levels, regarding climate change may affect our operations and those of our counterparties, and potentially limit our investments or affect their value' (AXA, 2019: 170). Such statements by insurers clearly indicate that regulatory requirements have influenced their climate change-related responses, and highlight that insurers have implemented coal exclusion policies partly to reduce their exposure to risks which arise as a result of increasing climate regulation.

However, regulatory uncertainty can hinder meaningful responses to climate change. In considering the diverging responses of European and American insurers to climate change, Haufler (2006: 10) refers to the 'paradoxical role' of the US government, which, on the one hand, has taken very little action in regard to climate change mitigation and, on the other, has insulated insurers from various risks through its national flood and crop insurance programmes. Haufler (2006: 10) argues that '[t]here is both an assumption by insurers that the US government will pick up the slack if the private sector does not provide insurance, and an awareness that any action by them on global warming issues probably would not elicit support from the government'. With regard to investment, insurers have cited the fragmentation of 'climate policies and regulations that impact investors' confidence' as a barrier to 'climate aware investing', which includes divestment (Golnaraghi, 2018: 22). Blyth et al. (2007: 5772) highlight the importance of policy certainty, stating that 'policy-makers need to be aware that [climate] policy uncertainty creates risk for private companies which can affect their investment behaviour'. This uncertainty can be reduced by strong climate policies (Skjærseth and Skodvin, 2001: 47).

Government laws and regulations that indicate that a business-as-usual carbon pathway will not be viable in the long term, for instance through the establishment of greenhouse gas emission reduction targets, the introduction of carbon pricing or the introduction of regulations mandating insurers to take account of and address climate-related risks, could encourage stronger responses by the insurance industry. Indeed, the Geneva Association (whose membership is made up of chief executive officers of the world's largest insurers) argues that governments could assist in removing barriers to insurers' efforts to contribute to climate change mitigation and adaptation, *inter alia*, by providing more clarity on national decarbonisation policies and phasing out fossil fuel subsidies (Golnaraghi, 2018: 25). Furthermore, in the context of investment, Bauer et al. (2018: 133) argue that '[i]f policymakers provide clear signals that strong climate policies will be imposed in the future, then divestment will reduce carbon lock-in and the low-carbon technology phase-in will ramp up earlier'.

Other influences shaping insurers' climate change responses

While regulation is the focus of this chapter, it is not the only driver of insurer behaviour. In addition to regulation, insurers have specifically acknowledged that the risk of stranded assets and reputation risk influenced their decisions to implement coal exclusion policies.

For instance, Storebrand stated in relation to its divestment decision: 'It was a financial and climate-related decision, and there was very much a consideration of stranded assets' (Morales, 2014). AXA (2016: 9) announced: 'In May 2015, following a careful analysis of this "stranded assets" hypothesis, AXA decided to divest from companies most exposed to coal-related activities'. Aegon has noted that 'poorly diversified thermal coal producers are most likely to be impacted by climate-related government regulation and therefore run the highest risk of their assets being stranded' (Aegon, 2017: 6). Swiss Re also reasoned as follows:

> Carbon-intense companies might … be confronted with higher taxes or tighter regulation on carbon emissions, which may lead to increased risk of impairment due to unanticipated or premature write-downs or asset devaluations. As such, the asset becomes potentially stranded, which triggers a higher investment risk.
>
> (Swiss Re, 2017: 27)

These insurer statements also indicate that the risk of stranded assets arises from the presence of climate-related government regulation.

With regard to reputation risk, as identified above, investors in France feel obliged to comply with article 173 of the French Energy Transition Law, which they do not consider to be prescriptive, 'for reputational reasons' (Brånå, 2017: 102). In its 'Group policy on coal mining and coal-based energy', which incorporated its divestment decision, AXA stated: 'Business links with certain activities or products may also endanger AXA's reputation' (AXA, undated). Furthermore, in its 2015 Annual Report, Munich Re America stated the following:

> The California Insurance Commissioner has asked all insurance companies doing business in California to voluntarily divest from their investments in thermal coal. ... In response, we are determining the exposure to coal in our portfolios on a regional basis, considering the reputational risk of being listed as a company which is not divesting.
>
> (Munich Re America Corporation, 2016: 4–5)

Furthermore, pressure exerted by, amongst others, rating agencies, civil society organisations and investors, may also influence insurers' climate change responses.

Certain rating agencies have started to pay attention to climate change in relation to insurers. Moody's has highlighted risks to insurers, including negative credit impacts and losses arising from climate change litigation, and concluded that '[c]limate change risks outweigh opportunities for P&C [property and casualty] (re)insurers' (Moody's, 2018: 1). Moody's views certain insurers' 'retreat from thermal coal as positive ... [as] [i]t reduces their exposure to potential climate change liability, and reduces the risk of their investment assets becoming stranded' (Moody's, 2020). Furthermore, Moody's assesses the thermal coal sector as 'elevated risk – intermediate', which reflects that 'the sector is already experiencing material credit implications as a result of environmental risks' (Moody's, 2019: 18). From mid-2015 to mid-2017, environment and climate concerns were factored into Standard & Poor's credit ratings in 717 cases and resulted in a change in rating in 106 cases. Thus, being proactive with regard to climate change responses could be beneficial from a credit rating perspective (Mathiesen, 2018: 455). Hecht (2008: 1611) argues that the scrutiny of rating agencies 'could push insurers toward addressing their climate risk exposure as they attempt to retain high ratings'.

Civil society organisations have arguably played an important role in the divestment movement, which has as its aim to 'shame, pressure, facilitate and encourage' investors to divest their fossil fuel holdings (Ayling and Gunningham, 2017: 132). This raises the potential for threats to reputation. The civil society initiative, Insure our Future (previously Unfriend Coal), has launched a focused campaign calling on insurers and reinsurers to divest from coal (and fossil fuels generally) and to stop underwriting the companies they no longer invest in. It is notable that following pressure from environmental groups, including the Insure our Future campaign, Allianz announced its decision to stop underwriting coal projects and to reduce its investment threshold to zero by 2040 (Alkousaa, 2018; Allianz, 2018).

With regard to investors, there have been an increasing number of share-holder resolutions regarding climate-related issues,[5] which 'illustrates that climate change has increasingly become of interest to shareholders' (Stechemesser et al., 2015: 557–558). In response to Munich Re's decision to continue to provide reinsurance to coal-related businesses, Munich Re investors stated that '[this] position could become increasingly untenable, though, as investors seek more detail from the companies they own, driven on by policymakers, particularly in Europe' (Jessop, Cohn and Sims, 2018). The following month, Munich Re lowered its divestment threshold from 50 per cent to 30 per cent and announced that it would no longer insure new coal-fired power plants or mines in industrialised countries (Gangcuangco, 2018). Notably, some insurers cited the lack of pressure from their inves-tors as a barrier to making progress in their climate strategies and stated that 'increased pressure from their investors would help provide a stronger internal mandate to drive progress on managing climate-related risks and opportunities' (Uhlenbruch, 2019: 40–41).

Discussion

The preceding sections have highlighted the importance of regulation in influencing insurers' climate-related responses; thus, regulators could, through laws and regulatory actions, encourage strong responses from insurers. Suggesting detailed regulatory reform is beyond the scope of this chapter; however, it is clear that regulators should be concerned that insurers are sufficiently prepared to manage climate change-related risks. Further, it is clear that insurers do respond to regulatory change itself, as well as the prospect of regulatory change. Mills suggests that regulators, *inter alia*, call for further research on weather-related losses and on the insurance-climate nexus; support more actuarial, risk-based pricing in the climate change context; support climate-friendly insurance products; sup-port improved building codes to enhance climate change adaptation; revise regulations to encourage climate-friendly investments and require public disclosure of climate risks (Mills, 2008: 147–157). Hecht supports this latter call, arguing that the disclosure of climate risk should be mandatory, which 'may motivate insurers to respond to peer pressure (from the competitive practices of other insurers) and market pressure to address climate risks' (Hecht, 2008: 1610).

In the context of investment, regulators should incentivise 'climate aware investing' by removing barriers to such investments and through better aligning insurance regulations with national climate change policies (Golnaraghi, 2018: 27). Paterson (1999: 29) notes that investment switching would be more viable if governments imposed carbon taxes and promoted renewable energy. Hecht (2008: 1610) also argues that '[t]o the extent that insurance regulators can focus on creating mechanisms to allow insurers to internalize the benefits of these public goods, they will make a significant contribution to addressing climate change'.

It is notable that insurers themselves have explicitly called for regulators to set higher prices for carbon, remove fossil fuel subsidies, incorporate climate risk considerations in the capital requirements of Solvency II and make Task Force on Climate-related Financial Disclosures reporting mandatory for investors and corporations (Uhlenbruch, 2019: 45–46). As noted above, the Geneva Association has argued that governments could assist in removing barriers to insurers' efforts to contribute to climate change mitigation and adaptation by, *inter alia*, providing more clarity on national decarbonisation policies and phasing out fossil fuel subsidies (Golnaraghi, 2018: 25). The implementation of such measures by regulators would go some way towards ensuring that 'the "systemic risk" of carbon is … correctly embedded into regulatory frameworks' so that it will not simply be a case of only 'a few responsible actors doing their best' (De Castries, 2015).

While focused on the influence of regulation, this chapter has highlighted other drivers of insurer behaviour, and this suggests at least the plausibility of alignments across key drivers of insurer behaviour. This is consistent with the findings of Sullivan and Gouldson (2017: 413 and 417) who argue that 'external governance pressures' (including government regulation as well as pressures from non-governmental organisations and investors), which are 'aligned, robust and of sufficient duration', can significantly influence internal governance processes and corporate strategies and actions—provided there is a clear business case.

The financial risks involved in failing to respond to climate change are increasingly being recognised by regulators (as discussed above) as well as large investors. A recent and prominent example of the latter is the decision taken by BlackRock—the world's largest asset manager—to stop investing in companies that earn more than 25 per cent of their revenue from thermal coal production. In a letter to its clients, BlackRock (2020) stated the following:

> Thermal coal is significantly carbon intensive, becoming less and less economically viable, and highly exposed to regulation because of its environmental impacts. With the acceleration of the global energy transition, we do not believe that the long-term economic or investment rationale justifies continued investment in this sector.

This followed the publication of a report by the Institute for Energy Economics and Financial Analysis, which found that BlackRock's investments in oil companies had resulted in an estimated loss of $90 billion in the last decade 'due largely to ignoring global climate risk' (Buckley, Sanzillo and Shah, 2019: 1).

The role that financial considerations play in influencing insurer responses to climate change cannot be overstated; and insurers have explicitly acknowledged that addressing climate change 'makes business sense'. Thus, Aviva (2015: 3) stated: 'Aviva is determined to make its own contribution to tackling climate change. This is not at odds with business or investment. In fact, it is a business imperative'. AXA has announced: 'Climate risk for us is neither an ideological or theoretical issue: it is a core business issue, as we are already seeing the impact of increasing weather-related disaster risks (De Castries, 2015). Allianz (2018) stated: 'We are convinced that our approach will further improve the risk/return profile of our portfolio in the long term, and that we will strengthen our position as a forward-looking investor'. Furthermore, Suncorp (2019: 3) stated: '[U]nderstanding weather change and climate risk and how this impacts our customers and our business makes not only good environmental sense but helps us protect and enhance shareholder value and makes good business sense'.

Thus, ensuring that a 'clear business case' for tackling climate change exists—including through ensuring that 'the "systemic risk" of carbon is ... correctly embedded into regulatory frameworks', more favourable treatment for longer-term investments (De Castries, 2015), and 'mechanisms to allow insurers to internalize the benefits of ... public goods' (Hecht, 2008: 1610)— would arguably serve to encourage stronger responses from insurers.

Concluding remarks

This review suggests the causes of insurer action and inaction are complex and multi-faceted and that no single condition is determinative. Beyond regulation, insurers note, for example, stranded asset and reputation risks as key considerations in guiding their behaviour. Nevertheless, there is an important role for government regulation in facilitating strong insurer responses to climate change. This is reflected in the uptake of coal exclusion policies in recent years: insurers internationally that have implemented coal exclusion policies are largely, though not exclusively, domiciled in countries with policy and regulatory frameworks that are more supportive of stronger climate mitigation actions, and insurers themselves have cited regulatory concern as a driver for their actions. In one instance, regulatory influence has also extended beyond insurers' domicile countries: in California, a major insurance market, action by the regulator has influenced the behaviour of insurers doing business in that market, even where they are domiciled elsewhere.

As Wright and Nyberg (2017: 1635) found, corporations generally are 'ill-suited' to addressing climate change. Buffett's suggestion that shareholders of Berkshire Hathaway need not be concerned about climate change as it did not pose a threat to profitability illustrates this argument well. Okereke and Russel (2010: 121) argue that 'only strong government regulation can ultimately induce radical action from business actors'. Whether or not there is alignment across external drivers of insurer behaviour, including reputation risk and stranded asset risk, government regulation has a crucial role to play in shaping, and strengthening, insurers' responses to climate change.

Notes

1. The insurance industry is comprised of, amongst others, insurers and reinsurers. The term 'insurers' is used to refer collectively to insurers as well as reinsurers.
2. This can be likened to the approach of insurers to fire prevention in the nineteenth century, which was focused on containing harm and damage 'rather than a more risk-based approach that prevented the initial outbreak of fire': see O'Malley and Hutchinson (2007: 377). An analysis of climate-related products and services that have been introduced by insurers is contained in Mills (2009).
3. The terms 'government regulation' and 'regulation' are intended to refer to regulation by national legislation as well as by insurance regulators.
4. *Loi relative à la transition énergétique pour la croissance verte*, which translates directly as 'The energy transition for green growth law'.
5. A database of climate-related resolutions is available at https://engagements. ceres.org/.

References

2° Investing Initiative. (2015). Decree Implementing Article 173-VI of the French Law for the Energy Transition: Challenges and First Recommendations. Available at: http://2degrees-investing.org/wp-content/uploads/2018/02/energy_transition_law_in_france_-_briefing_note_final.pdf [Accessed 30 July 2018].

Aegon. (2016). Aegon Strikes Coal Mining off Investment List. *Aegon Newsroom*, 25 May. Available at: https://www.aegon.com/newsroom/news/2016/Aegon-strikes-coal-mining-off-its-investment-list-/ [Accessed 13 March 2018].

Aegon. (2017). Aegon N.V. Responsible Investment Policy 2017. Available at: https://www.aegon.com/contentassets/a11467f650ae4f7087d9bdf75ab6217e/aegon-responsible-investment-policy-october-2017.pdf [Accessed 15 March 2018].

Alkousaa, R. (2018). Allianz Cuts Back on Coal Insurance after Environmental Criticism. *Reuters*, 4 May. Available at: https://www.reuters.com/article/us-allianz-climatechange/allianz-cuts-back-on-coal-insurance-after-environmentalist-criticism-idUSKBN1I511D [Accessed 15 June 2018].

Allianz. (2015). Allianz Statement on Coal-Based Investments. Available at: https://reporting.unpri.org/Download.aspx?id=85a6d2f1-35e5-434f-9747-89cbb1446037 [Accessed 19 March 2018].

Allianz. (2018). Allianz is Driving Change Toward a Low-Carbon Economy with an Ambitious Climate Protection Package [Press Release] 4 May. Available at: https://www.allianz.com/en/press/news/business/insurance/180504_allianz-announces-climate-protection-package/ [Accessed 4 May 2018].

AM Best. (2018). Best's Briefing: California Wildfires: The New Normal?. *Best's Insurance News & Analysis,* 8 August. Available at: http://news.ambest.com/PressContent.aspx?altsrc=14&refnum=26920 [Accessed 4 September 2019].

Aviva. (2015). *Aviva's Strategic Response to Climate Change.* London: Aviva. Available at: https://www.aviva.com/content/dam/aviva-corporate/documents/investors/pdfs/reports/2016/Avivas_strategic_response_to_climate_change_-_2016_update_ysSf6TN.pdf [Accessed 19 March 2018].

Aviva. (2017). *2016 Annual Review: Responsible Investment*. London: Aviva. Available at: https://www.avivainvestors.com/content/dam/aviva-investors/global/documents/Americas/2016_responsible_investment_annual_review_report.pdf [Accessed 7 August 2018].

Ayling, J. and Gunningham, N. (2017). Non-state governance and climate policy: The fossil fuel divestment movement. *Climate Policy*, 17(2), pp. 131–149.

AXA. (2016). *Award on Investor Climate-related Disclosures*. Paris: AXA. Available at: https://www-axa-com.cdn.axa-contento-118412.eu/www-axa-com%2Fcb46e9f7-8b1d-4418-a8a7-a68fba088db8_axa_investor_climate_report.pdf [Accessed 13 December 2018].

AXA. (2019). *Registration Document 2018: Annual Financial Report*. Paris: AXA. Available at: https://www-axa-com.cdn.axa-contento-118412.eu/www-axa-com%2F913d1869-3d11-4eb2-b013-4caedb747fab_axa-ddr2018b-en.pdf [Accessed 30 January 2020].

AXA. (n.d). *AXA Group Policy on Investments in Coal Mining and Coal-based Energy*. Paris: AXA. Available at: https://www-axa-com.cdn.axa-contento-118412.eu/www-axa-com%2Fab00881a-160f-434f-b76d-ef46d1b85843_axa_coal_policy_b.pdf [Accessed 15 March 2018].

Bachir, M., Gokhale, N. and Ashani, P. (2019). *Climate Risk: Regulators Sharpen their Focus*. New York: Deloitte Centre for Financial Services. Available at: https://www2.deloitte.com/content/dam/Deloitte/us/Documents/financial-services/us-fsi-climate-risk-regulators-sharpen-their-focus.pdf [Accessed 26 January 2020].

Bansal, P. and DesJardine, M. R. (2014). Business sustainability: It is about time. *Strategic Organization*, 12(1), pp. 70–78.

Bauer, N., McGlade, C., Hilaire, J. and Ekins, P. (2018). Divestment prevails over the green paradox when anticipating strong future climate policies. *Nature Climate Change*, 8, pp. 130–134.

Belsom, T., Kirjanas, P., Nagrawala, F., Hayward, S., Uhlenbruch, P. and Franklin, E. (2018). *Got it Covered? Insurance in a Changing Climate*. London: ShareAction. Available at: https://shareaction.org/wp-content/uploads/2018/06/AODP-GotItCovered.pdf [Accessed 29 May 2018].

BlackRock. (2020). *Sustainability as BlackRock's New Standard for Investing*. New York: BlackRock. Available at: https://www.blackrock.com/corporate/investor-relations/blackrock-client-letter [Accessed 15 January 2020].

Blyth, W., Bradley, R., Bunn, D., Clarke, C., Wilson, T. and Yang, M. (2007). Investment risks under uncertain climate change policy. *Energy Policy*, 35, pp. 5766–5773.

Bosshard, P. (2018). Insuring Coal No More: The 2018 Scorecard on Insurance, Coal and Climate Change. Unfriend Coal. Available at: https://unfriendcoal.com/wp-content/uploads/2018/11/Scorecard-2018-report-final-web-version.pdf [Accessed 3 December 2018].

Botzen, W. J. W., van den Bergh, J. C. J. M. and Bouwer, L. M. (2010). Climate change and increased risk for the insurance sector: A global perspective and an assessment for the Netherlands. *Natural Hazards*, 52, pp. 577–598.

Brånå, T. (2017). Investor Disclosure as Policy Response to Climate Change: Exploring the French Case of Mandatory Climate Disclosure for Institutional Investors. Unpublished Master's thesis, Norwegian University of Life Sciences, Ås, Norway.

Buckley, T., Sanzillo, T. and Shah, K. (2019). *Inaction is BlackRock's Biggest Risk during Energy Transition: Still Lagging in Sustainable Investing Leadership*. Cleveland,

OH: Institute for Energy Economics and Financial Analysis. Available at: http://ieefa.org/wp-content/uploads/2019/07/Inaction-BlackRocks-Biggest-Risk-During-the-Energy-Transition_August-2019.pdf [Accessed 15 January 2020].

Buffett, W. E. (2016). *To the Shareholders of Berkshire Hathaway Inc.* [Letter] 27 February. Omaha: Berkshire Hathaway Inc. Available at: http://www.berkshirehathaway.com/letters/2015ltr.pdf [Accessed 28 May 2018].

Campiglio, E., Dafermos, Y., Monnin, P., Ryan-Collins, J., Schotten, G. and Tanaka, M. (2018). Climate change challenges for central banks and financial regulators. *Nature Climate Change*, 8, pp. 462–468.

Carney, M. (2015). Breaking the Tragedy of the Horizon – Climate Change And Financial Stability. [Speech Given at Lloyd's of London] 29 September. Available at: https://www.bankofengland.co.uk/speech/2015/breaking-the-tragedy-of-the-horizon-climate-change-and-financial-stability [Accessed 19 January 2018].

Carney, M. (2016). Resolving the Climate Paradox. [Speech Given at the Arthur Burns Memorial Lecture, Berlin] 22 September. Available at: https://www.bankofengland.co.uk/speech/2016/resolving-the-climate-paradox [Accessed 19 January 2018].

Carney, M. (2018). A Transition in Thinking and Action. [Speech Given at the International Climate Risk Conference for Supervisors, De Nederlandsche Bank, Netherlands] 6 April. Available at: https://www.bankofengland.co.uk/speech/2018/mark-carney-speech-at-international-climate-risk-conference-for-supervisors [Accessed 9 April 2018].

California Department of Insurance. (2016). California Insurance Commissioner Dave Jones Calls for Insurance Industry Divestment from Coal. [Press release] 25 January. Available at: http://www.insurance.ca.gov/0400-news/0100-press-releases/2016/statement010-16.cfm [Accessed 27 August 2018].

California Department of Insurance. (n.d). *NAIC Climate Risk Disclosure Survey. California Department of Insurance.* Los Angeles: California Department of Insurance. Available at: http://www.insurance.ca.gov/0250-insurers/0300-insurers/0100-applications/ClimateSurvey/ (accessed 27 August 2018).

CSFI. (n.d.). *Insurance Banana Skins.* London: CSFI. Available at: http://www.csfi.org/insurance-banana-skins/ [Accessed 17 October 2018].

De Castries, H. (2015). Climate Change: It's No Longer About Whether, It's About When. *AXA Newsroom*, 22 May. Available at: https://www.axa.com/en/newsroom/news/about-whether-about-when [Accessed 22 March 2018].

De la Mare, W. T. J. (2013). Locality of harm: Insurance and climate change in the 21st century. *Connecticut Insurance Law Journal*, 20, pp. 189–272.

De Nederlandsche Bank. (2016). *Time for Transition: An Exploratory Study of the Transition to a Carbon-Neutral Economy.* Amsterdam: De Nederlandsche Bank. Available at: https://www.dnb.nl/en/binaries/tt_tcm47-338545.pdf [Accessed 14 February 2018].

De Nederlandsche Bank. (2017). *Waterproof? An Exploration of Climate-Related Risks for the Dutch Financial Sector.* Amsterdam: De Nederlandsche Bank. Available at: https://www.dnb.nl/en/binaries/Waterproof_tcm47-363851.pdf [Accessed 15 January 2018].

De Nederlandsche Bank. (2018). *2017 Annual Report.* Amsterdam: De Nederlandsche Bank. Available at: https://www.dnb.nl/en/binaries/DNB%202017%20Annual%20Report_tcm47-374121.pdf [Accessed 19 September 2018].

European Commission. (2015). Solvency II Overview – Frequently Asked Questions [Press release] 12 January. Available at: https://ec.europa.eu/commission/presscorner/detail/ro/MEMO_15_3120 [Accessed 21 January 2020].

Ericson, R. V., Doyle, A. and Barry, D. (2003). *Insurance as Governance*. Toronto: University of Toronto Press.

Ernst & Young. (2010). *Action Amid Uncertainty: The Business Response to Climate Change*. London: Ernst & Young. Available at: https://www.climate-expert.org/fileadmin/user_upload/PDF/EY_Action_amid_uncertainty_-_The_business_response_to_climate_change.pdf [Accessed 2 October 2018].

Froestad, J., Gjuvsland, K., Herbstein, T. and Shearing, C. (2011). Insurance as a Regulatory Mechanism Towards Sustainable Companies. Paper presented at *Towards Sustainable Companies: Identifying New Avenues*, Oslo, Norway, 29–30 August 2011.

Gangcuangco, T. (2018). Munich Re CEO Announces Approach to Coal. *Insurance Business*, 7 August. Available at: https://www.insurancebusinessmag.com/uk/news/environmental/munich-re-ceo-announces-approach-to-coal-108132.aspx [Accessed 8 August 2018].

Golnaraghi, M. (2018). *Climate Change and the Insurance Industry: Taking Action as Risk Mangers and Investors*. Zurich: The Geneva Association. Available at: https://www.genevaassociation.org/sites/default/files/research-topics-document-type/pdf_public//climate_change_and_the_insurance_industry_-_taking_action_as_risk_managers_and_investors.pdf [Accessed 23 January 2018].

Norwegian Ministry of Finance. (2016). *Guidelines for Observation and Exclusion from the Government Pension Fund Global*. Oslo: Norwegian Parliament. Available at: https://www.regjeringen.no/contentassets/7c9a364d2d1c474f8220965065695a4a/guidelines_observation_exclusion2016.pdf [Accessed 12 July 2018].

Haufler, V. (2006). Insurance and Reinsurance in a Changing Climate. Paper presented at *Climate Change Politics in North America*, Woodrow Wilson International Centre for Scholars, Washington DC, USA, 18–19 May 2006.

Hecht, S. B. (2008). Climate change and the transformation of risk: Insurance matters. *UCLA Law Review*, 55, pp. 1559–1620.

Herbstein, T. (2015). *Insurance and the Anthropocene: Like a Frog in Hot Water*. Unpublished PhD thesis, University of Cape Town, Cape Town, South Africa.

Herbstein, T., Froestad, J., Nel, D. and Shearing, C. (2013). Insurance, climate-risk and the barriers to change. In: T. A. Börzel and R. Hamann, eds., *Business and Climate Change Governance*. Hampshire: Palgrave Macmillan, pp. 156–172.

Grace, M. F. and Klein, R. W. (2009). Insurance regulation: The need for policy reform. In: M. F. Grace and R. W. Klein, eds., *The Future of Insurance Regulation in the United States*. Washington, DC: Brookings Institution Press, pp. 117–144.

International Association of Insurance Supervisors and Sustainable Insurance Forum. (2018). *Issues Paper on Climate Change Risks to the Insurance Sector*. Basel: International Association of Insurance Supervisors and Sustainable Insurance Forum. Available at: https://www.insurancejournal.com/research/app/uploads/2018/08/IAIS_and_SIF_Issues_Paper_on_Climate_Change_Risks_to_the_Insurance_Sector_-1.pdf [Accessed 31 August 2018].

Jessop, S., Cohn, C. and Sims, T. (2018). Munich Re Sticks With Coal Underwriting Despite Investor Pressure. *Reuters*, 6 July. Available at: https://www.reuters.com/article/us-munich-re-group-coal/munich-re-sticks-with-coal-underwriting-despite-investor-pressure-idUSKBN1JW1MY [Accessed 9 July 2018].

Jones, A. W. and Phillips, A. (2016). Voluntary business engagement in climate change: A study of the ClimateWise principles. *Journal of Cleaner Production*, 137, pp. 131–143.

Klein, R. W. (1995). Insurance regulation in transition. *The Journal of Risk and Insurance*, 62(3), pp. 363–404.

KLP. (2015). Decision on Changes in Companies Excluded on the Grounds of Coal-Based Business Operations. 8 December. Oslo: KLP. Available at: https://www.klp.no/en/corporate-responsibility-and-responsible-investments/exclusion-and-dialogue [Accessed 12 April 2018].

Leggett, J. (1993). *Climate Change and the Insurance Industry: Solidarity among the Risk Community?* 2nd ed. London: Greenpeace.

Mathiesen, K. (2018). Rating climate risks to credit worthiness. *Nature Climate Change*, 8, pp. 454–456.

Mills, E. (2005). Insurance in a climate of change. *Science*, 309(5737), pp. 1040–1044.

Mills, E. (2008). The role of U.S. Insurance regulators in responding to climate change. *Journal of Environmental Law*, 26, pp. 129–168.

Mills, E. (2009). A global review of insurance industry responses to climate change. *The Geneva Papers on Risk and Insurance – Issues and Practice*, 34, pp. 323–359.

Mills, E. (2012). The greening of insurance. *Science*, 338, pp. 1424–1425.

Mills, E., Lamm, T., Sukhia, S., Elkind, E. and Ezroj, A. (2018). *Trial by Fire: Managing Climate Risks Facing Insurers in the Golden State*. California: California Department of Insurance. Available at: http://www.insurance.ca.gov/0400-news/0100-press-releases/2018/upload/nr106TrialbyFire090618.pdf [Accessed 7 September 2018].

Moody's. (2018). *P&C Insurance and Reinsurance – Global: Climate Change Risks Outweigh Opportunities for P&C (Re)Insurers*. New York: Moody's Investors Service. Available at: https://www.law.berkeley.edu/wp-content/uploads/2018/06/Moodys-Climate-change-risks-outweigh-opportunities-for-PC-reinsurers.pdf [Accessed 30 August 2018].

Moody's. (2019). *Credit Outlook*. New York: Moody's Investors Services. Available at: https://www.moodys.com/researchdocumentcontentpage.aspx?docid=PBC_1169318 [Accessed 4 April 2019].

Moody's. (2020). *Moody's – Insurers' Retreat from Coal is Positive, Reducing Stranded Asset Risk, Limiting Liability Risk* [Research announcement] 24 February. New York: Moody's Investors Services. Available at: https://www.moodys.com/research/Moodys-Insurers-retreat-from-coal-is-positive-reducing-stranded-asset–PBC_1214543 [Accessed 5 March 2020].

Morales, A. (2014). 'Stranded Assets': Will Efforts to Counter Warming Render Energy Reserves Worthless? *Washington Post*, 4 December. Available at: https://www.washingtonpost.com/business/stranded-assets-will-efforts-to-counter-warming-render-energy-reserves-worthless/2014/12/05/ecbc73a6-7a45-11e4-9a27-6fdbc612bff8_story.html [Accessed 30 August 2018].

Morris, C. (2018). Camp Fire Forces Insurance Company Out of Business. *Fortune*, 4 December. Available at: https://fortune.com/2018/12/04/merced-camp-fire-insurance-company/ [Accessed 4 September 2019].

Munich Re America Corporation. (2016). *Annual Report for the Fiscal Year Ended December 31, 2015*. Princeton, NJ.: Munich Re America Corporation. Available at: https://www.munichre.com/site/mram-mobile/get/documents_E1511086199/mram/assetpool.mr_america/PDFs/2_About_us/MRAC_Financial_Report_2015.pdf [Accessed 4 April 2018].

Natixis. (2015). *Natixis to Cease Financing Coal Industries Worldwide* [Press release] 15 October. Paris: Natixis. Available at: https://www.natixis.com/natixis/upload/docs/application/pdf/2015-10/pr_natixis_15102015_eng.pdf [Accessed 12 April 2018].

Newell, P. and Paterson, M. (2010). *Climate Capitalism: Global Warming and the Transformation of the Global Economy* .Cambridge: Cambridge University Press.

O'Malley, P. and Hutchinson, S. (2007). Reinventing prevention: Why did 'crime prevention' develop so late? *British Journal of Criminology*, 47, pp. 373–389.

Okereke, C. and Russel, D. (2010). Regulatory pressure and competitive dynamics: Carbon management strategies of UK energy-intensive companies. *California Management Review*, 52(4), pp. 100–124.

Paterson, M. (1999). Global finance and environmental politics: The insurance industry and climate change. *IDS Bulletin*, 30(3), pp. 25–30.

Paterson, M. (2001). Risky business: Insurance companies in global warming politics. *Global Environmental Politics*, 1(4), pp. 18–42.

Phelan, L., Taplin, R., Henderson-Sellers, A. and Albrecht, G. (2011). Ecological viability or liability? Insurance system responses to climate risk. *Environmental Policy and Governance*, 21(2), pp. 112–130.

Phelan, L., Holley, C., Shearing, C. and du Toit, L. (2020). Insurance and climate change. In: A. Brisman and N. South, eds., *Routledge International Handbook of Green Criminology*, 2nd ed. New York: Routledge.

Pinson, L. (2018). Dirty Business: Insurance Companies Supporting the Growth of Polish Coal. Unfriend Coal. Available at: https://unfriendcoal.com/wp-content/uploads/2018/02/Dirty-Business_Unfriend-Coal.pdf [Accessed 8 February 2018].

Prudential Regulation Authority (PRA). (2015). *The Impact of Climate Change on the UK Insurance Sector: A Climate Change Adaptation Report by the Prudential Regulation Authority*. London: Bank of England Prudential Regulation Authority. Available at: https://www.bankofengland.co.uk/-/media/boe/files/prudential-regulation/publication/impact-of-climate-change-on-the-uk-insurance-sector.pdf [Accessed 19 July 2018].

Prudential Regulation Authority (PRA). (2019a). *Enhancing Banks' and Insurers' Approaches to Managing the Financial Risks from Climate Change* [Supervisory Statement | SS3/19]. London: Bank of England Prudential Regulation Authority. Available at: https://www.bankofengland.co.uk/-/media/boe/files/prudential-regulation/supervisory-statement/2019/ss319.pdf?la=en&hash=7BA9824BAC5FB-313F42C00889D4E3A6104881C44 [Accessed 3 September 2019].

Prudential Regulation Authority (PRA). (2019b). *Insurance Stress Test 2019* [Letter] 18 June. London: Bank of England Prudential Regulation Authority. Available at: https://www.bankofengland.co.uk/prudential-regulation/letter/2019/insurance-stress-test-2019 [Accessed 21 January 2020].

Robins, N. (2017). *Financing the Transition: How Climate Change Could Impact the Financial System*. Geneva: United Nations Environment Programme. Available at: https://www.fca.org.uk/publication/research/future-horizons-conference-financing-the-transition.pdf [Accessed 13 August 2018].

Shearing, C. (2015). Criminology and the anthropocene. *Criminology & Criminal Justice*, 15(3), pp. 255–269.

Skjærseth, J. B. and Skodvin, T. (2001). Climate change and the oil industry: Common problems, different strategies. *Global Environmental Politics*, 1(4), pp. 43–64.

Stechemesser, K., Endrikat, J., Grasshoff, N. and Guenther, E. (2015). Insurance companies' responses to climate change: Adaptation, dynamic capabilities and competitive advantage. *The Geneva Papers on Risk and Insurance – Issues and Practice*, 40, pp. 557–584.

Storebrand. (2013). *Storebrand Reduces Carbon Exposure in Investments – 19 Companies Excluded* [Press release] 2 July. Lysaker, Norway: Storebrand. Available at: https://www.storebrand.no/site/stb.nsf/Pages/newsdesk.html#/news/storebrand-reduces-carbon-exposure-in-investments-19-companies-excluded-62954 [Accessed 13 April 2018].

Sullivan, R. and Gouldson, A. (2017). The governance of corporate responses to climate change: An international comparison. *Business Strategy and the Environment*, 26, pp. 413–425.

Summerhayes, G. (2017a). *Australia's New Horizon: Climate Change Challenges and Prudential Risk*. [Speech presented at Insurance Council of Australia Annual Forum, Sydney] 17 February. Sydney: Australia Prudential Regulation Authority. Available at: https://www.apra.gov.au/media-centre/speeches/australias-new-horizon-climate-change-challenges-and-prudential-risk). [Accessed 6 February 2018].

Summerhayes, G. (2017b). The Weight of Money: A Business Case for Climate Risk Resilience. [Speech Presented at Centre for Policy Development, Sydney] 29 November. Available at: https://www.apra.gov.au/media-centre/speeches/weight-money-business-case-climate-risk-resilience [Accessed 6 February 2018].

Suncorp. (2019). Suncorp 2019 AGM Chairman's and Group CEO's Addresses. [ASX Announcement] 26 September. Available at: https://www.suncorpgroup.com.au/announcements-pdf/1248161 [Accessed 30 January 2020].

Swiss Re. (2017). *Responsible Investments: Shaping the Future of Investing*. Zurich: Swiss Re. Available at: http://media.swissre.com/documents/ZRH-17-11623-P1_Responsible%20Investments_WEB.PDF [Accessed 29 March 2018].

Thistlethwaite, J. and Wood, M. O. (2018). Insurance and climate change risk management: Rescaling to look beyond the horizon. *British Journal of Management*, 29, pp. 279–298.

Uhlenbruch, P. (2019). *Insuring a Low-Carbon Future*. London: ShareAction. Available at: https://aodproject.net/wp-content/uploads/2019/09/AODP-Insuring-a-Low-Carbon-Future-Full-Report.pdf [Accessed 17 September 2019].

UNEP-FI. (2012). *The Global State of Sustainable Insurance: Understanding and Integrating Environmental, Social and Governance Factors in Insurance*. Geneva: UNEP Finance Initiative Insurance Working Group. Available at: http://www.unepfi.org/psi/wp-content/uploads/2012/06/global-state-of-sustainable-insurance_01.pdf [Accessed 25 May 2018].

Wright, C. and Nyberg, D. (2017). An inconvenient truth: How organizations translate climate change into business as usual. *Academy of Management Journal*, 60(5), pp. 1633–1661.

8 Insurance in the Anthropocene

Exposure, solvency and manoeuvrability

Nicholas Philip Simpson[*]

Introduction

Buying insurance ostensibly makes one less vulnerable. It does not technically enhance capacity to endure harm, but it can fiscally compensate for that envisioned harm (Schwartz, 2019). The harm that insurance aims to safeguard against relates to our anticipation of a future and its anticipated risks. In this strict sense of exposure to harms, insurance does not protect or make safe. Yet, insurance is an industry that is fundamental to the security that individuals and companies require in order to invest, grow and avoid adverse disruption (de la Mare, 2013). Consequently, insurers are recognised as potential 'fulcrum institutions' with the ability to ameliorate the impact of environmental harms (Shearing, 2015), such as climate change, and influence public and private actions concerning associated risks (Phelan et al., 2020).

The insurance sector has been recognised as a critical actor in facilitating key mitigation and adaptation actions, and as a leading sector in terms of climate adaptation (CoastAdapt, 2018; Torabi, Dedekorkut-Howes and Howes, 2018). In addition, certain insurance products have been noted for their ability to set norms, for better or for worse (O'Hare, White and Connelly, 2016; Williamson and Nagashima, 2019), and in governing the lifestyles and behaviours of individuals and policyholders (Meyers and Van Hoyweghen, 2018; Beckie et al., 2019). This potentially affords the insurance industry access to influence people inside their home or business, where the power of the state and its potential role or ability to provide a securing function against harms has conventionally been expected to end (Froestad et al., 2011). Seifert and Lindberg (2012) observe that insurers can promote

[*] The author would like to acknowledge input from Dr Louise Du Toit (Global Risk Governance Programme, Law Faculty, University of Cape Town) who contributed to shaping the literature review and for her general perspective on mitigation-orientated innovations in the insurance sector in response to climate change. The author would also like to thank the editors for their constructive input during the review process of the chapter.

a more sustainable future through better risk-based modelling and product pricing, through innovative green products, through partnering with businesses for better environmental governance, through alliances with policy-makers and regulators to ensure voluntary market adjustments for risk and by championing the enforcement of building code efforts. This case study illustrates how one insurer in Africa (hereafter 'the Insurer'), is exploring how it can deal with a subset of these roles, through better risk-based modelling, product pricing and regulatory adjustments.

In light of the uncertainty associated with current environmental and climatic conditions, the insurance sector is, amongst other factors, currently facing technical challenges implementing envisioned proposals, by scholars like that of Seifert and Lindberg (2012) above, into business reality (Phelan, Henderson-Sellers and Taplin, 2010; Froestad et al., 2011; Herbstein, 2015). Further, exposure to more frequent and severe weather events, some of which are attributed to the Anthropocene (Keys et al., 2019; Schiermeier, 2019), give rise to more claims – reducing fiscal margins available for local innovation and research and development (Federation of European Risk Management Associations (FERMA), 2014; California Department of Insurance, 2018) and pose a threat to the ongoing viability of the insurance sector (Dlugolecki, 2008).

Uncertainty is a symptom of, and fundamental to, the current and anticipated future state of the Earth System in the Anthropocene (Mauelshagen, 2018; Steffen et al., 2018). Schwartz (2019: 87) has pointed out that although insurance cannot prevent harms, its conventional role in the governance of harms is securing 'a future by buying out uncertainty'. In Schwartz's (2019) view, insurance is traditionally based on a desire to reduce and control uncertainty. Critical of the apparently self-serving nature of the industry's response to augmented risks anticipated in the Anthropocene, Schwartz (2019: 88) believes insurers are not concerned with Anthropocene indicators, such a loss of biodiversity, starvation or mass migration and that rather their concern is 'diminishing predictability'.

Responding to calls for greater empirical understanding of how insurers are responding to enhanced risk (Berz, 1999; Paterson, 1999; Phelan et al., 2011), Herbstein (2015) identified how the commercial insurance industry responds under conditions of increasing uncertainty, particularly in light of 'debounded' risks. By 'debounded', Herbstein (2015) references Beck's (2010, 1992) notion of risk, which conceptualises augmented risks in a globalised and interconnected world, a notion of risk which fits well with the current understanding of the scale and unpredictability of risks scholars anticipate in the Anthropocene (Keys et al., 2019), where risks and their perception transcend temporal and geographical boundaries, potentially making them uninsurable (Bouwer, 2019). Herbstein's work has further highlighted the need for empirical understanding of how insurers in developing regions of the world are responding to the emerging challenges they face (Herbstein, 2015). Although largely ignored till recently, such areas have become increasingly important to scholars, considering the global reach of insurers for the governance of climate shocks.

Insurers have two sources of revenue: underwriting and investments. There is a longstanding assumption that the most straightforward approach for insurers to respond to Anthropocene risks might be management of investment portfolios (ClimateWise, 2019). However, Herbstein (2015) identified how commercial insurers have mainly responded to climate risk through adaptation of their business – mainly through the use of what he calls 'defensive underwriting' to limit their exposure to financial risk, rather than investment portfolio changes. Herbstein (2015) notes that insurers are finding their existing risk assessment tools progressively out-dated in a world where risk is no longer as predictable as it once was. In effect, Herbstein (2015) found insurers are pursuing responses focused largely on tweaking their existing ways of engaging risk, including managing their own risks by incentivising others to manage theirs.

Scholars have pointed to the way insurers govern how people (should) act, who qualifies for protection, how to allocate blame and responsibility and help to develop systems of surveillance, monitoring and policing (Ericson et al., 2003; Ericson and Doyle, 2004). Although recent regulatory advances hold potential benefits for the general robustness and solvency of the industry (such as those recently proposed by the California Department of Insurance (2018)), political pressure on their role and function can result in artificially low insurance premiums in order to please stakeholders such as property developers or local municipalities (Herbstein, 2015). Following Hurricane Katrina, for example, regulators in Florida, under pressure from the local electorate facing sharply higher insurance premiums, forced the industry to maintain rates at well below sustainable levels. This led to many insurers withdrawing from the market, impacting not only their own operations, but also the vulnerability of local homeowners, many whom were left without adequate cover (Grace, Klein and Liu, 2005).

Globally, 2017 and 2018 brought the costliest back-to-back years on record for both economic losses solely due to weather-related events ($653 billion), and for insured losses across all perils ($237 billion) (AON, 2019: 1). Of 349 individual events, AON identified 42 individual billion-dollar natural disaster events that occurred in 2018 (AON, 2019: 1). Climate change has thus become a multi-faceted material risk for the $4.6-trillion global insurance industry (California Department of Insurance, 2018). In less developed parts of the world, victims often have little to no insurance cover. Munich Re have recently highlighted that poorer countries that have experienced disasters often take years to recover (Munich Re, 2019). The loss in Mozambique after Cyclone Idai is equivalent to around one-tenth of the country's gross domestic product (Munich Re, 2019).

Some global insurers have begun partnering with the scientific community to perform basic research and help build forward-looking risk models that take climate change into account. Since 1999, reinsurers have been driving this research agenda through the Resilience Alliance and this has resulted in a number of industry-wide innovations, such as the Carbon Disclosure Project (CDP, 2020), Principles for Sustainable Investing (UNEP-Fi and PSI, 2019) and the Task Force on Climate-related Financial Disclosures (TCFD) (TCFD, 2017). However, these notable examples of progress in the industry can detract from the underwhelming lack of progress called for regarding climate risk attribution. Despite significant endeavours (for some examples, Phelan, 2011; Phelan et al., 2011; UNEP-Fi and PSI, 2019), 20 years later insurers' modelling techniques remain unable to provide usable models that integrate the broad implications of climate risk (Spreng, Sovacool and Spreng, 2016; Thistlethwaite and Wood, 2018).

This chapter focuses on an insurer faced with a variety of socio-economic stressors in its base in South Africa, together with operations in 32 African countries and 3 Asian countries, including India. Its short-term division is currently engaging with understanding, responding to and anticipating the material risks of climate change. The analysis here acknowledges calls by Herbstein (2015) and others (Bougen, 2003; O'Malley, 2003) for clarification of how insurers are responding to enhanced risk. The Insurer's short-term division was chosen in part due to the ongoing research access it provides to our research group at the Global Risk Governance Programme, but also as it allows for analysis of a particular type of risk carrying and risk management – one that responds to claims at a high frequency (monthly and annual terms) – to be more concretely explored. It is hypothesised, in light of an absence of insurers' mitigative actions concerning their investment portfolios (Phelan, Henderson-Sellers and Taplin, 2010; Phelan et al., 2011; Herbstein, 2015), that actions taken by short-term insurers – those ostensibly cognisant of emerging increases in the frequency of climate-related claims – might provide insight into how insurers are adaptively managing risk and therefore illustrate the risk governance role some insurers may be beginning to play in the Anthropocene.

Local responses: A case study from South Africa

The African insurance market is underdeveloped (KPMG, 2018) and, in total, the African insurance industry accounts for just under 1.2 per cent ($0.06 trillion) of insurance premiums written globally (PWC, 2018: 12). The African market is dominated by South Africa, which accounts for 74 per cent of the total (PWC, 2018: 12). Even so, at only 17 per cent insured, the South African market is under-insured by global standards (PWC, 2018: 12). This has led to calls to speed up insurance penetration to the un(der)insured across the continent (PWC, 2018).

Compared to the rest of Africa, the South African insurance market is highly competitive and more mature, dominated by a few large players, aided by relatively strong institutions and a sound regulatory environment (PWC, 2018). As such, the South African Insurance Association (2018: 4) claims the industry has an important role to play as a 'safety net and risk adaptation partner' to customers and other stakeholders. The Insurer under investigation here accounts for approximately 25 per cent of the South African insurance market, positioning it as the largest insurer in the largest and most comprehensive insurance market on the continent (Insurer, 2019).

The Insurer was the first in Africa to mobilise the short-term insurance industry in response to increasing climate and weather risk (Insurer, 2017). In 2009, the Insurer embarked on an 'Ecocentric Journey' as growing awareness of environmental concerns matched an increase in climate-related losses (Herbstein, 2015). Hosting an 'Ecocentric Journey' conference for the industry that year, the Insurer positioned itself publicly as a leader in issues relating to climate risk. It sees climate-related catastrophe events, particularly when coupled with developmental concerns such as rapid urban growth, municipality capacity constraints and insufficient infrastructure development, to have a potentially severe impact on its business and the industry at large (Insurer, 2017). In recent years, the company had been exposed to a number of environmental perils that have caused significant losses. This included floods and droughts, fires, coastal erosion and increasingly frequently, from lightning strikes and hailstorms. Between 2003 and 2008, more than R 2.5 billion ($222 million) worth of total economic losses occurred, of which R 60 million ($5.4 million) was paid out, via insurance claims, by the Insurer alone (Herbstein, 2015). Unprecedented losses have also recently been experienced in South Africa with the 'worst catastrophe event in South African insurance history' accounting for R 823 million (approximately $60 million) paid out for damage caused by wildfires in Knysna and freak storms in Cape Town in 2017 (Insurer, 2018: 8). A further R1.1bn (approximately $80 million) was paid out for floods and hailstorms that year (Insurer, 2018: 8). As a result, South Africa is no longer considered a benign natural catastrophe territory by international reinsurers, who have raised the price of reinsurance (South African Insurance Association (SAIA), 2018). The Insurer's underwriting margin decreased slightly between 2016 and 2018 as the group was significantly affected by these catastrophe claims and large commercial claims (KPMG, 2018).

The Insurer understands climate change to be one of the future drivers shaping its business model and a risk that poses an existential threat to the industry (Insurer, 2019). In 2007, the organisation explicitly listed pace of adaptation to climate change as one of the key 'material matters' relevant to the company and stakeholders, demonstrating how the organisation kept pace with emerging global thinking around climate change and insurance at the time (such as that of Mills, 2007), subsequently listing climate change as a significant strategic risk in their *Integrated Reports* from 2017 onwards (Insurer, 2018: 15–16). It is acknowledged that the 'material matter' of climate change and its effects directly affect the 'ability of [The Insurer] to be agile in responding to emerging challenges and opportunities' (Insurer, 2018: 14).

In order to illustrate the decision-making tests the Insurer faces, the following section sets out three challenges: (i) climate risk exposure, (ii) solvency and (iii) manoeuvrability. These challenges were observed during discussions at the Insurer's climate risk workshops and interviews with risk managers carried out in the first half of 2019. These themes are relevant beyond the Insurer's own deliberations: climate risk exposure (Insurance Business, 2018; AON, 2019; ClimateWise, 2019), solvency (Steffen, 2008; Turnbull, 2018) and manoeuvrability (Glaas, Keskitalo and Hjerpe, 2017), have been identified as key challenges to the industry the world over. In addition, the Insurer has a globally recognised leadership role related to climate risk. This positions its decision making and actions at the forefront of what African insurers are doing.

In January 2019, in an externally facilitated two-day workshop, the Insurer explored material risks relating to their commitments to the TCFD. In March 2019 a group of scientists from the University of Cape Town's Climate Systems Analysis Group (CSAG), African Climate Development Initiative (ACDI) and Global Risk Governance Programme deliberated with the Insurer's risk professionals over a further two-day workshop, exploring the available climate science data and models, as well as the Insurer's approaches to risk and modelling. The workshop explored how the respective risk data and models can be used to understand the current and future climate risk impacts on the Insurer's business and its stakeholders, and to develop future scenarios to assist in the determination of the appropriate governance, strategy, risk management and targets and responses for the Insurer. In addition to engaged participant observation of the presentations, risk identification activities, discussions and feedback sessions at the two workshops, one-on-one interviews were conducted with four senior risk managers during and after the second workshop with those risk managers who expressed day-to-day engagement with innovating the Insurer's risk assessment and management of flood risk. Interviews concentrated on themes of climate risk exposure and what actions the Insurer is taking in response to enhanced climate risk.

Exposure

The Insurer has made a number of responses to climate risk exposure, most of which relate to taking a leadership role in the industry on climate risk (TCFD, 2017; UNEP-Fi, 2019), as well as managing proximate risks in the municipalities where they are exposed (Insurer, 2017, 2019). Workshop discussions confirmed that despite progress in climate modelling (Dosio et al., 2019), current climate models can only provide high-level probabilities at temporal scales of decades, covering vast regional geographies, while short-term insurers require information to make decisions commonly within an annual timeframe and require that information to be as locally specific as possible as they insure buildings, cars, ports and farms. Current models (such as the CORDEX model, Dosio and Panitz, 2016), are currently insufficient as an information base for short-term insurer's decision making at property scale (Mechler et al., 2019).

In line with TCFD expectations, the Insurer is supposed to 'demonstrate responsibility and foresight in their consideration of climate issues' (TCFD, 2017: 2). Risk identification therefore holds potential to signal the kinds of harmscapes insurers are anticipating. Fleshing out the physical and broader indirect physical impacts, the Insurer has identified and categorised how risks are or will likely manifest with direct impact on their insurance business as well as on their clients. Herbstein (2015) had previously found that the Insurer had been forced to redefine flood lines from 1-in-50 to 1-in-10 year events, in order to accommodate shifts in flood frequencies. Herbstein (2015) observed that, from an underwriting perspective, Geographic Information System (GIS) models were quickly identified as an ideal response to the inherent weakness of the actuarial models to the challenges the Insurer was facing. However, one of the shortfalls of the GIS models they applied was that, although they started to identify the properties likely to be most impacted by specific Anthropocene perils, such as flooding, they failed to account for how or why the floods occurred in the first place, how the risks were likely to change over time, as the variables shifted and how the perils could be better managed (Herbstein, 2015).

Interviews with flood risk managers demonstrated that the endeavour for more fine grain and adaptive GIS-based modelling is evolving within the organisation through their approach to geocoding risk and development of a vast flood lines data set. Hydrologists and risk managers developing this programme revealed that this programme is still in its infancy, as insurance premiums are still generally calculated according to more coarsely-grained proxy indicators, such postal code or suburb, rather than directly on geophysical risks at such spatial scales. However, as Figure 8.1 shows, the Insurer is exploring how flood lines and other physical characteristics can be spatially integrated to risk assessment and management.

Figure 8.1 indicates a hypothetical 20km cross-section of a suburb that includes an estuary. Previously there was no way for insurers to systematically nor proactively differentiate between degrees of risk across this profile, apart from on a claim-by-claim basis. However, being able to map slope and flood lines are critical for flooding and land subsidence calculations. This is achieved through a two-step process, as indicated in Figure 8.1.

Step 1 suggests that analysis of historical loss data can be mapped onto such a transect, or along selected topographies, affording risk managers the opportunity to identify high- and low-risk areas and make more informed calculations of risk. Step 2 is a scenario-building exercise that can be used to anticipate shifts in risk across a topographical profile. Of great interest to risk managers is (a) identifying areas of stability and low risk, such as those hypothetically indicated on the right side of Step 2, (b) understanding areas of transitional risk and (c) identifying high-risk areas, which either

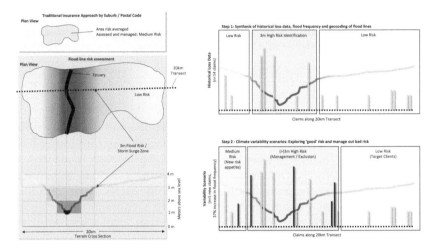

Figure 8.1 Geocoding risk.

need to be priced accordingly or managed off their books. This endeavour aims to calculate risk and cost of premiums with greater accuracy. It potentially allows the Insurer to avoid exposure to the riskiest assets, make use of deductibles and excesses, diversify its risk exposure or simply withdraw from the highest risk markets altogether (Herbstein, 2015). An example of this was displayed in an interview, which revealed that the municipality of Cape Town had called in one of the Insurer's senior flood risk managers to informally request the Insurer to stop 'managing' risk (withdrawing cover from particular zones), as their actions were affecting property prices and the municipality's rates base in the Strand region of Cape Town. Although anecdotal, there is good reason to expect such moves by a local government. Generally, flooding in coastal areas lowers property values (McGregor and Spicer, 2016; Belanger and Bourdeau-Brien, 2018). If flood risks were directly related to costs, there should be a reduction in land and housing values in such floodplains (Lamond and Proverbs, 2008). However, Armbruster, Zischg and Andreas (2018) found that when insurance is available for such areas, on the contrary occurs. When flood hazard maps are introduced into legally binding municipal land use planning in multiple jurisdictions across the world, municipality assessed property prices increase (Armbruster, Zischg and Andreas, 2018). There is likely many reasons for this increase (land buyers imperfectly foresee the construction process of houses and relevant flood risks, when they buy land and people commonly underestimate flood risk) (Armbruster, Zischg and Andreas, 2018), but it is likely that revenue collection for the municipality plays an important role. Such actions, however, by local governments can induce moral hazard, increasing the eventual cost of flooding to the wider community (Lamond and Proverbs, 2008).

This approach highlights the role of GIS in the Insurer's move towards a more centralised approach to risk assessment and management, as it aims to both improve the quality of data collected and automate as many parts of the underwriting process as possible. Herbstein (2015: 75) observed the Insurer's initial transition away from a large network of semi-autonomous regional offices and brokerages (conventionally decentralised), to one of more central 'control', where they might be 'more consistent underwriting results and to gain access to all the data it needed to fully understand the changing risk landscape it was being exposed to'.

In mature insurance markets, regulators will generally attempt to prevent a scarcity of available insurance, and one way they do so is by disallowing an insurer to leave a particular market on the threat that if the insurer does so, the commissioner may penalise or discontinue the insurer's license to write any line of insurance (de la Mare, 2013). However, market penetration in Africa is so low, insurers and their regulators face a unique arrangement. For example, South Africa has the highest rate of short-term insurance in Africa, and yet only 17 per cent of South Africans are insured (KPMG, 2018). In light of the regulator's conventional role to facilitate available insurance, it will be interesting to see how insurers manage their exposure while attempting to expand insurance markets and to what extent regulators will allow insurers to manage out 'bad' climate risk. In their current formulation, it is unlikely that such actions by insurers would have a positive effect for distributive justice (Grace, Klein and Liu, 2005; Bouwer, 2019).

Solvency

Climate risk and its harmscapes present a solvency challenge to insurers, challenging the amount and sources of capital in the business, as well as potential future regulatory capital requirements in response to climate perturbations of the insurance market. During workshop discussions, the Insurer's Head of Strategy flagged climate risk to be a question of solvency and one serious enough to threaten the existence of the organisation within a decade. Price (the premium that should be charged to a policyholder), reserves (the amount set aside in order to pay claims) and capital coverage ratio (or solvency amount: the capital requirement for regulatory solvency purposes considering both the liability and assets of insurers) are all monitored through the Insurer's quarterly Group risk appetite, which is drawn up by the Enterprise Risk Management (ERM) and Financial Risk Management (FRM) teams, then approved quarterly by the Insurer's Board (Insurer, 2017). In general terms, the Insurer acknowledges that climate change will impact their operating environment. However, deliberations in the workshops revealed that active risk management, like its geocoding exercises discussed above, although cognisant of experienced variations in historical loss data, was not calculated in accordance with specific climatic scenarios and rather based on loss ratios and price of premiums of the previous year and in light of general historical loss data.

This solvency imperative brings sharply into focus that climate variability and climate change will likely pose an existential threat to those insurers not making provision for such enhanced risk. Further it opens up a challenging new praxis of establishing and justifying what this solvency amount could or should be, what a commensurate risk appetite should be, and how capital coverage ratios relate to or are informed by climate prediction probabilities and uncertainties.

de la Mare (2013: 235) has cautioned that:

> [a]s the pressures of climate change increase, if the global insurance system does not develop the necessary internal structures to spread risk as efficiently as possible, two possible outcomes will emerge: insurers will become insolvent due to not being allowed to charge adequate premiums, or they will have to leave markets due to the markets being unable to afford the actuarially-true premiums.

The Insurer group's economic capital requirement, at 31 December 2017, amounted to R 6 billion ($430 million), an economic capital coverage ratio of 158 per cent (Insurer, 2018). The Insurer's board of directors generally targets an economic capital coverage ratio of between 130 per cent and 170 per cent (Insurer, 2018). An amount determined to be 'excess capital' is maintained (i) to make an allowance for risk based on the complexity of the underlying business, (ii) to maintain a margin over the current regulatory capital requirements, (iii) to maintain the Insurer's insurer financial strength credit ratings and (iv) to fund business growth and allow for any corporate actions (Insurer, 2018). These four stated capital allocations are imperative for the sustainability of a conventional insurer business model, yet each is subject to unpredictable climate risks. The organisation's commitment to 'efficient capital management' may need to be revised to allow for an enhanced margin. Philosophically and pragmatically, imperatives of 'capital efficiency', allocating capital to its most productive ends (Reuss, Russ and Wieland, 2015), run contrary to and rarely tolerate holding large reserve capacities that risk-based solvency frameworks such as Solvency II now require (Reuss, Russ and Wieland, 2015). Yet, in the face of uncertainty, climate risks are increasingly alerting risk managers, from a diverse range of fields with responsibility for the sustainable finance of an entity, to consider revising their approach and assumptions of how much and what type of reserves are needed (Simpson et al., 2019). Although the identification of solvency challenges was a noted outcome of the workshops, how the Insurer will make such provision calculations remains to be determined.

There have been global calls for the development of comprehensive legal structures to address climate change risks, together with warnings that a failure to enact such a structure may leave the insurance industry unable to deal with catastrophic loss from climate change-related risk (de la Mare, 2013). Recent regulatory developments in South Africa have demanded insurers' solvency and capital requirements correspond to international standards (Insurer, 2018; KPMG, 2018). At time of writing, the Insurer is still undergoing the regulatory accommodations of Solvency II (such as a revision of the Insurer's solvency capital requirement) and the organisation recognises that the global industry faces tighter regulatory regimes (Insurer, 2019). While the South African regulator imposes new standards on the domestic industry (not necessarily specific to climate risk), regulators across the world are setting new precedents for insurers to quantify their climate risk.

One noteworthy example internationally has been in response to wild fires in California, where the Californian Insurance Commissioner led as the first United States financial regulator to undertake climate-related scenario stress testing of insurers' reserves (California Department of Insurance, 2018). This came out of the regulator's recognised 'responsibility for monitoring the financial condition of insurers, including both their assets and their liabilities and risks thereto, and helping maintain the availability, affordability and adequacy of insurance for consumers' (California Department of Insurance, 2018: 5). It remains to be seen whether these kinds of strength tests and climate-related scenario testing will become the norm and expected by regulators and prudential authorities more widely.

Manoeuvrability

In short-term or retail insurance contexts, customers generally do not understand climate risk as a contributing component of the premium they pay (Botzen and Van Den Bergh, 2008; Hudson et al., 2016; Li et al., 2017). This militates against one insurer increasing premium costs in order to price climate risk into short-term insurance products, when competitors do not also do so. The Insurer explained that the insurance market, particularly in under-insured markets like South Africa, is often a 'race to the bottom', where competitor insurers aim to marginally undercut each other and convince clients of the value of their product offering. Clients will often switch between neither insurers based on price without full consideration of the comprehensiveness of the cover offered nor the risk factors behind that pricing of premiums. It therefore makes it very challenging for one insurer to act alone, based on their internal understanding of climate risk and increase premiums in accord with their calculation of the full risk. Further, if these calculations are based on climate scenarios and people are notoriously unaware of their present, let alone future risk, such costs would likely be seen as exhorbitant by the consumer. The Insurer expressed therefore that they could not risk pricing their products outside the status quo of the non-climate priced insurance market.

During workshop discussions it was identified that this is further hampered through regulatory controls designed to prevent collusion; these same regulations prevent insurers from acting in concert, for example, to include a percentage of premiums for climate risk, which could be passed on to the consumer. This is thought to present proactive and climate risk-aware insurers with a first mover disadvantage. In addition to a threat of losing clients, it can also create a market niche for predatory insurers with higher risk appetites prepared to consider climate risk without the same degree of caution in their risk management approach. It is conceivable that such insurers could simply declare bankruptcy rather than honour claims when major insured climate losses manifest. Workshop participants were quick to point out how two insurers in South Africa did not survive the 2017 claims season for this very reason (see CFO South Africa, 2018). In light of these developments, the degree to which consumer choice may change with greater climate risk awareness will be an increasingly important research agenda for insurers with lower risk appetites.

One potential way that has been proposed to overcome this lack of manoeuvrability and pricing flexibility for insurers, acting alone or in collusion, is for the regulator to place a range of climate risk governance demands on all insurers within their jurisdiction, such as those proposed by the Californian Insurance Regulator (California Department of Insurance, 2018). In such a case, premiums may not explicitly have climate risk priced into them but premiums will likely rise in cost, reflecting increases in due diligence burdens common to all in the market. Climate risk can then be indirectly priced into the business model with costs past onto the market.

Conclusion

This chapter illustrated the challenges of climate exposure, solvency and manoeuvrability for a short-term insurer as it grapples to accommodate and implement current climate knowledge into their business. These challenges have been presented as they emerged out of the Insurer's deliberations on climate risk, together with consideration of associated regulatory developments. Although regulation is the number 'one factor influencing underwriting, and the number one factor in terms of risk severity' (de la Mare, 2013: 247), and one of the most notable challenges currently facing insurers, particularly South African insurers (KPMG, 2018), this case exemplifies what has been noted elsewhere: that climate risks globally and their governing responses by short-term insurers have generally outpaced the development of prudential regulatory or legal frameworks in most regimes (de la Mare, 2013).

The enhanced unknowns of climate variability and change of the Anthropocene present augmented challenges to the insurance sector as a whole as it contemplates the implications of evolving climate risk. This case has illustrated how historic data is still used in risk assessment and management, yet becomes increasingly less helpful for insurers (Nel, Shearing and Reyers, 2011; Bouwer, 2019). This elevates the importance of cautions that the insurance industry may find itself unable to effectively analyse the risks it faces, undermining both the profitability of industry and the role it plays in society (de la Mare, 2013). In the workshop and interviews participants identified how climate change presents novel and future risks, with a range of associated harmscapes, which do not match well with the insurer's conventional and existing risk assessment calculation practices. Although highly desired, the interpretability and translatability of current climate science into the insurer's business is demonstrated in this case to be a far more complex and problematic task than previously assumed. The Insurer demonstrates that this potentially requires a multitude of risk-specific recalibrations to find where 'good risk' is in the Anthropocene, and dynamic modelling of where it might emerge or change. The case demonstrates entrenchment and elaboration of what Herbstein (2015), in a thesis with the instructive sub-title, *Like a Frog in Hot Water*, identified as 'defensive underwriting' in the Insurer's response to climate risk through adaptation of their business.

The potential manoeuvrability of one insurance company, acting alone and proactively is displayed in this case to be significantly constrained by market competition as well as global insurance pricing trends. Such constraints highlight the potential role of insurance regulators, client awareness, carbon disclosures and cooperation with other market players in order to accommodate such pricing shifts or flexibility. A shift in insurance coverage may have larger societal risk management implications, particularly for African countries with low insurance penetration rates. At a time when society requires greater insurance penetration, likely at higher premiums, the potential vulnerability of currently uninsured entities militates against their future coverage and protection against climate harms.

References

AON. (2019). *Weather, Climate & Catastrophe Insight: 2018 Annual Report*. London: AON. Available at: http://bit.ly/if-annual-report-2018 [Accessed 24 April 2020].

Armbruster, Stephanie, Beat, Zischg and Hintermann, Andreas. (2018). The Effects of Flood Events on Land and Housing Value: Evidence from the Swiss Real Estate Market. Submission to SURED Conference, Monte Verita, June 3–7, 2018. Available at: https://ethz.ch/content/dam/ethz/special-interest/mtec/cer-eth/resource-econ-dam/documents/research/sured/sured-2018/65-Hintermann-The_effects_of_flood_events.pdf. [Accessed 25 April 2020].

Beck, Ulrich. (1992). *Risk Society: Towards a New Modernity*. London: Sage Publications.

———. (2010). Climate for change, or how to create a green modernity? *Theory, Culture and Society*, 27(2), pp. 254–266. https://doi.org/10.1177/0263276409358729.

Beckie, Hugh J., Smyth, Stuart J., Owen, Micheal D. K. and Gleim, Savannah. (2019). Rewarding best pest management practices via reduced crop insurance premiums. *International Journal of Agronomy*, pp. 1–11. https://doi.org/10.1155/2019/9390501.

Belanger, Philippe and Bourdeau-Brien, Michael. (2018). The impact of flood risk on the price of residential properties: The case of England. *Housing Studies*, 33(6), pp. 876–901. https://doi.org/10.1080/02673037.2017.1408781.

Berz, Gerhard A. (1999). Catastrophes and climate change: Concerns and possible countermeasures of the insurance industry. *Mitigation and Adaptation Strategies for Global Change*, 4, pp. 283–293. https://doi.org/https://doi.org/10.1023/A:1009663605118.

Botzen, W. J. W. and Van Den Bergh, J. C. J. M. (2008). Insurance against climate change and flooding in the Netherlands: Present, future, and comparison with other countries. *Risk Analysis*, 28(2), pp. 413–426. https://doi.org/10.1111/j.1539-6924.2008.01035.x.

Bougen, Philip D. (2003). Catastrophe risk. *Economy and Society*, 32(2), pp. 253–274. https://doi.org/10.1080/03085140032000073428.

Bouwer, Laurens M. (2019). Observed and projected impacts from extreme weather events: Implications for loss and damage. In: R. Mechler, L. Bouwer, T. Schinko, S. Surminski and J. Linnerooth-Bayer, eds. *Loss and Damage from Climate Change: Concepts, Methods and Policy Options*. Cham: Springer, pp. 63–82. https://doi.org/10.1007/978-3-319-72026-5.

California Department of Insurance. (2018). *Trial by Fire: Managing Climate Risks Facing Insurers in the Golden State*. Los Angeles: California Department of Insurance. Available at: https://www.law.berkeley.edu/wp-content/uploads/2018/09/Trial-by-Fire-September-2018.pdf [Accessed 25 April 2020].

Carbon Disclosure Project (CDP). (2020). *Climate Change*. London: Carbon Disclosure Project (CDP). Available at: https://www.cdp.net/en/climate. [Accessed 25 April 2020].

CFO South Africa. (2018). Lion of Africa Insurance Winds down Operations Voluntarily. CFO South Africa. [News Bulletin] 19 November. Available at: https://cfo.co.za/article/lion-of-africa-insurance-winds-down-operations-voluntarily. [Accessed 25 April 2020].

ClimateWise. (2019). *Physical Risk Framework: Understanding the Impacts of Climate Change on Real Estate Lending and Investment Portfolios*. Cambridge: University of Cambridge Institute for Sustainability Leadership (CISL).

CoastAdapt. (2018). *Role of Insurance in Adaptation*. Canberra: CoastAdapt. Available at: https://coastadapt.com.au/role-of-insurance. [Accessed 25 April 2020].

Dlugolecki, Andrew. (2008). Climate change and the insurance sector. *The Geneva Papers on Risk and Insurance-Issues and Practice*, 33(1), pp. 71–90.

Dosio, Alessandro, Jones, R., Jack, C., Lennard, C., Nikulin, G. and Hewitson, B. (2019). What can we know about future precipitation in Africa? Robustness, significance and added value of projections from a large ensemble of regional climate models. *Climate Dynamics*, July, pp. 5833–5858. https://doi.org/10.1007/s00382-019-04900-3.

Dosio, Alessandro and Panitz, Hans Jürgen. (2016). Climate change projections for CORDEX-Africa with COSMO-CLM regional climate model and differences with the driving global climate models. *Climate Dynamics*, 46(5–6), pp. 1599–1625. https://doi.org/10.1007/s00382-015-2664-4.

Ericson, R.V. and Doyle, A. (2004). *Uncertain Business: Risk, Insurance and the Limits of Knowledge*. Toronto: University of Toronto Press.

Ericson, R.V., Doyle, A., Barry, D. and Ericson, D. (2003). *Insurance as Governance*. Toronto: University of Toronto Press.

Federation of European Risk Management Associations (FERMA). (2014). *European Risk and Insurance Report*. Brussels: Federation of European Risk Management Associations. Available at: http://www.eosrisq.com/publications/FERMA_ BenchmarkingSurvey_2014.pdf. [Accessed 25 April 2020].

Froestad, Jan, Gjuvsland, Kjersti, Herbstein, Tom and Shearing, Clifford. (2011). Insurance as a regulatory mechanism towards sustainable companies. *Risk and Insurance*, August, pp. 29–30.

Glaas, Erik, Keskitalo, Carina H. and Hjerpe, Mattias. (2017). Insurance sector management of climate change adaptation in three Nordic countries: The influence of policy and market factors. *Journal of Environmental Planning and Management*, 60(9), pp. 1601–1621. https://doi.org/10.1080/09640568.2016.1245654.

Grace, Martin F., Klein, Robert Warren and Liu, Zhiyong John. (2005). Increased hurricane risk and insurance market responses. *Journal of Insurance Regulation*, 24(2), pp. 2–32. https://ssrn.com/abstract=2670910.

Herbstein, Tom Philip. (2015). Insurance and the Anthropocene: Like a Frog in Hot Water. Unpublished PhD thesis, University of Cape Town, Cape Town. Available at: https://open.uct.ac.za/bitstream/handle/11427/16571/thesis_law_2015_herbstein_ tom_philip.pdf;sequence=1. [Accessed 24 April 2020].

Hudson, Paul, Botzen, W. J. Wouter, Feyen, Luc and Aerts, Jeroen C. J. H. (2016). Incentivising flood risk adaptation through risk based insurance premiums: Trade-offs between affordability and risk reduction. *Ecological Economics*, 125, pp. 1–13. https://doi.org/10.1016/j.ecolecon.2016.01.015.

Insurance Business. (2018). Lloyd's of London Reveals Toronto's Greatest Loss Exposures. *Insurance Business*. [News Bulletin] 27 June. Available at: https://www. insurancebusinessmag.com/ca/risk-management/news/lloyds-of-london-reveals-to-rontos-greatest-loss-exposures-104414.aspx. [Accessed 25 April 2020].

Insurer. (2017). The Insurer ClimateWise Report. Cape Town. [On file with the author].
———. (2018). The Insurer's Integrated Report 2017. Cape Town. [On file with the author].
———. (2019). The Insurer's Integrated Report 2018. Cape Town. [On file with the author].

Keys, Patrick W., Galaz, Victor, Dyer, Michelle, Matthews, Nathanial, Folke, Carl, Nyström, Magnus and Cornell, Sarah E. (2019). Anthropocene risk. *Nature Sustainability*, July, pp. 1–8. https://doi.org/10.1038/s41893-019-0327-x.

KPMG. (2018). *Financial Services: The South African Insurance Industry Survey 2018*. Johannesburg: KPMG. Available at: https://home.kpmg/content/dam/ kpmg/za/pdf/2018/October/Insurance%20survey-FINAL-web.pdf. [Accessed 25 April 2020].

de la Mare, William de. (2013). Locality of harm: Insurance and climate change in the 21st century. *Connecticut Insurance Law Journal*, 20(1), pp. 189–272. https:// heinonline.org/HOL/P?h=hein.journals/conilj20&i=199.

Lamond, J. E. and Proverbs, D. G. (2008). Flood insurance in the UK – A survey of the experience of floodplain residents. *WIT Transactions on Ecology and the Environment*, 118(10), pp. 325–334. https://doi.org/10.2495/FRIAR080311.

Li, Sen, Juhász-Horváth, Linda, Harrison, Paula A., Pintér, László and Rounsevell, Mark D. A. (2017). Relating farmer's perceptions of climate change risk to adaptation behaviour in Hungary. *Journal of Environmental Management*, 185, pp. 21–30. https://doi.org/10.1016/j.jenvman.2016.10.051.

Mauelshagen, Franz. (2018). The age of uncertainty: The challenges of climate change for the insurance business. In: Claus Leggewie and Franz Mauelshagen, eds., *Climate Change and Cultural Transition in Europe*, 4th ed. Leiden, The Netherlands: Brill Academic Publishers, pp. 301–319. https://doi.org/https://doi.org/10.1163/9789004356825_012.

McGregor, Michael and Spicer, Zachary. (2016). The Canadian home-voter: Property values and municipal politics in Canada. *Journal of Urban Affairs*, 38(1), pp. 123–139. https://doi.org/10.1111/juaf.12178.

Mechler, R., Bouwer, L., Schinko, T., Surminski, S. and Linnerooth-Bayer, J. (2019). *Loss and Damage from Climate Change: Concepts, Methods and Policy Options*, Cham: Springer, pp. 63–82. https://doi.org/10.1007/978-3-319-72026-5.

Meyers, Gert and Van Hoyweghen, Ine. (2018). Enacting actuarial fairness in insurance: From fair discrimination to behaviour-based fairness. *Science as Culture*, 27(4), pp. 413–438. https://doi.org/10.1080/09505431.2017.1398223.

Mills, Evan. (2007). Synergisms between climate change mitigation and adaptation: An insurance perspective. *Mitigation and Adaptation Strategies for Global Change*, 12(5), pp. 809–842. https://doi.org/10.1007/s11027-007-9101-x.

Munich Re. (2019). Thunderstorms, Cyclones and Heatwaves: The Natural Disaster Figures for the First Half of 2019. [Press release] 30 July. Available at: https://www.munichre.com/content/dam/munichre/global/content-pieces/documents/20190730_NatCat_HJ2019_en.pdf/_jcr_content/renditions/original./20190730_NatCat_HJ2019_en.pdf [Accessed 25 April 2020].

Nel, D. C., Shearing, Clifford and Reyers, B. (2011). Insurers could help address climate risks. *Nature*, 476, p. 33.

O'Hare, Paul, White, Iain and Connelly, Angela. (2016). Insurance as maladaptation: Resilience and the 'Business as Usual' paradox. *Environment and Planning C: Government and Policy*, 34(6), pp. 1175–1193. https://doi.org/10.1177/0263774X15602022.

O'Malley, Pat. (2003). Governable catastrophes: A comment on Bougen. *Economy and Society*, 32 (2), pp. 275–279. https://doi.org/10.1080/0308514032000073437.

Paterson, Matthew. (1999). Global finance and environmental politics climate change. *Ids Bulletin*, 30(3), pp. 25–30. https://doi.org/10.1111/j.1759-5436.1999.mp30003004.x.

Phelan, Liam. (2011). Managing climate risk: Extreme weather events and the future of insurance in a climate-changed world. *Australasian Journal of Environmental Management*, 18(4), pp. 223–232. https://doi.org/10.1080/14486563.2011.611486.

Phelan, Liam, Henderson-Sellers, Ann and Taplin, Ros. (2010). Climate change, carbon prices and insurance systems. *International Journal of Sustainable Development and World Ecology*, 17(2), pp. 95–108. https://doi.org/10.1080/13504500903541806.

Phelan, Liam, Holley, Cameron, Shearing, Clifford D. and du Toit, Louise. (2020). Insurance and climate change. In: Avi Brisman and Nigel South, eds., *Routledge International Handbook of Green Criminology*, 2nd ed. London and New York: Routledge, pp. 680–700.

Phelan, Liam, Taplin, Ros, Henderson-Sellers, Ann and Albrecht, Glenn. (2011). Ecological viability or liability? Insurance system responses to climate risk. *Environmental Policy and Governance*, 21(2), pp. 112–130. https://doi.org/10.1002/eet.565.

PWC. (2018). *Reay and Willing: African Insurance Industry Poised for Growth.* Luxembourgh: PWC. Available at: https://www.pwc.co.za/en/assets/pdf/south-african-insurance-2018.pdf. [Accessed 25 April 2020].

Reuss, Andreas, Russ, Jochen and Wieland, Jochen. (2015). Participating life insurance contracts under risk based solvency frameworks: How to increase capital efficiency by product design. In: Kathrin Glau, Matthias Scherer and Rudi Zagst, eds., *Innovations in Quantitative Risk Management.* Heidelberg: Springer, pp. 185–208. https://doi.org/DOI 10.1007/978-3-319-09114-3_11.

South African Insurance Association (SAIA). (2018). *Accelerating Our Journey to Future-Proofing Our Industry.* Cape Town: South African Insurance Association. Available at: https://saia.co.za/assets/ebook/ebook/AR2018/files/basic-html/page23.html. [Accessed 25 April 2020].

Schiermeier, Quirin. (2019). Climate change made Europe's mega-heatwave five times more likely. *Nature*, 571, p. 155. https://doi.org/10.1038/d41586-019-02071-z.

Schwartz, Scott W. (2019). Measuring vulnerability and deferring responsibility: Quantifying the anthropocene. *Theory, Culture and Society*, 36(4), pp. 73–93. https://doi.org/10.1177/0263276418820961.

Seifert, Deborah L. and Lindberg, Deborah L. (2012). Managing climate change risk: Insurers can lead the way. *Risk, Hazards & Crisis in Public Policy*, 3(2), pp. 1–16. https://doi.org/10.1515/1944-4079.1109.

Shearing, Clifford. (2015). Criminology and the anthropocene. *Criminology and Criminal Justice*, 15(3), pp. 255–269.

Simpson, Nicholas Philip, Simpson, Kayleen Jeanne, Shearing, Clifford D. and Cirolia, Liza Rose. (2019). Municipal finance and resilience lessons for urban infrastructure management: A case study from the Cape Town drought. *International Journal of Urban Sustainable Development*, 11(3), pp. 257–276. https://doi.org/https://doi.org/10.1080/19463138.2019.1642203.

Spreng, Connor P., Sovacool, Benjamin K. and Spreng, Daniel. (2016). All hands on deck: Polycentric governance for climate change insurance. *Climatic Change*, 139(2), pp. 129–140. https://doi.org/10.1007/s10584-016-1777-z.

Steffen, Thomas. (2008). Solvency II and the work of CEIOPS. *Geneva Papers on Risk and Insurance: Issues and Practice*, 33(1), pp. 60–65. https://doi.org/10.1057/palgrave.gpp.2510162.

Steffen, Will, Rockström, Johan, Richardson, Katherine, Lenton, Timothy M., Folke, Carl, Liverman, Diana, Summerhayes, Colin P., Barnosky, Anthony D., Cornell, Sarah E., Crucifix, Michel, Jonathan, F., Ingo Fetzer, Donges, Lade, Steven J., Scheffer, Marten, Winkelmann, Ricarda and Schellnhuber, Hans Joachim. (2018). Trajectories of the Earth system in the anthropocene. *Proceedings of the National Academy of Sciences of the United States of America*, 115(33), pp. 8252–8259. https://doi.org/10.1073/pnas.1810141115.

Task Force on Climate-related Financial Disclosures (TCFD). (2017). *Recommendations of the Task Force on Climate Related Financial Disclosures.* New York: Task Force on Climate-related Financial Disclosures (TCFD). Available at: https://www.fsb-tcfd.org/wp-content/uploads/2017/06/FINAL-2017-TCFD-Report-11052018.pdf. [Accessed 25 April 2020].

Thistlethwaite, Jason and Wood, Michael O. (2018). Insurance and climate change risk management: Rescaling to look beyond the horizon. *British Journal of Management*, 29(2), pp. 279–298. https://doi.org/10.1111/1467-8551.12302.

Torabi, Elnaz, Dedekorkut-Howes, Aysin and Howes, Michael. (2018). Adapting or maladapting: Building resilience to climate-related disasters in coastal cities. *Cities*, 72 (December 2018), pp. 295–309. https://doi.org/10.1016/j.cities.2017.09.008.

Turnbull, C. (2018). Some notes on approaches to regulatory capital assessment for insurance firms. *British Actuarial Journal*, 23(6), pp. 1–10. https://doi.org/10.1017/S1357321718000016.

UNEP-Fi. (2019). African Insurance and UN Leaders Meet in Lagos to Drive Collaborative Action for Sustainable Development. Geneva: UNEP-Fi. Available at: https://www.entrepreneur.com/article/333221. [Accessed 25 April 2020].

UNEP-Fi and PSI. (2019). UN Environment and World's Insurers Join Forces to Raise Ambition in Tackling Global Sustainability Challenges. [News Bulletin] 12 March. Geneva: UNEP-Fi and PSI. Available at: http://www.unepfi.org/psi/wp-content/uploads/2019/03/PSI-Allianz-event-Post-event-message-Mar-2019-final.pdf. [Accessed 24 April 2020].

Williamson, Piers R. and Nagashima, Miori. (2019). Imagining insurance in Japanese high schools during the era of rapid modernisation: From "distrust" to the Japanese "spirit". *Social Science Japan Journal*, July. pp. 229–246. https://doi.org/10.1093/ssjj/jyz012.

9 Finance actors and climate-related disclosure regulation

Logic, limits, and emerging accountability

Megan Bowman and Daniel Wiseman[*]

Introduction

Climate-related corporate disclosure has become a favoured regulatory tool for addressing climate risk to financial and market stability. This is notably so since the advent of the final recommendations of the TaskForce on Climate-related Financial Disclosures (TCFD) established by the international Financial Stability Board (TCFD, 2017), legislative proposals arising from the European Commission's *Sustainable Finance Action Plan* (European Commission, 2018), and policy directions in the United Kingdom (UK) *Green Finance Strategy* (HM Government, 2019). These initiatives promote forward-looking reporting by companies of the climate-related risks and opportunities that face their business. More specifically, such reporting ought to 'be useful to investors, lenders and insurance underwriters in understanding material risk' (TCFD, 2017: iii) when making investment decisions in an increasingly carbon-constrained economy.

To a large extent, using non-financial reporting as a modality to enhance transparency and mitigate risk is not new. Such corporate reporting has been used for many years to document corporate greenhouse gas emissions (the international benchmark being the GHG Protocol Corporate Standard) and is also employed in analogous social fields such as human rights in business supply chains (e.g. UK Modern Slavery Act 2015, section 54). Yet what cannot be understated is the influence of recent regulatory initiatives such as the TCFD as well as interventions by financial regulators such as the UK Prudential Regulatory Authority (PRA), in *changing the corporate narrative on climate change* by recasting climate change as a strategic and financial risk and no longer a peripheral ethical issue.

[*] We are grateful to Klaudia Dadasiewicz for her valuable research assistance through the 2019 King's Undergraduate Research Fellowships scheme. Daniel Wiseman would like to acknowledge Stephanie Morton's work in preparing the ClientEarth complaints discussed in this chapter.

These initiatives have also intensified scrutiny of the climate readiness of supervised firms, namely banks and insurers. By the very nature of their businesses, banks and insurers are naturally accomplished at measuring, mitigating and managing risk, which includes peering into the future to analyse foreseeable business and investment risks and also opportunities caused by climate change. Moreover, insurers and reinsurers in particular may face drastic potential economic consequences due to the physical impacts of climate change. Yet, despite recent exhortations by prudential and market regulators (e.g. PRA, 2015, 2018a, 2018b) these finance actors are not yet living up to their potential to lead an orderly market transition to a low-carbon economy.

It is becoming apparent that more attention needs to be given to the role and forms of accountability mechanisms to help fulfil the logic of climate-related disclosure. To be effective, climate-related reporting must be given consequence not only by regulators but also by market actors and other stakeholders. Indeed, non-state accountability measures are emerging through various actions of shareholders, civil society, and third-sector organisations that seek improved disclosure and responsibility from both companies and regulators. Notably, environmental law charity ClientEarth has reported numerous companies to UK financial regulators in recent years for alleged failures to disclose material information about climate-related trends and risks in their annual reports. The companies targeted in those complaints have spanned a wide variety of sectors, including oil and gas companies, airlines, manufacturers, infrastructure owners and operators, and insurers (ClientEarth, 2019). In each of these cases, the complaints alleged that the company in question had breached the law by failing to adequately disclose climate-related information and requested that the financial regulators take remedial action.

This chapter analyses the logic of disclosure and uses ClientEarth complaints against three insurance companies as a case study for examining legal innovation, notions of accountability, and likely regulatory direction of travel in this emerging area. In so doing, it makes clear that climate change comprises much more than a peripheral Environmental, Social and Governance (ESG) consideration but rather embodies a material financial risk that ought to sit front and centre on the legal and strategic agendas of company Boards and be addressed explicitly in financial reports. Further, the chapter provides first-hand insight into the least-discussed category of climate risk known as 'liability risk', which sits within the tripartite taxonomy of physical risks, transition risks, and liability risks associated with climate change (PRA, 2018b). Liability risk has received relatively little attention in scholarly or industry literature to date. When it is discussed, especially in industry sources, it is usually described as the risk of being sued for contributing to climate change through greenhouse gas emissions (e.g. Aviva, 2018). Yet the case study in this chapter demonstrates that companies (and finance actors in particular) have responsibility, at the very least, to disclose climate-related risks and opportunities in accordance with existing reporting regulation. In this way, we propose that 'liability risk' of corporate actors is moving beyond the current narrow conception of liability for directly causing carbon pollution.

This chapter proceeds as follows. The next part conceptualises a three-pronged logic of disclosure to combat climate risk at macro, meso, and micro levels, and outlines regulatory responses that have precipitated closer scrutiny of banks and insurers in particular. It also explores current challenges regarding variability and uptake of climate-related reporting, and the need for a whole-of-market approach to accountability that engages a spectrum of stakeholders. The third part provides detailed analysis of ClientEarth's insurance-related complaints, including the relevant legal requirements, factual basis and outcomes. It focuses on conceptions of materiality and principle risks in the context of current reporting duties and the PRA's tripartite taxonomy of climate risks. The chapter then provides analysis and forward-looking discussion focusing particularly on regulatory direction of travel, materiality thresholds, and auditing for accountability. Prior to concluding, it highlights the need for complementary regulatory design in order to make the logic of reporting a reality.

Disclosure regulation: Logic and limits

The zeitgeist of climate-related disclosure is best summarised by Geoff Summerhayes, former Chair of the Sustainable Insurance Forum and Board Member of the Australian Prudential Regulatory Authority:

> The weight of money, through consumer demand, investor decisions, and regulatory responses, is pushing the transition to a low carbon economy relentlessly forward... but to make good decisions, governments, regulators, businesses and investors need access to timely, reliable and sufficiently granular information.
>
> (Summerhayes, 2019)

A disclosure-based approach puts market and regulatory pressure on investors to invest in a way that mitigates business and market risks arising from climate change. A disclosure-based approach the 'right' choices is hard for investors to do without the information they need, which necessitates a theoretical exploration of the logic of disclosure.

The logic of disclosure and regulatory responses

We might consider the logic of disclosure as a trident with three 'prongs'.

The first prong embodies the macro-economic level. In 2015 Mark Carney, then-Governor of the Bank of England and Head of the Financial Stability Board, was the first financial regulator to publicly herald that climate change presents systemic financial risks with potential to destabilise markets and induce a new global financial crisis (Carney, 2015; Fisher, 2017). Carney's landmark speech at Lloyd's of London highlighted the importance of avoiding a 'Minsky moment' brought on by sudden repricing of fossil fuel and carbon-intensive assets that would trigger a fire sale by distressed investors with disastrous whole-of-market consequences due to the interconnected nature of the global economy. Thus, the logic of this prong is that, - when investors have more information-, then markets can price risks earlier, with the result of a more orderly or graduated series of smaller price corrections over time (Fisher, 2019). Moreover, for regulators, enhanced disclosure and transparency ought to enable assessment of whether supervised firms (banks and insurers) are 'financially viable, well-governed, regulatory compliant and resilient' (Summerhayes, 2019) and thus regulators can evaluate the status of market health generally.

This leads into the second prong of disclosure logic, which points to the meso-market level. For investors, access to accurate information regarding the past performance and future prospects of companies can inform capital allocation decisions and share prices. The logic here is that, in a carbon-constrained world, a virtuous feedback loop can be perpetuated whereby: (a) investors increasingly invest in low-carbon targets; and (b) companies that provide additional 'green' assurances to the market receive competitive advantage in attracting investment (Carney, 2019; Fisher, 2019). Moreover, investors and shareholders are likely to agitate for more and better information and, eventually, better climate action from companies (Eccles and Krzus, 2017).

The third prong embodies the micro individual company level, best summarised by the old accounting adage that 'what gets measured gets managed'. In other words, firms need to internalise the externalities by putting them on the balance sheet and making them explicit. In this way the company itself can see its own inputs, outputs, and impacts, and make informed decisions about where the inflection points for internal change reside. This prong is little discussed in the literature. However, it will likely garner attention as reporting practice gains momentum and the attendant benefits and challenges become more apparent to firms and regulators alike.

It is the first and second prongs of disclosure logic that have been driving recent and unprecedented interventions by financial regulators around the world. These interventions are best exemplified by creation of the Central Banks and Supervisors Network for Greening the Financial System (NGFS), which is a voluntary network of more than 40 global members and observers contributing to the development of climate risk management in the finance sector, mainstreaming finance to support the low-carbon transition, and defining and promoting best practices for in-country implementation by member banks (NGFS, 2018). More specifically, Carney has categorised climate-related risks into a tripartite taxonomy of physical risks, transition risks, and liability risks, which the UK PRA and other authorities have since noted will likely manifest as credit, market, and operational risks for banks and insurers (e.g. PRA, 2018b). These risks are detailed in the third part, below.

Importantly, climate-related reporting has become the most prominent regulatory tool for addressing those risks since the release of the 2017 final recommendations of the G20 Financial Stability Board's Taskforce on Climate-related Financial Disclosures (TCFD, 2017). The TCFD was established in 2015 as an international initiative comprising a series of widely spread public consultations to produce final voluntary recommendations for corporate reporting on the financial implications of climate change. These reporting recommendations apply to all corporate and financial entities, including banks, insurance firms, investors, asset managers, and intermediaries, such as ratings agencies. Specifically, the recommendations encourage individual firms to provide information to stakeholders (investors, lenders, and insurers) on risks and opportunities posed to their business by climate change using forward-looking scenario analysis regarding governance, strategy, risk management, and metrics and targets.

Naturally, this heightened activity by financial regulators has precipitated closer scrutiny of the firms they supervise, namely banks and insurers.[1] Indeed, the first country to do so was France, which enacted the *2015 French Energy Transition and Green Growth Law* ahead of the Paris Agreement on climate change and TCFD recommendations. Article 173 of this French legislation mandates enhanced climate-related financial disclosure specifically from banks and insurers (see generally Webster, 2020). The intense gaze on banks and insurers is also exemplified by the UK PRA final supervisory statement (PRA, 2019), *Enhancing Banks' and Insurers' Approaches to Managing the Financial Risks from Climate Change* (hereafter PRA SS3/19). Pursuant to this supervisory statement, the PRA expects supervised firms to establish strategic plans that, amongst other things, enhance transparency through a robust disclosure approach, delineate clear roles and responsibilities for Boards regarding management of climate risk, use scenario analysis, and incorporate financial risks from climate change into risk management practice.

Explicitly requiring climate-related disclosures by banks and insurers – as a discrete subset of corporate actor – is quite radical. These actors are not regarded as producing high greenhouse gas emissions or a notable environmental footprint and, in market economies at least, have not been traditionally subject to special scrutiny by environmental law, let alone financial regulation, on the issue of climate change. While the integral role of private finance actors to redressing sustainability and climate change have been identified previously in select regulatory scholarship (Richardson, 2006; Alexander, 2014; Bowman, 2015), it is a new endeavour by prudential and market regulators to spotlight this sector as essential for an orderly transition to a low-carbon and climate-resilient economy.

Limitations and challenges

Despite the warm reception of these initiatives, there are shortcomings in uptake and implementation to date. In short, two key challenges are emerging: the highly variable quality of disclosure; and low uptake whereby some companies are not addressing climate risk at all in their annual reports. In response to these challenges, much of the burgeoning climate disclosure literature has focused on whether disclosure, especially the TCFD requirements, ought to be voluntary or mandatory to ensure efficacy (Hahn, Reimsbach and Schiemann, 2015). This is an extensive and intensive debate that can only be summarised here. Proponents of voluntary reporting regard it as preferable for ensuring the right balance between free market principles and the need for appropriate risk-pricing (e.g. Campiglio et al., 2018). The main fear is that legislating disclosure rules would curtail innovation and collaboration (e.g. Henderson, 2009; also Knox-Hayes and Levy, 2011) whereas voluntary schemes, such as the Carbon Disclosure Project (CDP), are nimble at advancing and diffusing new standards of climate awareness in business (Andrew and Cortese, 2011) without stunting flexibility. In contrast, there is growing sentiment that only mandatory reporting can ensure high enough levels of reliability, comparability, credibility, and, perhaps most importantly, mass uptake to be effective (e.g. Harper Ho, 2017; Ioannou and Serafeim, 2017; Jackson et al., 2017). Indeed, several industry commentators who are well-acquainted with financial regulators opine that disclosure will inevitably become mandatory because, in the words of Paul Fisher, ex-economist of the Bank of England, 'those with the biggest exposures – which are most difficult to reduce [and therefore may cause the most harm] – are the most likely not to volunteer' (Fisher, 2019; also Summerhayes, 2019).

The voluntary/mandatory debate is not easy to reconcile. In the UK at least, the government has committed to 'exploring' mandatory reporting and there is an expectation that all listed companies and large asset owners will disclose consistently with TCFD recommendations by 2022 (HM Government, 2019) and preference has been shown for a 'comply or explain' model as per the UK Corporate Governance Code (House of Commons Environmental Audit Committee, 2018; Financial Conduct Authority, 2018). Nonetheless, empirical evidence regarding Article 173 of the French Energy Transition and Green Growth Law, 2015 has shown that even this form of mandatory disclosure does not guarantee compliance and that discretionary methods of reporting have produced highly variable reporting quality (see e.g. FourTwentySeven, 2018).

More specifically, neither banks nor insurers are yet doing enough to support an orderly transition. Overwhelmingly, industry reports reveal that insurers and banks are lagging behind other sectors when it comes to addressing climate change (e.g. Environmental Finance, 2016; French Treasury, Banque de France and ACPR, 2017; Aviva, 2018; Boston Common Asset Management, 2018). Specific studies show the extent of this unreadiness.

For example, a 2018 PRA survey of the majority of the UK banking sector, representing over £11 trillion in assets, found that only 10 per cent of respondent banks were taking a strategic, board-level approach to identify and measure long-term financial risks posed by climate risk (PRA, 2018b), which raises questions about the attitudes and abilities of the other 90 per cent of respondents. More tellingly, a 2019 report from the UK Institute and Faculty of Actuaries found that only a minority of sampled large publicly listed insurance companies (and large local government pension schemes) were reporting on their actions to mitigate climate risk, let alone in a way that aligns with TCFD recommendations (Klumpes et al., 2019).

The disclosure literature cited above rarely explains *why* companies are producing inadequate reports or not disclosing at all. There is a strong argument based on previous empirical research that sector-wide voluntary uptake of climate measures by finance actors will be impeded by entrenched cultural-cognitive norms (Bowman, 2014). Yet that thesis needs exploration in the context of climate disclosure to elucidate potential solutions. Nonetheless, it is apparent that, for the logic of disclosure to fulfil its promise, heightened attention needs to focus on not only the soft elements of awareness-raising and education at the front end but also the hard aspects of accountability and enforcement at the back or pointy end.

The pointy end of regulating disclosure

Adjudication and accountability are essential but little discussed aspects of 'climate finance regulation'. This is perhaps unsurprising given the nascency of the field generally, and the fact that financial regulators in most jurisdictions are not yet mandating climate-related disclosure specifically (Summerhayes, 2019). Importantly, most financial regulators do not currently have the resources or remit to enforce it (Bowman and Steenmans, 2019). Moreover, in the case of recommendations such as the TCFD, we currently have the conundrum of attempting to enforce a *voluntary* initiative.

Nonetheless, scholarship in regulatory theory demonstrates that accountability extends beyond a 'bureaucratic mode of public accountability' (Dowdle, 2017: 199) by state enforcement of black letter law. In the context of regulating global business generally (Braithwaite and Drahos, 2000) and various markets specifically, ranging from water (Holley and Sinclair, 2018) to free range eggs (Parker et al., 2017) to finance (MacLeod and Park, 2011; Richardson, 2015; Ayling and Gunningham, 2017), complex 'interactions' amongst participants can be discerned (Eberlein et al., 2014) that can ensure – or undermine – accountability and integrity.

When reflecting on the logic of disclosure, it is clear that climate-related reporting – whether voluntary or mandatory – can only be effective if it is acted upon and thus given consequence by market actors and other stakeholders, which includes but is certainly not limited to financial regulators. Jackson et al. (2019) write that disclosure is only likely to produce substantial changes in corporate actions if stakeholders reward or punish firms' activities, and the UK Institute and Faculty of Actuaries (Klumpes et al., 2019) has highlighted the sensitivity of insurance companies to reputation risk in particular.

Indeed, in the context of climate disclosure, we see non-state accountability measures emerging through civil society campaigns and shareholder activism, such as resolutions to Boards seeking more and better disclosure (e.g. International Investor Group on Climate Change, 2019), litigation against companies for inadequate disclosure (*Abrahams v Commonwealth Bank of Australia*, 2017), and even calls for investors to vote directors off the Boards of companies that fail to act on climate change (Landell-Mills, 2019). We also see third sector organisations pushing for improved accountability from both companies and regulators by making legal complaints for deficient disclosure compliance (e.g. ClientEarth, 2018a, 2018b, 2018c) and producing empirical research on disclosure practices (e.g. Evain, Cardona and Nicol, 2018; FourTwentySeven, 2018).

Importantly, a compelling argument can be made that climate-related disclosure is *already* mandatory by virtue of the *materiality* of climate risk (Staker and Garton, 2018; Fisher, 2019). That is, where climate change presents a *material financial risk* to a company, then directors of that company must report on it pursuant to their general directors' duties in corporate legislation and reporting regulations. This legal obligation is rooted in the general fiduciary duty enshrined in most market economy jurisdictions – that a director must act in good faith to promote the best interests of the company and/or its members (e.g. UK Companies Act, 2006, section 172(2); Australian Corporations Act, 2001, section 180(1); fiduciary duties of care and loyalty at common law in the US; Black, 2001).[2] In the context of climate disclosure, this 'materiality' argument circumnavigates the voluntary/mandatory debate regarding efficacy and enforceability of guidelines such as the TCFD recommendations.

With these considerations front and centre, ClientEarth initiated complaints in the UK against three insurance companies for allegedly breaching their legal obligations to adequately disclose climate-related information. These legal actions and arguments are detailed next.

Emerging accountability: ClientEarth complaints against insurers

In August 2018, ClientEarth submitted three separate complaints to the UK's Financial Conduct Authority (FCA) regarding the failure by three insurance companies to adequately disclose information about climate-related risks in their annual reports (the Complaints) (ClientEarth, 2018c). The insurers subject to the Complaints were Admiral Group plc (Admiral), a well-known motor and house insurer; Lancashire Holdings Limited (Lancashire), a specialty property and casualty insurer; and Phoenix Group

Holdings (Phoenix), a life insurer. The Complaints alleged that by failing to make any mention at all about climate change in their annual reports, these companies had breached the law by omitting the disclosure of a 'principal risk or uncertainty' facing their business. The complaints requested that the FCA impose a financial penalty on the companies and require them to take corrective action.

Summary of legal requirements

Beyond mandatory requirements for listed companies to report annual greenhouse gas (GHG) emissions pursuant to the Companies Act 2006 (Strategic Report and Directors' Report) Regulations 2013, primary legislation in the UK does not explicitly require the disclosure of climate-related information. Nonetheless, for listed companies, there are numerous general reporting requirements where climate-related information may need to be disclosed where relevance and materiality thresholds are met. For certain companies incorporated in the UK, this includes requirements under the Companies Act 2006 (Companies Act), which mandate disclosure of the principal risks and uncertainties facing the company; the company's strategy, objectives, and business model; environmental matters, including the impacts of the company's business; performance metrics to assess progress against objectives, strategy, and impacts (Companies Act, 2006, Chapter 4A); and the viability and prospects of the company over the long term (UK Corporate Governance Code, [C.2.2]).

In addition to the Companies Act requirements, companies with a public listing on a UK stock exchange (even those incorporated elsewhere) must comply with requirements under the *Financial Conduct Authority Handbook* (hereafter *FCA Handbook*), many of which directly implement European Union (EU) Directives aimed at harmonising public disclosures by listed companies (see, e.g. EU Transparency Directive, 2004/109/EC). Most relevant amongst these is a requirement to 'provide a description of the principal risks and uncertainties' facing the company (*FCA Handbook, DTR 4.1.8 R*); and to take 'all reasonable care' to ensure that any information disclosed in the Annual Report 'is not misleading, false or deceptive and does not omit anything likely to affect the import of the information (*FCA Handbook, DTR 1A.3.2 R*)'.

While some of the Companies Act requirements may have been applicable, the ClientEarth complaints against the insurers were based exclusively on the requirements in the *FCA Handbook*. This was for two reasons. Firstly, two of the companies, despite their UK listing, were not incorporated in the UK and therefore the Companies Act requirements may not have applied directly. And secondly, the FCA has primary responsibility for enforcement of requirements under the *FCA Handbook*, whereas supervision and enforcement of the reporting requirements under the Companies Act have traditionally fallen within the remit of another regulator, the Financial Reporting Council (FRC), which has more limited enforcement powers.

On that basis, the substance of ClientEarth's Complaints against each of the insurance companies was that the failure to disclose any information at all about climate change was a failure to disclose a 'principal risk' facing the business and therefore a breach of DTR 1A.3.2 R and DTR 4.1.8 R under the *FCA Handbook*, which would deprive shareholders of relevant information to support their investment decision-making. For breaches of this sort, the FCA has extensive powers to impose financial penalties (Financial Services and Markets Act, 2000 (FSMA), section 91(1ZA)), and to require the companies to publish corrective information (*FCA Handbook, LR 1.3.2 R*). These were the powers which ClientEarth requested the FCA to exercise as part of their investigation of the Complaints. Relevantly, the FCA accepts complaints from investors and the public regarding breaches of its rules (FCA, 2016) but has a policy of not making public its decisions about the status of its investigations, except in exceptional circumstances (*FCA Handbook, EG 6.1*).

What is a 'principal risk'?

The key interpretative question to be addressed in the complaints was therefore whether or not climate change was a 'principal risk' for these companies. Unfortunately, the DTRs do not themselves provide a definition of the term 'principal risks and uncertainties' and the FCA has never provided any explicit guidance on this particular requirement. However, the *FRC Guidance on the Strategic Report* (*FRC Guidance*), does provide guidance on the equivalent requirement under the Companies Act. For this reason, the Complaints asserted that the *FRC Guidance* was the most authoritative indication as to how the term 'principal risks', as contained in the *FCA Handbook*, should be interpreted: 'the terms "key" ... and "principal" ... refer to facts or circumstances that are (or should be) considered material to a shareholder's understanding of the development, performance, position or future prospects of the business' (FRC Guidance, 2014, [5.7] (now superseded); and '[i]nformation is material if its omission or misrepresentation could influence the economic decisions shareholders take on the basis of the annual report as a whole' (FRC Guidance, 2014, [5.1] (now superseded)).

On the basis of this guidance, two main arguments were submitted:

- The subject companies' Annual Reports must include a description of *all* of the principal risks and uncertainties facing the company; and
- A true and accurate understanding of 'principal risks and uncertainties' means 'material' facts or circumstances which a reasonable director would consider 'could influence the economic decisions which shareholders would take on the basis of the annual report as a whole' (ClientEarth, 2018c).

Evidence of the materiality of climate-related risks to insurers

In order to substantiate the claim that the risks associated with climate change were material to the subject companies, and would have been considered by a reasonable director to be so, the Complaints detailed evidence of the financial implications of climate change to the insurance business in general and to the specific companies in particular. Amongst other things, this included evidence from peer companies, industry bodies and regulators regarding the significance of climate change-related risks to the insurance sector.

Over the past few years, there has been a growing awareness of the risks that climate change poses to the insurance sector. In September 2015, the UK PRA published a highly influential paper, *The Impact of Climate Change on the UK Insurance Sector*, which provided an overview of some of these risks and identified that 'there is potential for climate change to present a substantial challenge to the business model of insurers' (PRA, 2015: 5). This paper also adopted the now widely used taxonomy of 'physical risks', 'transition risks', and 'liability risks' to describe the economic impacts of climate change on firms. Accordingly, this was also the approach adopted in the Complaints as described below.

Physical risks

There is now widespread evidence of the potential economic consequences of the physical impacts of climate change on insurance firms. The broad scientific consensus is clear that increasing global temperatures will have a significant impact on weather-related natural catastrophes and will account for an increasing proportion of natural catastrophe losses (IPCC, 2015).

These risks are increasingly manifesting in urban areas with high potential property losses. On this point, the *Lloyds' City Risk Index* discusses the economic consequences of climate change for the cities in its index. It anticipates that climate events will cost those cities $122.98 billion every year, and that this sum will grow as extreme weather events become more frequent and severe (Lloyds of London, 2018). Recent weather events provide an insight into the magnitude of the problem. Lloyd's of London estimated that the storm surge from Hurricane Sandy increased surge losses by 30 per cent due to the 20 cm sea level rise since 1950. All these risks are likely to lead to increased claims where they cause direct damage to insured property. Indeed, insured losses from catastrophes in 2017 were the highest on record; at around $140 billion (Swiss Re Institute, 2018). Accordingly, the increased level of claims is becoming deeply challenging for many insurers' business models.

Beyond payouts for more frequent claims, the physical risks from climate change will likely negatively impact the value of insurers' investment portfolios. For example, the value of real estate is expected to fall in flood-prone areas. The Union of Concerned Scientists considers that 'the cliff's edge of a real estate market deflation due to flooding and sea level rise is already visible for many communities' (Union of Concerned Scientists, 2018: 25). Additionally, credit downgrades have been anticipated for municipalities that do not engage in addressing climate change threats. Local governments are considered more likely to default where they suffer direct financial losses due to climate change and sea level rise, potentially threatening the strength of municipal bonds, which form significant portions of insurers' portfolios (Miller, 2018).

The correlation of these risks on both sides of the balance sheet only compounds the problem. Moody's, the credit rating agency, considers that this correlation results in a negative credit impact for property and casualty (re)insurers. Its view is that 'the property and casualty insurance and reinsurance sector have significant exposure to the economic consequences of climate change' (Moody's, 2018: 1). Consequently, the physical risks from climate change go to the heart of insurance. As ClimateWise have recently recognised, 'growing physical risks driven by climate change and an increasing population vulnerable to these risks means insurers need to rethink the traditional insurance model' (ClimateWise, 2017: 5).

In the Complaints, this evidence was set out in greater detail, including direct links to the business models of each of the different insurers. In the context of Admiral, for example, the Complaint highlighted the specific physical risks facing the car and household insurance sector. This included evidence about the impacts of increasing severe weather events on car and household insurance claims as identified by other insurers and Admiral in previous annual reports and outside of its annual report (ClientEarth, 2018d).

Transition risks

If the world is to achieve the objectives of the Paris Agreement, a significant shift in the trajectory of carbon emissions will be required (International Energy Agency (IEA), 2017). This transition to a low-carbon economy could have a significant impact on the value of financial assets and their capital returns as a result of policy changes, legal actions, technological changes, market responses, and reputational considerations.

Thus, transition risks could impact both sides of insurers' balance sheets. Firstly, these risks could reduce demand for insurance from carbon-intensive sectors. Secondly, they could detrimentally impact the value of insurers' investment portfolios. Partly as a response to concerns raised by the Bank of England, Lloyd's of London released a report on how stranded asset risk may affect the assets and liabilities of the (re)insurance sector. Its view was that 'physical environmental change and societal response to these changes could potentially strand entire regions and global industries within a very short timeframe, with direct and indirect impacts on international insurance markets' (Lloyds of London, 2017: 4).

A recent analysis was also conducted by the California Department of Insurance with regard to insurers' investments. This revealed that Californian insurers were heavily exposed to the stranded asset risks associated with coal as their portfolios were consistent with a trajectory of greater than 3°C of warming (California Department of Insurance, 2018). This over-exposure is unlikely to be confined to Californian insurers, and insurers globally should be assessing and managing their exposure to high-risk sectors such as coal.

Alongside further detail on this general evidence, the Complaints also highlighted more specific risks identified by financial regulators and peers in the sector as evidence of materiality. This included statements by other major insurers, such as AXA and Aviva. Aviva, for example, had identified climate change as a principal risk in its 2017 annual report, stating that climate change could result in 'higher than expected weather-related claims (including business continuity claims) and inaccurate pricing of general insurance risk, as well as adversely impacting economic growth and investments markets' (Aviva, 2017: 26).

Liability risks

The final category of risk detailed in the Complaints related to 'liability risks'. If parties suffer losses as a result of climate-related risks, they may seek to recover those sums from those they allege are responsible. As a result, the insurance industry faces the prospect of increased third-party liability claims. Although climate litigation is highly varied, the cases relevant to insurers can be broadly categorised as follows:

a claims for failing to mitigate the impacts of climate change;
b claims for failing to adapt to the impacts of climate change; and
c claims for failing to disclose climate-related risks, or to comply with legislation or regulation.

As set out in the Lancashire Complaint in most detail, these liability risks may impact insurance companies in two ways. Firstly, they may lead to increased claims under liability policies. Secondly, such claims could be brought directly against an insurance company and/or its directors where that company has failed to disclose or adequately adapt to climate change risks (ClientEarth, 2018e). Given the rapid rate at which climate-related litigation is now developing, the insurance industry is potentially exposed to significant losses as these claims increase in volume and sophistication (Brooke and Beresford, 2019).

Outcomes

Despite the substantial evidence provided, the FCA ultimately decided not to take any public enforcement action against any of the companies subject to the Complaints (ClientEarth, 2019). However, the Complaints did prompt direct engagement by the FCA with the subject companies. The result being that each of the companies' subsequent annual reports disclosed significantly more information about climate change-related risks, indicating internal efforts to analyse the likely effects within the businesses.

Admiral, for example, subsequently identified that it 'is exposed to the risk of high losses due to the occurrence of man-made catastrophes or natural weather events, potentially increased in frequency and severity due to climate change'; and that it is 'considering the impact of climate change across its business' (Admiral, 2018: 53). Phoenix noted that it is '[e]xpanding the Group's programme of qualitative and quantitative scenario analysis to take account of the potential impact of climate change scenarios; and to ensure this is appropriately reflected in the Group's risk management framework' (Phoenix, 2018: 57). And Lancashire asserted that it will 'consider and adapt to the risks and opportunities arising from climate change through the analysis of the associated physical, transitional and liability risks' (Lancashire, 2018: 36).

In and of themselves these disclosures provide limited additional information to inform investors' decision-making. They do, however, indicate that climate-related risks and impacts have been elevated to board level and are being addressed more strategically. In addition, these modest disclosures can pave the way for more detailed and meaningful reporting to follow, especially as investors and regulators increase their expectations in coming years.

Analysis and discussion

Regulatory direction of travel

It is arguable that, beyond instigating direct changes at individual company level and broader stakeholder awareness through industry and legal media (e.g. LaCroix, 2018), a significant impact of the ClientEarth Complaints has been their contribution to and reinforcement of UK financial regulator responses, which will shape market behaviour by raising the expected standard of climate-related reporting for all listed companies in the UK. In this respect, while it is difficult to evidence direct causation, all three UK financial regulators – the FCA, FRC, and PRA – have now broadly mirrored the arguments set out in the Complaints in their updated statements and guidance to the market.

For example, the FRC, in response to the announcement of the UK government's *Green Finance Strategy* (HM Government, 2019), issued a statement setting out its expectations of company reporting duties in relation to climate change-related risks:

> The Boards of UK companies have a responsibility to consider their impact on the environment and the likely consequences of any business decisions in the long-term. They should therefore address, and where relevant report on, the effects of climate change (both direct and indirect). Reporting should set out how the company has taken into account the resilience of the company's business model and its risks, uncertainties and viability in both the immediate and longer-term in light of climate change.
>
> (FRC, 2019a)

This is the clearest expression to date of the FRC's views on the duties of companies to address climate-related risk under existing legal requirements, and reflects the assertions made in the ClientEarth Complaints. Moreover, a recent report from the FRC Financial Reporting Lab on Climate Change-Related Reporting identifies that although 'there is no requirement to report on climate change specifically, there are many reporting requirements that may require companies to address climate-related issues' (FRC, 2019b: 81).

Similarly, the FCA recently announced the launch of a consultation proposing new disclosure rules for certain issuers aligned with the TCFD's recommendations and clarifying existing disclosure obligations relating to climate risks. Moreover, as discussed earlier, PRA *Supervisory Statement SS3/19* requires insurers and banks to comply with the obligation to disclose principal risks and uncertainties under the Companies Act (PRA, 2019).

The direction of travel is further clarified by the UK government and FCA publicly stating their intention to introduce new disclosure requirements directly aligned with the TCFD recommendations, as detailed in the second part of this chapter. In light of these increasingly definitive statements from UK financial regulators, the expectation on companies to consider and disclose detailed information about climate-related risks under existing laws is clearly mounting.

The materiality threshold

It is important to note that materiality is a complex legal issue that could easily comprise a chapter in itself, but given its salience to the way forward we provide some insights here to signpost more detailed analysis in future work. The first point to appreciate is that prior to interventions by the TCFD and financial regulators, such as the Bank of England, climate change was regarded as a peripheral environmental consideration, to be delegated to the corporate social responsibility department or relegated to a secondary ESG report. Now, it is strongly arguable that climate change is deemed a material financial risk. As such, corporate attitudes to climate-related disclosure, especially by banks and insurers, ought to reflect this reality. In short, climate risk ought to sit squarely on Boards' agendas and in the Directors' report regarding forward-looking projections about the health of the company and the prudence of its activities and investments in a carbon-constrained world.

For financial regulators and the finance sector, Summerhayes sounds the wake-up call:

> The idea that taking action to address climate change is a luxury or a financial burden is redundant. To the contrary, it's a financial necessity...US electricity giant PG&E Corp. filed for bankruptcy in the face of an estimated $30 billion liability caused by California's devastating wildfires. It will not be the last company to fold as the physical, transitional and liability risks of global warming bite ever more sharply in years to come.
>
> (Summerhayes, 2019)

Nonetheless, the second point to appreciate is that the definition of materiality is an unresolved issue, as revealed by the ClientEarth Complaints discussed in this chapter. Currently in the UK (and several comparable jurisdictions) the concept of 'materiality' is not defined in legislation or EU Directives so company directors in their discretion (but within legal boundaries of best interests of the corporation) decide which risks are material to their individual firm and thus which risks need to be disclosed. The issue for climate disclosure is clear: if a Board decides that climate risk is not material to their particular business then they do not need to report on it.

Yet in a carbon-constrained world, this is creating an ever-widening gap between what companies are disclosing and what investors need to know (Henderson, 2009; Sjåfjell and Wiesbrock, 2015; Haque, Deegan and Inglis, 2016). Indeed, a 2019 global survey of investors and companies on the materiality of climate risk for financial reporting revealed that while the majority of investors deemed climate risk as financially material through regulatory and liability risks, the majority of companies did not (Amel-Zadeh, 2019; also, FourTwentySeven, 2018). This gap undermines transparency and accountability given that, as Lipskyte and Koster argue, 'the principles of transparency and completeness have come to be seen as underlying thresholds for the importance of data reported within the materiality concept' (Lipskyte and Koster, 2018: 4).

In practice, one of the key questions regulators and directors will need to start considering is how best to determine the materiality of climate change to individual firms. The most basic but significant step for directors in acquitting their duties will be to facilitate compilation and evaluation of the firm's exposure to climate risks through scenario analysis and stress testing. Moreover, to be fully accurate, the evaluations ought to include secondary exposure through that of suppliers and even customers (Fisher, 2019).

Going forward, as indicated by a recent intervention from the International Accounting Standards Board (IASB), it may also become more common for directors and regulators to test materiality thresholds against the reasonable expectations of shareholders and other stakeholders, which may further assist in closing the current expectation gap (IASB, 2019).

Auditing for accountability

As mentioned previously, disclosure as a regulatory tool can only be effective if investors and other stakeholders act upon the information provided. Amongst other things, that requires users to trust the information provided. In this respect, auditors and assurance providers could help play a critical role to ensure reliability and therefore integrity of climate-related disclosures.

Scholars have highlighted the importance of auditors and assurers to enhancing credibility of voluntary schemes, such as in the US (Harper Ho, 2017), and also mandatory schemes, such as the EU *Non-financial Reporting Directive* (La Torre et al., 2018). Yet, in practice, empirical legal and accounting studies have shown that the level of assurance in non-financial reporting processes is uneven. This is because external parties rarely verify corporate social responsibility reports (Michelon, Pilonato and Ricceri, 2014) and, where assurance is given, there is no uniform standard unlike in financial auditing (Harper Ho, 2017) and assurance tends to favour managerial interests 'thereby eroding transparency' (Lipskyte and Koster, 2018: 3). For reasons of materiality, it is arguable that climate-related financial disclosure is a weightier creature than non-financial reporting (which manifests as ESG or corporate social responsibility reporting); yet they are often conflated, which begs the question whether climate-related financial disclosure will be treated more conscientiously by firms and their auditors.

Moreover, the prudence of auditors, alongside the banks and insurers they assure, has come under scrutiny in the aftermath of the 2008 Global Financial Crisis (Jones, 2011; Financial Times, 2018). In the context of climate disclosure, pro-stewardship investors are now asserting that shareholders ought to vote against using auditors who do not demonstrate prudent accounting of material climate risks (Landell-Mills, 2019). Even despite the malleability of 'materiality' in the assurance industry (Edgley, Jones and Atkins, 2015), in a carbon-constrained world it can now be argued that prudence entails at least providing a true and fair evaluation of the economic health of fossil fuel companies and eradicating material misrepresentations of climate impacts (Landell-Mills, 2019).

Indeed, in the context of the above Complaints and others, ClientEarth requested clarification from the Big Four auditors about how they address climate-related issues in light of recently introduced UK legal requirements regarding audits (e.g. ClientEarth, 2018b). In the UK, auditors are now required to provide an opinion on whether or not 'other information' included in a company's annual report is consistent with the financial statements, and has been prepared in accordance with applicable legal requirements (Companies Act, 2006, section 496(1)(a)). They are also required to confirm that they have not identified material misstatements in this information (Companies Act, 2006, section 496(1)(b)). While the relevant standards indicate that these requirements do not amount to a full audit of this information, they do make clear that auditors must pay heed to obtain necessary satisfaction to provide these opinions (FRC, (2016)).

A recent UK government enquiry into the future of audit also indicates that there is a significant likelihood that the scope of the full audit may be extended in future to include all information in the annual report, including climate-related disclosures (HM Government, 2019). Given the demand from major institutional investors for investment-grade climate-related information this would be an important driver of greater accountability around disclosure and the risk management, governance and strategic decision-making processes necessary to put in place to produce them.

Climate-related reporting beyond risk disclosure and scenario analysis

In addition to regulators increasingly asserting the need for companies to disclose climate-related risks under existing laws, and governments indicating clear appetite to mandate the TCFD recommendations, investors are moving ahead with their own demands. In particular, shareholders are now starting to request that companies disclose detailed strategies of how they are planning to align their business with the overall temperature objectives of the Paris Agreement, including disclosures of detailed 'Paris-aligned' emission reduction targets and capital expenditure plans. Initially, investors' focus has been directed at major oil and gas and diversified mining companies (International Investor Group on Climate Change, 2019), however there may be growing appetite to target cornerstone financial services firms in the near future.

Concluding remarks

The need for greater public information about the risks and impacts of climate change on business and financial service providers is now widely seen as a critical piece of the overall climate governance landscape. Governments, regulators, investors, and companies are all rapidly moving ahead with new frameworks and practices for disclosure. As experimentation continues and market and regulatory expectations mature, however, what is also becoming clear is that appropriate accountability and enforcement mechanisms will be essential if the information that is produced is to be trusted and effective in meaningfully changing behaviour and mitigating climate change-related risks in financial markets and the real world. While initial accountability mechanisms have so far centred around private ordering between investors and companies under existing generalised disclosure regimes and voluntary frameworks, as climate-related disclosures become increasingly mandatory and detailed there will be a much clearer role for financial regulators, auditors and civil society to hold companies responsible for the accuracy and completeness of disclosed information. In this respect, the ClientEarth Complaints and increased regulatory guidance from financial regulators indicate a clear direction of travel.

Importantly, in addition to sanctions and other accountability mechanisms explored in this chapter, the promise of reporting can be made real by ensuring it is complemented by other climate finance regulatory instruments (Bowman and Steenmans, 2018) and 'smart' regulatory design (Gunningham et al., 1998). Specifically, law-makers and regulators can utilise a two-fold typology of regulatory options and legal forms to mobilise climate finance through an integrated regulatory framework of 'financial mechanisms' and 'facilitative modalities' (Bowman, 2018; Bowman and Steenmans, 2018). Financial mechanisms directly mobilise or leverage private finance through, for example, blended finance, carbon pricing, tax incentives, green bonds, feed-in tariffs, and subsidies. In contrast, facilitative modalities help *indirectly* mobilise private finance by improving knowledge transfer, project pipeline, and capacity building. This includes enhancing prudential regulation, corporate reporting, matchmaking and training schemes, and taxonomies for defining 'green' investments. Both type of options – financial and facilitative – are essential and complementary for mainstreaming green markets and mobilising climate finance at scale.

Disclosure is not a panacea; it is just another tool in the regulatory toolbox. Acknowledging the full spectrum of tools available and utilising them complementarily will be required to facilitate real change.

Notes

1. The PRA defines supervised firms as 'all UK insurance and reinsurance firms and groups, ie those within the scope of Solvency II including the Society of Lloyd's and managing agents ("Solvency II firms") and non-Solvency II firms, (collectively referred to as "insurers"), banks, building societies, and PRA-designated investment firms (collectively referred to as "banks")' (PRA, 2019: 1).
2. See Staker and Garton (2018) for an excellent analysis of the climate materiality issue in UK corporate law; also see Bowman (2015: 32–149) regarding several market economy jurisdictions.

References

Abrahams v Commonwealth Bank of Australia (2017) Notice of Filing VID879.2017. Available at: https://envirojustice.org.au/sites/default/files/files/170807%20Concise%20Statement%20(as%20filed).pdf [Accessed 22 April 2020].

Admiral Group plc. (2018). *Annual Report 2018*. Cardiff, Wales: Admiral Group plc.

Alexander, Kern. (2014). *Stability and Sustainability in Banking Reform: Are Environmental Risks Missing in Basel III?* Cambridge: Cambridge/UNEP. Available at: https://www.researchgate.net/publication/279259466_Stability_and_Sustainability_in_Banking_Reform_Are_Environmental_Risks_Missing_in_Basel_III [Accessed 28 April 2020].

Amel-Zadeh, Amir. (2019). The Materiality of Climate Risk. Available at: https://papers.ssrn.com/sol3/papers.cfm?abstract_id=3295184 [Accessed 22 April 2019].

Andrew, Jane and Cortese, Corrine L. (2011). Carbon disclosures: Comparability, the carbon disclosure project and greenhouse gas protocol. *Australasian Accounting Business and Finance Journal*, 5, pp. 5–18.

Ayling, Julie and Gunningham, Neil. (2017). Non-state governance and climate policy: The fossil fuel divestment movement. *Climate Policy*, 17(2), pp. 131–149.

Aviva. (2017). *Annual Report and Accounts 2017*. London: Aviva.

Aviva. (2018). *Aviva's Climate-Related Financial Disclosure 2018*. London: Aviva.

Black, B. S. (2001). The Principal Fiduciary Duties of Boards of Directors. [Presentation at Third Asian Roundtable on Corporate Governance, Singapore, 4 April 2001], Available at: https://www.oecd.org/corporate/ca/corporategovernanceprinciples/1872746.pdf. [Accessed 22 April 2020].

Bowman, Megan. (2014). The Limitations of Business Case Logic for Societal Benefit and Implications for Corporate Law: A Case Study of 'Climate Friendly' Banks. Available at: https://papers.ssrn.com/sol3/papers.cfm?abstract_id=2489116 [Accessed 22 April 2020].

Bowman, Megan. (2015). *Banking on Climate Change: How Finance Actors and Regulatory Regimes Are Responding*. Den Haag: Kluwer.

Bowman, Megan. (2018). Legal Readiness for Public-Private Climate Finance: Final Options Paper for UN Environment. [Unpublished Report. On file with the author].

Bowman, Megan and Steenmans, Katrien. (2019). *Legal Readiness for Climate Finance: Private Sector Opportunities. Report and Findings of Roundtable Held at King's College London 25 January 2019*. London: King's College London. Available at: https://www.kcl.ac.uk/law/research/centres/climate-law-and-governance/docs/climate-finance-law-report-2019.pdf [Accessed 28 April 2020].

Bowman, Megan and Steenmans, Katrien. (2018). *Climate Finance Law: Legal Readiness for Climate Finance. Report and Findings of Workshop Held at King's College London 9-11 March 2018*. London: King's College London. Available at: https://www.kcl.ac.uk/law/research/centres/climate-law-and-governance/climate-finance-law-report-update.pdf [Accessed 28 April 2020].

Boston Common Asset Management. (2018). *Banking on a Law-Carbon Future: Are the World's Largest Banks Stepping Up to the Risks & Opportunities of Climate Change?* Boston, MA: Boston Common Asset Management.

Braithwaite, John and Drahos, Peter. (2000). *Global Business Regulation*. Cambridge: Cambridge University Press.

Brooke, Nigel and Beresford, Neil. (2019). Climate change - the evolving landscape of litigation. Available at https://resilience.clydeco.com/articles/climate-change-liability-risks [Accessed 22 April 2020].

California Department of Insurance. (2018). 2° Scenario Analysis: Insurance Companies Operating in California. Available at: https://interactive.web.insurance.ca.gov/apex_extprd/cdi_apps/r/250/files/static/v54/2018_full_report.pdf [Accessed 28 April 2020].

Campiglio, Emmanuel, Dafermos, Yannis, Monnin, Pierre, Ryan-Collins, Josh, Schotten, Guido and Tanaka, Misa. (2018). Climate change challenges for central banks and financial regulators. *Nature Climate Change*, 8, pp. 462–468.

Carney, Mark. (2015). Breaking the Tragedy of the Horizon – Climate change and Financial Stability. [Speech Given at Lloyd's of London, 29 September]. Available at: https://www.mainstreamingclimate.org/publication/breaking-the-tragedy-of-the-horizon-climate-change-and-financial-stability/ [Accessed 28 April 2020].

Carney, Mark. (2019). A New Horizon. [Speech given at the European Commission Conference: A global approach to sustainable finance, 21 March 2019]. Available at: https://www.bankofengland.co.uk/-/media/boe/files/speech/2019/a-new-horizon-speech-by-mark-carney.pdf?la=en&hash=F63F8064E0408F038CABB1F29C58F B1A0CD0FE25 [Accessed 28 October 2020]

ClientEarth. (2019). UK Financial Regulators Are Missing in Action on Company Failures to Disclose Material Climate-Related Information. Available at: https://www.documents.clientearth.org/library/download-info/uk-financial-regulators-are-missing-in-action-on-company-failures-to-disclose-material-climate-related-information/ [Accessed 1 May 2020].

ClientEarth. (2018a). Complaint to the FRC Conduct Committee: EasyJet PLC. Available at: https://www.documents.clientearth.org/wp-content/uploads/library/2018-09-07-complaint-to-the-frc-conduct-committee-easyjet-plc-ce-en.pdf [Accessed 28 April 2020].

ClientEarth. (2018b). Letter to KPMG Regarding the Company's Audit of Balfour Beatty PLC. Available at: https://www.documents.clientearth.org/wp-content/uploads/library/2018-09-05-letter-to-kpmg-regarding-balfour-beatty-plc-audit-ce-en.pdf [Accessed 28 April 2020].

ClientEarth. (2018c). Insurance Firms Could Face Fines over Climate Reporting Failure. Available at: https://www.clientearth.org/insurance-firms-could-face-fines-over-climate-reporting-failure/ [Accessed 01 May 2020].

ClientEarth. (2018d). Complaint to the FCA: Admiral Group plc. Available at: https://www.documents.clientearth.org/library/download-info/fca-complaint-admiral-group-plc/ [Accessed 01 May 2020].

ClientEarth. (2018e). Complaint to the FCA: Lancashire Holdings Limited. Available at: https://www.documents.clientearth.org/library/download-info/fca-complaint-lancashire-holdings-limited/ [Accessed 1 May 2020].

ClimateWise. (2017). Insurable Cities: ClimateWise Principles Independent Review 2017. Available at: https://www.cisl.cam.ac.uk/resources/publication-pdfs/climatewise-principles-review-2017.pdf [Accessed 28 April 2020].

Dowdle, Michael W. (2017). Public accountability: Conceptual, historical and epistemic mappings. In: P. Drahos, ed., *Regulatory Theory: Foundations and Applications*. Canberra: ANU Press, pp. 197–216.

Eberlein, Burkard, Abbott, Kenneth W., Black, Julia, Meidinger, Errol and Wood, Stepan. (2014). Transnational business governance interactions: Conceptualization and framework for analysis. *Regulation & Governance*, 8, pp.1–21.

Eccles, Robert G. and Krzus, Michael P. (2017). An Analysis of Oil & Gas Company Disclosures from the Perspective of the Task Force on Climate-related Financial Disclosures. Available at: https://ssrn.com/abstract=3091232 [Accessed 22 April 2020].

Edgley, Carla, Jones, Michael and Atkins, Jill. (2015). The adoption of the materiality concept in social and environmental reporting assurance. *British Accounting Review*, 47, pp. 1–18.

Environmental Finance. (2016). Insuring in a Changing Climate. Environmental Finance, 10 October.

European Commission. (2018). Communication from the Commission to the European Parliament, the European Council, the Council, the European Central Bank, the European Economic and Social Committee and the Committee of the Regions. Action Plan: Financing Sustainable Growth, 8 March. COM/2018/097 final. Available at: https://ec.europa.eu/info/publications/180308-action-plan-sustainable-growth_en [Accessed 22 April 2020].

Evain, Julie, Cardona, Michel and Nicol, Morgane. (2018). Article 173: Overview of Climate-Related Financial Disclosure after Two Years of Implementation. Available at: https://www.i4ce.org/download/article-173-overview-of-climate-related-financial-dislosure-after-two-years-of-implementation/ [Accessed 28 April 2020].

Financial Conduct Authority (FCA). (2018). Climate Change and Green Finance. Available at: https://www.fca.org.uk/publication/discussion/dp18-08.pdf [Accessed 28 April 2020].

Financial Conduct Authority (FCA). (2016). Make a Complaint Against an Issuer. Available at: https://www.fca.org.uk/markets/primary-markets/contact/complaint-against-issuer [Accessed 28 April 2020].

Financial Reporting Council (FRC). (2016). *International Standard on Auditing (UK and Ireland) 720: The Auditor's Responsibilities Relating to Other Information in Documents Containing Audited Financial Statements.* London: Financial Reporting Council. Available at: https://www.frc.org.uk/getattachment/11b5e047-a2d7-4674-8281-cc57ec3d5e66/ISA-(UK)-720_Revised-June-2016.pdf [Accessed 28 April 2020].

Financial Reporting Council (FRC). (2019a). FRC Statement on the Government's Green Finance Strategy. [News]. Available at: https://www.frc.org.uk/news/july-2019/frc-statement-on-the-government's-green-finance-st [Accessed 22 April 2020].

Financial Reporting Council (FRC). (2019b). Climate Change-Related Corporate Reporting: Where to Next? Available at: https://www.frc.org.uk/getattachment/22ee8a43-e8ca-47be-944b-c394ecb3c5dd/Climate-Change-v9.pdf [Accessed 22 April 2020].

Financial Times. (2018). The Big Flaw: Auditing in Crisis, 5-Part Series, *Financial Times.* Available at: https://www.ft.com/content/bdaf51da-9ae6-11e8-ab77-f854c65a4465 [Accessed 22 April 2020].

Fisher, Paul. (2017). Comment: Could Climate Cause The Next Financial Crisis? *IPE Magazine*, 29 June. Available at: https://www.ipe.com/comment-could-climate-cause-the-next-financial-crisis/10019641.article [Accessed 22 April 2020].

Fisher, Paul. (2019). Why Climate Related Financial Disclosures Matter. *London Institute of Banking* [News Bulletin], 18 July. Available at: https://www.ipe.com/comment-could-climate-cause-the-next-financial-crisis/10019641.article [Accessed 22 April 2020].

FourTwentySeven. (2018). Article 173, Lessons Learned from Climate Risk Disclosures in France. [Newsletter] 21 March. Available at: http://427mt.com/2018/03/21/art-173-lessons-learned-climate-risk-disclosures-france/ [Accessed 28 April 2020].

French Treasury, Banque de France and ACPR. (2017). *Assessing Climate Change-Related Risks in the Banking Sector.* Paris: French Treasury.

Gunningham, Neil, Grabosky, Peter and Sinclair, Darren (1998) 'Smart Regulation: Designing Environmental Policy'. Oxford UK: Clarendon Press.

Hahn, Rudiger, Reimsbach, Daniel and Schiemann, Frank. (2015). Organizations, climate change and transparency: Reviewing the literature on carbon disclosure. *Organization & Environment*, 28(1), pp. 80–102.

Haque, Shamima, Deegan, Craig and Inglis, Robert. (2016). Demand for, and impediments to, the disclosure of information about climate change-related corporate governance practices. *Accounting and Business Research*, 46(6), pp. 620–664.

Harper Ho, Virginia. (2017). 'Comply or Explain' and the future of nonfinancial reporting. *Lewis & Clark Law Review*, 21(2), pp. 318–355.

Henderson, Gail Elizabeth. (2009). The Materiality of Climate Change and the Role of Voluntary Disclosure. *Osgoode Hall Law School Comparative Research in Law & Political Economy Research Paper Series,* Research paper No 47. York University, Toronto. Available at: https://digitalcommons.osgoode.yorku.ca/cgi/viewcontent.cgi?article=1155&context=clpe [Accessed 28 April 2020].

HM Government (UK). (July 2019). Green Finance Strategy: Transforming Finance for a Greener Future. Available at: https://assets.publishing.service.gov.uk/government/uploads/system/uploads/attachment_data/file/820284/190716_BEIS_Green_Finance_Strategy_Accessible_Final.pdf [Accessed 11 May 2020].

Holley, Cameron and Sinclair, Darren, eds. (2018). *Reforming Water Law and Governance: From Stagnation to Innovation in Australia*. Berlin: Springer.

House of Commons Environmental Audit Committee (UK). (2018). Greening Finance: Embedding Sustainability in Financial Decision Making. Available at: https://publications.parliament.uk/pa/cm201719/cmselect/cmenvaud/1063/1063.pdf [Accessed 28 April 2020].

International Energy Agency (IEA). (2017). Energy Technology Perspective 2017: Catalysing Energy Technology Transformations, Executive Summary. Available at: https://webstore.iea.org/download/summary/237?fileName=English-ETP-2017-ES.pdf [Accessed 28 April 2020].

Intergovernmental Panel on Climate Change (IPCC). (2015). *Climate Change 2014: Synthesis Report. Contribution of Working Groups I, II and III to the Fifth Assessment Report of the Intergovernmental Panel on Climate Change* [Core Writing Team, R. K. Pachauri and L. A. Meyer, eds.]. Geneva: IPCC. Available at: https://www.ipcc.ch/site/assets/uploads/2018/05/SYR_AR5_FINAL_full_wcover.pdf [Accessed 28 April 2020].

Ioannou, Ioannis and Serafeim, George. (2017). The Consequences of Mandatory Corporate Sustainability Reporting. *Harvard Business School* [Research Working Paper No. 11-100]. Available at: https://papers.ssrn.com/sol3/papers.cfm?abstract_id=1799589 [Accessed 22 April 2020].

International Accounting Standards Board (IASB). (2019). IFRS Standards and Climate-related Disclosures. Available at https://www.ifrs.org/news-and-events/2019/11/nick-anderson-ifrs-standards-and-climate-related-disclosures/ [Accessed 6 November 2020].

International Investor Group on Climate Change (IIGCC). (2019). Climate Change Resolution at BP AGM from Climate Action 100+ Investors Passes with over 99% Shareholder Support. [Press Release] 21 May. Available at: https://www.iigcc.org/news/climate-change-resolution-at-bp-agm-from-climate-action-100-investors-passes-with-over-99-shareholder-support/ [Accessed 22 April 2020].

Jackson, Gregory, Bartosch, Julia, Avetisyan, Emma, Kinderman, Daniel and Knudsen, Jette Steen. (2019). Mandatory non-financial disclosure and its influence on CSR: An international comparison. *Journal of Business Ethics*, 162: 323–342, https://doi.org/10.1007/s10551-019-04200-0.

Jones, Adam. (2011). Auditors Criticized for Role in Financial Crisis. *Financial Times*, 30 March.

Klumpes, Paul, Acharyya, Madhu, Kakar, Gautam and Sturgess, Emily. (2019). *Climate Risk Reporting Practices by UK Insurance Companies and Pension Schemes*. London: Institute and Faculty of Actuaries.

Knox-Hayes, Janelle and Levy, David. (2011). The politics of carbon disclosure as climate governance. *Strategic Organization*, 9, pp. 91–99.

Lacroix, Kevin. (2018). Three U.K. Insurers Hit with Complaints Over Alleged Climate Change-Related Disclosure Omissions. *The D&O Diary,* 7 August. Available at: https://www.dandodiary.com/2018/08/articles/climate-change/three-u-k-insurers-hit-complaints-alleged-climate-change-related-disclosure-omissions/ [Accessed 28 April 2020].

Lancashire Holdings Ltd. (2018). *Annual Report and Accounts 2018*. Hamilton, Bermuda: Lancashire Holdings Ltd.

Landell-Mills, Natasha. (2019). Investors Should Fire Directors Who Fail to Take Climate Action. *Financial Times,* 29 January. Available at: https://www.ft.com/content/8403fb3a-22df-11e9-b20d-5376ca5216eb [Accessed 28 April 2020].

La Torre, Matteo, Sabelfield, Svetlana, Blomkvist, Marita, Tarquinio, Lara and Dumay, John. (2018). Harmonising non-financial reporting regulation in Europe: Practical forces and projections for future research. *Meditari Accountancy Research*, 26(4), pp. 598–621.

Lipskyte, Justina and Koster, Harold. (2018). Evaluation of sustainability reporting under EU directive 2014/95. *International Company and Commercial Law Review*, 29(8), pp. 522–534.

Lloyd's of London. (2018). Lloyd's City Risk Index: Executive Summary. Available at: https://cityriskindex.lloyds.com/wp-content/uploads/2018/06/Lloyds_CRI2018_executive%20summary.pdf [Accessed 28 April 2020].

Lloyd's of London. (2017). Stranded assets: The transition to a low carbon economy. *Overview for the Insurance Industry - Emerging Risk Report 2017*. London: Lloyd's of London.

Lloyd's of London. (2014). *Catastrophe Modelling and Climate Change*. London: Lloyd's of London. Available at: https://www.lloyds.com/news-and-risk-insight/risk-reports/library/natural-environment/catastrophe-modelling-and-climate-change [Accessed 28 April 2020].

MacLeod, Michael and Park, Jacob. (2011). Financial activism and global climate change: The rise of investor-driven governance networks. *Global Environmental Politics*, 11(2), pp. 54–74.

Michelon, G., Pilonato, S. and Ricceri, F. (2014). CSR reporting practices and the quality of disclosure: An empirical analysis. *Critical Perspectives on Accounting*, 33, pp. 59–78.

Miller, John A. (2018). Credit Downgrade Threat as a Non-regulatory Driver for Flood Risk Mitigation and Sea Level Rise Adaptation. *Master of Environmental Studies Capstone Projects,* 73. Available at: https://repository.upenn.edu/mes_capstones/73 [Accessed 28 April 2020].

Moody's. (2018). *Sector In-Depth: P&C Insurance and Reinsurance – Global. Climate Change Risks Outweigh Opportunities for P&C (Re)Insurers*. New York: Moodys. Available at: https://www.law.berkeley.edu/wp-content/uploads/2018/06/

Moodys-Climate-change-risks-outweigh-opportunities-for-PC-reinsurers. pdf [Accessed 28 April 2020].

Network for Greening the Financial System (NGFS). (2018). First Progress Report. Available at: https://www.banque-france.fr/sites/default/files/media/2018/10/11/818366-ngfs-first-progress-report-20181011.pdf [Accessed 28 April 2020].

Parker, Christine, Carey, Michael, De Costa, Josephine and Scrinis, Gyorgy. (2017). Can the hidden hand of the market be an effective and legitimate regulator? The case of animal welfare under a labeling for consumer choice policy approach. *Regulation & Governance*, 11, pp. 368–387.

Phoenix Group. (2018). *Annual Report and Accounts 2018*. London: Phoenix Group.

Prudential Regulation Authority (PRA). (2015). *The Impact of Climate Change on the UK Insurance Sector: A Climate Change Adaptation Report by the Prudential Regulation Authority*. London: Bank of England, Prudential Regulation Authority. Available at: https://www.bankofengland.co.uk/-/media/boe/files/prudential-regulation/publication/impact-of-climate-change-on-the-uk-insurance-sector.pdf [Accessed 28 April 2020].

Prudential Regulation Authority (PRA). (2018a). *Transition in Thinking: The Impact of Climate Change on the UK Banking Sector*. London: Bank of England, Prudential Regulation Authority. Available at: https://www.bankofengland.co.uk/prudential-regulation/publication/2018/transition-in-thinking-the-impact-of-climate-change-on-the-uk-banking-sector [Accessed 28 April 2020].

Prudential Regulation Authority (PRA). (2018b). *Enhancing Banks' and Insurers' Approaches to Managing the Financial Risks from Climate Change*. London: Bank of England, Prudential Regulation Authority. Available at: https://www.bankofengland.co.uk/prudential-regulation/publication/2018/enhancing-banks-and-insurers-approaches-to-managing-the-financial-risks-from-climate-change [Accessed 28 April 2020].

Prudential Regulation Authority (PRA). (2019). *Supervisory Statement SS3/19 Enhancing Banks' and Insurers' Approaches to Managing the Financial Risks from Climate Change*. London: Bank of England, Prudential Regulation Authority. Available at: https://www.bankofengland.co.uk/-/media/boe/files/prudential-regulation/supervisory-statement/2019/ss319 [Accessed 11 May 2020].

Richardson, B. J. (2015). Financial markets and socially responsible investing. In: B. Sjåfjell and B. J. Richardson, eds., *Company Law and Sustainability: Legal Barriers and Opportunities*. Cambridge: Cambridge University Press, pp. 226–274.

Richardson, B. J. (2006). Sustainable finance: Environmental law and financial institutions. In: B. J. Richardson and S. Wood, eds., *Environmental Law for Sustainability*. Oxford: Hart Publishing, pp. 309–340.

Beate Sjåfjell and Anja Wiesbrock, eds. (2015). *The Greening of European Business Under EU Law: Taking Article 11 TFEU Seriously*. London: Routledge.

Staker, Alexia and Garton, Alice. (2018). Directors' Liability and Climate Risk: United Kingdom – Country Paper. *Commonwealth Climate and Law Initiative*, April. Available at: https://www.smithschool.ox.ac.uk/research/sustainable-finance/publications/CCLI-UK-Paper-Final.pdf [Accessed 22 April 2020].

Summerhayes, Geoff. (2019). Financial Exposure: The Role of Disclosure in Addressing the Climate Data Deficit. *ClimateWise and University of Cambridge Institute for Sustainable Leadership*, [News Bulletin] 22 February. Available at:

https://www.cisl.cam.ac.uk/news/news-pdfs-or-prs/financial-exposure-geoff-summerhayes.pdf [Accessed 28 April 2020].

Swiss Re Institute. (2018). Natural Catastrophes and Man-Made Disasters in 2017: A Year of Record-Breaking Losses. *Sigma*, 1. Available at: https://www.swissre.com/dam/jcr:1b3e94c3-ac4e-4585-aa6f-4d482d8f46cc/sigma1_2018_en.pdf [Accessed 22 April 2020].

Task Force on Climate-Related Financial Disclosures (TCFD). (2017). *Final Recommendations*. Basel: Task Force on Climate-Related Financial Disclosures. Available at: https://www.fsb-tcfd.org/publications/final-recommendations-report/ [Accessed 28 April 2020].

Union of Concerned Scientists. (2018). *Underwater: Rising Seas, Chronic Floods, and the Implications for US Coastal Real Estate*. Cambridge, MA. Union of Concerned Scientists. Available at: https://www.ucsusa.org/sites/default/files/attach/2018/06/underwater-analysis-full-report.pdf [Accessed 28 April 2020].

Webster, Emily. (2020). Information disclosure and the transition to a low-carbon economy: Climate-related risk in the UK and France. *Journal of Environmental Law*, 32(2), pp. 279–308.

10 Towards attribution-based climate insurance

Redefining who should pay for weather-related insurance[†]

*Mark New[*], Sylvia Dorbor,
Romaric Odoulami, and David Maslo*

Introduction

In this chapter we explore how determining the relative influence of human forcing of climate on weather risk and losses could be used as a basis for calculating equitable contributions to weather insurance premiums in Africa. This is important for three reasons. Firstly, losses through climate-implicated weather events are rising, including in agriculture (Coronese et al., 2019) and many African countries have limited capacity to finance disaster risk reduction and recovery, including insurance premiums (e.g., Matera et al., 2018). Secondly, the key international environmental agreements on climate change establish a basis for common but shared responsibilities for climate change, as a framework for developed countries to contribute financially to developing countries' climate change adaptation efforts (e.g., United Nations General Assembly, 1994; UNFCCC, 2015). Thirdly, it is technically feasible to attribute at least some extreme weather and seasonal climate events to climate change (Allen et al., 2007). We use drought-related agricultural losses in Malawi as a case study because it provides a clear example of climate change-implicated weather losses, and because Malawi is a developing country with limited capacity to pay increasing insurance premiums, with some arguing that sovereign insurance is not the most appropriate financial channel for building climate resilience (Reeves, 2017).

[†] This work was funded through the AXA Research Fund. We thank Blessing Siewela from ARC for his support in the use of ARV, and ARC Ltd. for enabling use of ARV and the involvement of ARC staff in the research. Any opinions expressed are those of the authors alone.

[*] MN conceived the research problem, collaborated with SD, DM, and RO regarding the design of the research methodology, and undertook the risk model simulations with SD and RO. MN wrote the final manuscript with input from all authors.

Weather-related disasters dominate the losses from natural perils globally. For example, AON (2019: 1) estimate that 90 per cent of the $225 billion annual average economic losses from natural disasters in the decade ending 2018 were due to weather and climate events. While many of these losses were in developed countries, it is likely that losses in developing countries are underestimated (Osuteye, Johnson and Brown, 2017). The leading loss-causing weather-related disasters globally are tropical cyclones, floods, drought, fire, and a basket of other severe weather events, including tornadoes and winter weather (AON, 2019).

As per the Secretariat of the United Nations International Strategy for Disaster Reduction (UNISDR, 2017), managing disaster risk typically requires action on four fronts: (i) prevention, through avoiding hazards altogether (e.g., relocating exposed people and assets away from a hazard, such as flood risk); (ii) mitigation, by reducing the hazard impact (e.g., by constructing flood defences or planting drought resistant crops); (iii) preparedness, where those affected and those responsible for reacting to disasters are able to respond and recover quickly to disasters (e.g., early warning systems), and; (iv) risk transfer, where the resources required for recovery are obtained from other entities, either formally or informally. Insurance is the most common approach to risk transfer and our focus for this chapter.

Insurance has traditionally provided risk transfer for specific assets, such as infrastructure and property, often for multiple perils. This form is typically termed indemnity insurance (Jarzabkowski et al., 2019) and supports the rebuilding of assets. In the last few decades, a new form of insurance – parametric or index-based insurance – has become increasingly popular for natural disaster-related perils (McGee, Phelan and Wenta, 2014; Marr et al., 2016; Jensen and Barrett, 2017; Broberg, 2019; Singh and Agrawal, 2019). A parametric insurance product provides payouts triggered by one or more indices specific to the type and severity of the disaster; this is distinct from traditional insurance approaches that require confirmation of losses and their value, a process that takes some time and cost. One advantage of parametric insurance is that it offers a way to quickly provide financial resources, and this can be particularly helpful in the wake of natural disasters.

A major challenge regarding insurance as a risk transfer mechanism is the risk protection gap, defined as the difference between actual economic loss from disasters and that which is covered by insurance. It is estimated that in low- and middle-income countries this gap – or shortfall in insurance coverage compared to the financial value of losses – is 90 per cent, while in Organisation for Economic Cooperation and Development[1] countries it is lower, but still considerable, according to South African Insurance Association at about 50 per cent (SAIA, 2019). Reasons for this lack of protection include low insurance penetration, losses from risks beyond the limits of insurability and losses from emerging risks (Centre for Financial Inclusion, 2018; Howard, 2018). Insurance penetration is particularly low in Africa. For example, across eight sub-Saharan African countries, personal insurance of any kind ranged from 1 to 8 per cent (Schlemmer and Rinehart-Smit, 2020). Reasons for this lack of penetration are many, including awareness and trust, access to products, affordability, perception of risk, as well as cultural norms for risk transfer.

Climate change can act to exacerbate the underlying drivers of risk protection gaps in several ways. Firstly, as climate change alters the likelihood and severity of weather-related disasters, traditional approaches to modelling risk will deliver inaccurate results. A typical risk model used for underwriting will use historic climate data to estimate risk, but a changing climate means that data from further in the past are biasing risk profiles away from true present-day distributions. If coverage is agreed using a risk profile that does not represent the true risk, the purchased coverage and ceilings may be wrong, increasing (or in some instances, decreasing) the protection gap. Secondly, if the risk profiles on which underwriting are based are wrong, the pricing for coverage will also be wrong. If pricing is underestimated, then insurance companies may be exposed to claims that exceed their ability to pay, and therefore their financial viability. Finally, if a changing climate is partially or fully incorporated into risk models – and therefore underwriting – in areas where risk is increasing, the cost of insurance will also increase. This might in some instances lead to insurance – at least for coverage levels that are meaningful – to become unaffordable (Phelan et al., 2011).

The potentially higher cost of insurance in developing countries due to climate change has important practical and ethical implications. Where penetration is already low, one of the main reasons is the high cost of insurance relative to income, whether it is at the national level for sovereign insurance or the household level for personal or community insurance (Centre for Financial Inclusion, 2018). If premiums increase, fewer are likely to purchase cover, increasing an already large protection gap. Ethically, we can ask whether it is fair that states and individuals in developing countries pay more for weather loss insurance: the higher cost from increases in climate risk is largely a result of historic emissions from the developed world (Matthews et al., 2014). In broad terms, the principle of 'common but differentiated responsibilities' in the UNFCCC (United Nations General Assembly, 1994) and echoed in the Paris Agreement (UNFCCC, 2015) notes developing countries' vulnerability to climate impacts. The Paris Agreement specifically calls for developed countries to provide financial support to developing countries, recognising that developed countries have both played a greater role historically in creating climate change (the contribution of sub-Saharan African states is, for example, negligible) and have greater financial capacity to respond to the common challenge climate change presents.

Climate change attribution offers a potential route to apportioning the cost of weather risk insurance between that due to natural weather events and that added due to human influence on the weather of today and the future. Attribution aims to quantify the relative influence of human forcing (greenhouse gases, aerosols, land-use change) and natural forcing (solar insolation, volcanic aerosols) on different diagnostics of the climate system (Stott et al., 2010; Hegerl and Zwiers, 2011) or on the impacts of climate trends and variations on social and ecological systems (Rosenzweig and Neofotis, 2013).

In the next sections we explore how climate change attribution approaches can be applied to insurance risk models that are used for underwriting calculations, and ultimately the costing of insurance policies. We do this for the specific case of index-based drought insurance with the risk model used by Africa Risk Capacity Insurance Company Ltd. (ARC Ltd.) to develop sovereign insurance offerings for African nations. ARC Ltd. is the financial affiliate to ARC Specialised Agency of the African Union, which carries out commercial insurance functions of risk pooling and risk transfer in accordance with national regulations for parametric weather insurance. Firstly, we provide an overview of climate change attribution using climate models, and then a description of the Africa *RiskView* (ARV) model used by ARC Ltd. Next, we describe our approach to coupling climate model attribution data with ARV. We then present some illustrative results from a case study in Africa: Malawi. We conclude by discussing the implications of our results for development of more equitable insurance products for developing countries.

Climate change attribution

Methods in climate change attribution initially evolved in response to the question: 'to what extent [can] human influence on climate be "blamed" for observed weather trends and specific weather events such a floods, storms, or heat waves' (Allen et al., 2007)? Successive reports of the Intergovernmental Panel on Climate Change (IPCC) have assessed the evidence on the causes of observed changes in temperature, as well as other measured characteristics of the climate system, such as ocean heat temperature, precipitation, mountain glaciers and arctic sea ice, and atmospheric circulation from global to regional scales (Bindoff et al., 2013: 932–939, Table 10.1). More recently, testing for a human influence on individual extreme events, such as heat waves, heavy precipitation, drought, and wildfire weather has become possible (Stott et al., 2016) with over 200 events having been studied by 2018 (Schiermeier, 2018).

The most common approach in climate change attribution is to use global climate models (GCMs) to test the response of the modelled climate system to a set of hypothesised causes of climate change (Hegerl and Zwiers, 2011). Typical hypothesised causes that have been evaluated are anthropogenic – the major greenhouse gases and aerosol pollutants – and natural – solar insolation and volcanic aerosols – as well as unforced internal variability of the climate system. Simulations with the observed historic levels of these drivers, usually with multiple GCMs from different climate modelling centres, are then statistically compared to the observed climate change metric. The statistical match between drivers – or combinations of drivers – and

Table 10.1 Factors that affect underwriting for ARC Ltd.'s sovereign index-based insurance and the effects of the counterfactual risk profile in Malawi

Risk transfer parameter	Description	Effect on premium	Effect of risk profile in counterfactual world (i.e., a world without anthropogenic climate change)
Attachment Point	Payout triggered when MDRC exceeds this point. Default is the MDRC with a one in five- year return period, but can be adjusted higher or lower by negotiation.	Reducing the attachment point increases the premium as the frequency of payout increases.	Frequency a given attachment point is exceeded will be lower. Premium for any given attachment point will be lower.
Exhaustion Point	The maximum payout, set by ARC Ltd. as the maximum MDRC.	A lower exhaustion point will reduce the maximum payout, and reduce the premium.	Lowers the exhaustion point. Premium for any given ceding percentage will be lower.
Coverage Limit	The maximum that ARC Ltd. is normally willing to insure, currently USD 30 million. Exhaustion point cannot exceed coverage limit.	If negotiated higher, will increase the premium.	Exhaustion point less likely to exceed coverage limit. A greater proportion of risk can be transferred for a given premium.
Ceding Percentage	Proportion of the potential risk transfer (exhaustion point minus attachment point) that will be covered by ARC Ltd.	A higher ceding percentage will increase the premium.	Ceding percentage for any given premium will be higher.

the observed climate record allow for confidence statements about different hypothesised causes of climate change to be made. Therefore, the most recent IPCC assessment report (IPCC, 2013: 17) stated that '[i]t is *extremely likely* that human influence has been the dominant cause of the observed warming since the mid-20th century'; the term 'extremely likely' corresponds to a confidence level of 95 per cent (Mastrandrea et al., 2011), which arises from the statistical analysis of the underlying climate model attribution simulations.

Attributing the impacts of climate change on natural and social systems is much harder (Cramer et al., 2014; Hansen and Stone, 2016). The main challenge is that many confounding factors can also influence observed changes in these systems. For instance, species range-shifts or extinctions might be partly driven by factors such as land-cover change, harvesting, pollution, as well as climate change. Further, our ability to model these complex systems is limited, so the kinds of model-based attribution studies that have been undertaken for physical climate variables, such as temperature, are much rarer. Most impact attribution studies assessed in the most recent IPCC report (Cramer et al., 2014) tended to assess whether observed changes in a system were consistent with observed changes in climate, rather than attributing causative links. Some studies have adopted a modelling approach: for example, mortality during the 2003 European heatwave (Mitchell et al., 2016). These typically take a well-established model – such as an epidemiological, hydrological, or agricultural model – and simulate the response using two sets of climate model outputs, representing the climate system with and without historically observed human forcing due to greenhouse gases and aerosols.

African Risk Capacity Ltd. and the Africa *RiskView* model

The African Risk Capacity Ltd. (ARC) is a specialised agency of the African Union, established to provide sovereign-level insurance against climate and weather-related risks, which are offered to African countries, including through the African Risk Capacity Insurance scheme (ARC, 2018). The aim of this insurance scheme is to develop a risk-pooling and transfer instrument using weather-based index insurance to pre-finance disaster risks for affected member parties in Africa (ARC, 2018). The insurance currently deals with drought-related events; models for other extreme events such as floods and tropical cyclones are being developed (ARC, 2018). As of 2018, insurance had been acquired by nine African countries: Senegal, Mali, Niger, the Gambia, Mauritania, Burkina Faso, Cote d'Ivoire, Kenya, and Malawi (ARC, 2019). Each country intending to join the risk pool is required to develop a contingency plan for drought response, which includes outlining how the funds, if paid, will be distributed to the population affected. While ARC Ltd. operates at a sovereign level, it seeks to reduce disaster risk at the individual level; thereby ensuring that the mechanism for the distribution of funds or other relief materials to the number of people affected from a disaster is an important part of the overall insurance agreement.

ARC Ltd. has developed ARV (see ARC, 2016) to estimate an historical risk profile for a country that is considering joining the risk pool. The modelled risk profiles from ARV – expressed as population affected by drought in each year for which there are historical climate data – are then used as an input to the underwriting process for any insurance contract. ARV uses historical ten-day rainfall to calculate the seasonal evolution of a drought index, the Water Requirement Satisfaction Index (WRSI), at 1 km resolution across any country in sub-Saharan Africa. The index serves as an indicator of crop performance based on the amount of water available to a crop during a growing season. WRSI ranges from 0 to 100, with 100 indicating no water deficit and an excellent growing season, and larger departures below 100 indicating increasingly severe water deficit. To determine if the drought conditions are more severe than expected at the end of a growing season, the aggregated WRSI is compared to its expected level, the 'benchmark'. The default benchmark in ARV is the median WRSI value of the previous five years (ARC, 2016).

The WRSI is aggregated and overlaid onto district-level vulnerability parameters to estimate the likelihood of crop failure. These parameters are defined using in-country expertise to represent the crop-type and farming practices across a country. The parameters comprise four crop impact thresholds: a drought detection point, and three increasingly severe impact points. If the WRSI is above the drought detection point, the assumption is there is no crop failure. Between the drought detection point and the third (most severe) impact point, the proportion of people experiencing crop failure increases towards 100 per cent; if the third impact point is reached, then all people in that district are assumed to have experienced complete crop failure. The proportion of the population experiencing crop failure is then multiplied by population density to estimate the number of people affected by drought at each district in the country; this is then aggregated to a national total.

The final calculation in ARV estimates the response costs needed to assist the estimated drought-affected population. This step is by far the simplest in the modelling as it involves a straightforward multiplier of the estimated population affected by response cost per person. The default response cost per person for a rainfall season is $100 per person for countries with unimodal rainy seasons and $50 per person for countries with bimodal rainy seasons. However, the final response cost per person often varies across countries and requires discussion that involves governments and insurance partners. The national modelled drought response costs underlie the basis of the parametric insurance products. Figure 10.1 illustrates the final output from ARV, showing the estimated population at risk in Malawi and the

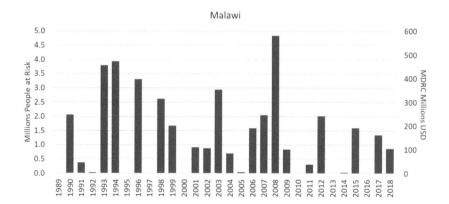

Figure 10.1 Illustrative risk profile output from ARV for Malawi, showing modelled population at risk and the MDRC from drought-related crop failure from 1989 to 2018.

estimated response cost (MDRC or modelled drought response cost), for each year from 1989 to 2018.

Attribution of climate impact on risk profiles and insurance premiums

To assess the attributable impacts of climate change on risk profiles in ARV, we utilise rainfall outputs from a set of 15 GCM attribution simulations archived by the 5th Coupled Model Intercomparison Project (CMIP5) (Taylor, Stouffer and Meehl, 2012). For each GCM, two simulations were used: a 'natural run', where the model is forced only with natural (solar insolation and volcanic aerosols) drivers of climate and an 'historical run' where the model is forced with both natural and societal (greenhouse gases and aerosols) drivers. Each pair of GCM simulations therefore represents one realisation of the climate with and without human influence, commonly termed the factual and counterfactual. Daily rainfall from each simulation was post-processed to match the standard ten-day rainfall input format to ARV. This included conversion to the spatial and temporal resolution required, bias correction so that the statistical properties of the GCM data match the observational rainfall data used in ARV, as well as evaluation of the processed GCM data against observations. Dorbor (2020) provides details of the data pre-processing and evaluation.

The pairs of factual and counterfactual rainfall data were applied to ARV, using the case study of Malawi, resulting in 15 risk profiles estimated for a world with and without human influence on climate (Figure 10.2). In the world without human influence on climate, the risk profile is markedly lower. For example, in the counterfactual world around 2.6 million people (median across models) would be at risk 10 per cent of the time (corresponding to a one in ten-year drought) while in today's world, the median estimate of the people at risk is 4.75 million. While there is overlap in the spread of risk profiles across the 15 GCMs (dashed lines in Figure 10.2), at least half of the realisations in the counterfactual world lie outside the 90th percentile of those in the factual world, indicating there is a significant shift in the risk profile.

These different risk profiles have large implications for underwriting parametric insurance coverage offered by ARC Ltd. and other insurers. The interaction of four factors is critical to the cost of insurance such as that offered by ARC Ltd.: (i) the attachment point, (ii) the exhaustion point, (iii) the coverage limit, and (iv) the ceding percentage (see Table 10.1); of these, the first two depend fundamentally on the modelled risk profile. In the case of Malawi, where the MDRC profile in the counterfactual world is shifted towards lower values for a given return period, the effect would have been to reduce the cost of insurance. If the risk transfer parameters are determined according to default values used by the ARC Ltd.'s insurance scheme, and assuming 100 per cent coverage, then the insurance premium based on the ARV attachment and exhaustion points in the world with human influence on climate

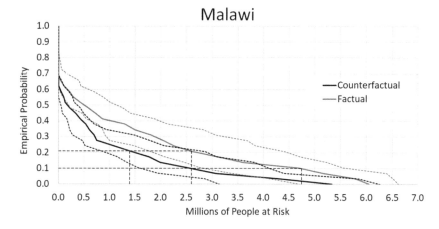

Figure 10.2 The risk profile for Malawi in worlds with (factual) and without (counterfactual) human influence on climate, expressed as millions of people at risk. (The profile for MDRC is a simple multiple of the people at risk. Solid lines show the median across all 15 models, while the heavy dashed lines show the 10th and 90th percentiles of the exceedance probabilities. The dashed horizontal and vertical lines show equivalent median MDRC-probability relationships between the factual and counterfactual worlds).

would decrease by a median value of 63 per cent. Of the 15 realisations with GCMs, two result in an increase in premium, while 13 result in a premium decrease. More robust estimates are possible through use of additional climate model experiments, as well as more sophisticated probabilistic modelling of the risk profiles (New et al., 2020). Different risk transfer parameter choices would alter the premiums, but not the fact that the premium for the same level of coverage would be lower in the counterfactual world.

Common but differentiated responsibilities: Insurance premiums

The analysis for Malawi illustrates an approach to estimating how human influence on climate has altered the cost of sovereign drought insurance. In the case of Malawi, and using a limited set of GCM attribution simulations, the best estimate of the increase in cost due to anthropogenic climate change, using the ARC Ltd.'s standard parameter values for underwriting, is 63 per cent.

For a developing country such as Malawi, with limited resources for disaster management, climate change has made it more expensive, and therefore more difficult, to use risk transfer through insurance as one of its strategies to respond to climate-related disasters. Using attribution methods to estimate the contribution of anthropogenic climate change to the cost of parametric insurance offers possibilities for a sharing of the premium between the country – which might be expected to be responsible for the cost of coverage in a world without climate change – and a global climate fund such as the Green Climate Fund – which could cover the additional cost due to climate change. This kind of support is consistent with Articles 7, 8, and 9 of the Paris Agreement (UNFCCC, 2015), which focus specifically on the need for technical and financial support for adaptation and loss and damage, including: 'Risk insurance facilities, climate risk pooling and other insurance solutions' (Article 8.4(f)) and that 'developed country Parties should continue to take the lead in mobilizing climate finance from a wide variety of sources, instruments and channels' (Article 9.3). While ARC Ltd. was established with capital – in the form of interest-free loans – from developed country development aid,[2] this support was not specifically from bilateral climate funds; further the capital has to be repaid, and so ARC Ltd. has to make a profit from its insurance offerings to meet this repayment requirement. Additionally, the support from these international development agencies has not been calculated with reference to the increased cost of drought insurance in Africa attributable to climate change.

Elsewhere in the world, regional insurance schemes for developing countries are established (e.g., in the Caribbean – see McGee, Phelan and Wenta, 2014) or proposed (e.g., the South Pacific – see UN Development Program, 2019) with the provision for developed countries to make financial contributions. In Africa, a similar approach to multi-party purchase of index-based insurance has already been operationalised with a different, but applicable focus by the World Food Program (WFP), through its ARC Replica project (WFP, 2018). The WFP partnered with ARC Ltd. to match the sovereign insurance taken up by Mauritania in 2018, effectively doubling the coverage available. The Replica partner also assists with the development and implementation of national technical capacities and systems in emergency preparedness and response, targeting the use of the insurance payout. Using attribution-based approaches can assist with a fairer approach to replication; in Malawi, for example, the replication amount should have been twice that taken out by Malawi, and the WFP and other partners might have been able to leverage climate finance to support the replication.

Even as the principle of 'common but differentiated responsibilities' is intended for universal application, an attribution-based approach to determining responsibility for the cost of index-based weather disaster insurance, such as that offered by ARC Ltd., would need to reflect regional differences. For example, for drought insurance – a primary consideration in Africa – the shifts in seasonal rainfall attributable to climate change vary across the continent (Figure 10.3). Over Southern Africa and West Africa the simulated reduction in rainfall would suggest that a risk model such as ARV would show an increase in MDRC compared to a world without climate change, and an increase in the cost of insurance. In the Gulf of Africa and in parts of East Africa, the MDRC would have decreased, and there would not be a case

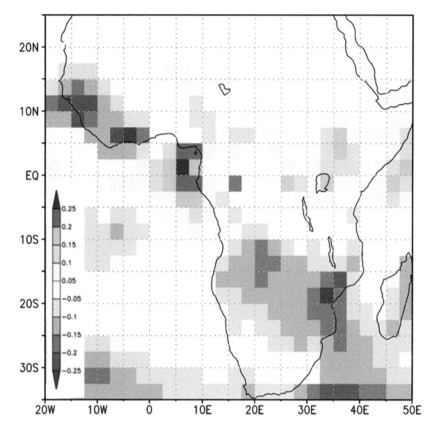

Figure 10.3 Multi-model average simulated differences in annual rainfall across Africa compared to a world without human influence on climate, derived from the CMIP5 GCM historic and natural attribution simulations (authors own analysis). (Areas that are red show decreased rainfall (increased drought risk) and areas that are blue show increased rainfall (and decreased drought risk)).

for a contribution from international climate funds. Nevertheless, broadly speaking, anthropogenic climate change is exacerbating loss-causing weather events, in terms of frequency and severity, and will continue to do so. As such, an attribution-based approach to insurance premiums could provide an increasingly important opportunity for equitable financing of adaptation to climate change.

Conclusion

Insurance is an important component of climate disaster risk management, supporting risk transfer of damage costs that cannot be avoided or covered through other mechanisms. While it is not a silver bullet, it is being pushed by a range of international actors – multi-lateral banks, development donors, and the insurance industry itself – and there are major efforts to increase penetration at all levels in developing countries.

Without properly accounting for how anthropogenic climate change is affecting climate-related disaster risk, and therefore the cost of insurance, developed countries who push for greater penetration are also shifting responsibility onto developing countries. They are, in effect, expecting developing countries to cover the ever-increasing cost of risk transfer. This increased risk layer can already be quite large, as shown for Malawi in this study: the climate change already accounts for around 60 per cent of the cost of a relatively standard drought insurance offering.

Using climate change impact attribution methods offers a way of estimating the fair share of insurance against climate risk. These estimates can either be used qualitatively to make the case for more meaningful contributions from developed countries for climate risk management, for example by converting ARC Ltd.'s capital loan to a donation, which would reduce premiums; or in supporting other areas of risk reduction, such as farm-based adaptation and capacity building (Reeves, 2017). If insurance is going to continue to encouraged – as seems to be the case – then the approach we pilot here could be used to determine fair contributions from international climate funds towards the cost of insurance. While estimates derived in this manner will always have associated uncertainty, the same is true of any underwriting process, and this has not prevented insurance companies from building this uncertainty into their pricing.

Notes

1. That is, developed countries.
2. Primarily the UK and Germany.

References

African Risk Capacity Ltd. (ARC). (2016). Africa RiskView Methodology Technical Note: Drought. p. 29. Available at: http://africariskview.org/Content/Technical-Note_en.pdf [Accessed January 2019].

African Risk Capacity Ltd. (ARC). (2018). African Risk Capacity: Transforming Disaster Risk Management & Financing in Africa. Available at: https://africanriskcapacity.org [Accessed March 2020].

African Risk Capacity Ltd. (ARC). (2019). African Risk Capacity Insurance Limited to Issue $738,835 Payout to Cote d'Ivoire. [African Risk Capacity Updates] Available at: https://africanriskcapacity.org/page/2 [Accessed January 2020].

Allen, M., Pall, P., Stone, D., Stott, P., Frame, D., Min, S. K., Nozawa, T. and Yukimoto, S. (2007). Scientific challenges in the attribution of harm to human influence on climate. *University of Pennsylvania Law Review*, 155(6), pp. 1353–1400.

AON. (2019). *Weather, Climate and Catastrophe Insight: 2018 Report*. p. 88. London: AON. Available at: http://catastropheinsight.aon.com [Accessed February 2020].

Bindoff, N. L., Stott, P. A., AchutaRao, K. M., Allen, M. R., Gillett, N., Gutzler, D., Hansingo, K., Hegerl, G., Hu, Y., Jain, S., Mokhov, I. I., Overland, J., Perlwitz, J., Sebbari, R. and Zhang, X. (2013). Detection and attribution of climate change: From global to regional. In: T. F. Stocker, D. Qin, G.-K. Plattner, M. Tignor, S. K. Allen, J. Boschung, A. Nauels, Y. Xia, V. Bex and P. M. Midgley, eds. *Climate Change 2013: The Physical Science Basis. Contribution of Working Group I to the Fifth Assessment Report of the Intergovernmental Panel on Climate Change*. Cambridge, UK and New York :Cambridge University Press, pp. 867–952.

Broberg, M. (2019). Parametric loss and damage insurance schemes as a means to enhance climate change resilience in developing countries. *Climate Policy*, early online, pp. 1–11.

Centre for Financial Inclusion. (2018). *Inclusive Insurance: Closing the Protection Gap for Emerging Customers*. Washington, DC and Cambridge, MA: Centre for Financial Inclusion, p. 49. Available at: https://www.centerforfinancialinclusion. org/inclusive-insurance-closing-the-protection-gap-for-emerging-customers-2 [Accessed February 2020].

Coronese, M., Lamperti, F., Keller, K., Chiaromonte, F. and Roventini, A. (2019). Evidence for sharp increase in the economic damages of extreme natural disasters. *Proceedings of the National Academy of Sciences*, 116(43), pp. 21450–21455, doi: 10.1073/pnas.1907826116.

Cramer, W., Yohe, G. W., Auffhammer, M., Huggel, C., Molau, U., Dias, M. A. F. S., Solow, A., Stone, D. A. and Tibig, L. (2014). Detection and attribution of observed impacts. In: C. B. Field, V. R. Barros, D. J. Dokken, K. J. Mach, M. D. Mastrandrea, T. E. Bilir, M. Chatterjee, K. L. Ebi, Y. O. Estrada, R. C. Genova, B. Girma, E. S. Kissel, A. N. Levy, S. MacCracken, P. R. Mastrandrea and L. L. White, eds., *Climate Change 2014: Impacts, Adaptation, and Vulnerability. Part A: Global and Sectoral Aspects. Contribution of Working Group II to the Fifth Assessment Report of the Intergovernmental Panel of*, Yohe, G. W., Auffhammer, M., Huggel, C., Molau, U., Dias, M. A. F. S., Solow, A., Stone, D. A. and Tibig, L. *Climate Change*. Cambridge, UK and New York: Cambridge University Press, pp. 979–1037.

Dorbor, S. D. (2020). Attribution-Based Parametric Insurance: Towards Affordable Premiums. MSc Thesis, University of Cape Town.

Hansen, G. and Stone, D. (2016). Assessing the observed impact of anthropogenic climate change. *Nature Climate Change*, 6(5), pp. 532–537, doi:10.1038/nclimate2896.

Hegerl, G. and Zwiers, F. (2011). Use of models in detection and attribution of climate change. *Wiley Interdisciplinary Reviews: Climate Change*, 2(4), pp. 570–591.

Howard, L. S. (2018). Insurance Protection Gap Is Growing Global Problem: Swiss Re, RenRe & WTW Comment, Journal, I. Available at: https://www.insurancejournal. com/news/international/2018/01/17/477266.htm [Accessed March 2020].

Intergovernmental Panel on Climate Change (IPCC). (2013). Summary for policymakers. In: T. F. Stocker, D. Qin, G.-K. Plattner, M. Tignor, S. K. Allen, J. Boschung, A. Nauels, Y. Xia, V. Bex and P. M. Midgley, eds., *Climate Change 2013: The Physical Science Basis. Contribution of Working Group I to the Fifth Assessment Report of the Intergovernmental Panel on Climate Change*. Cambridge, UK and New York: Cambridge University Press.

Jarzabkowski, P., Chalkias, K., Clarke, D., Iyahen, E., Stadtmueller, D. and Zwick, A. (2019). *Insurance for Climate Adaptation*. [Background Paper for the Global Commission on Adaptation]. Rotterdam and Washington, DC: Global Commission on Adaptation. Available at: www.gca.org [Accessed November 2019].

Jensen, N. and Barrett, C. (2017). Agricultural index insurance for development. *Applied Economic Perspectives and Policy*, 39(2), pp. 199–219, doi:10.1093/aepp/ppw022.

Marr, A., Winkel, A., van Asseldonk, M., Lensink, R. and Bulte, E. (2016). Adoption and impact of index-insurance and credit for smallholder farmers in developing countries: A systematic review. *Agricultural Finance Review*, 76(1), pp. 94–118, doi:10.1108/AFR-11-2015-0050.

Mastrandrea, M. D., Mach, K. J., Plattner, G.-K., Edenhofer, O., Stocker, T. F., Field, C. B., Ebi, K. L. and Matschoss, P. R. (2011). The IPCC AR5 guidance note on consistent treatment of uncertainties: A common approach across the working groups. *Climatic Change*, 108(4), p. 675, doi:10.1007/s10584-011-0178-6.10.1007/s10584-011-0178-6.

Matera, M., Dana, J., de Moura, F. S., Alton, L., Sampainho, J. and Chavana, X. A. (2018). *Financial Protection Against Disasters in Mozambique*. New York: Global Facility for Disaster Reduction and Recovery. Available at: https://www.gfdrr.org/sites/default/files/publication/bm-brochura-pfc-en.pdf [Accessed March 2020].

Matthews, H. D., Graham, T. L., Keverian, S., Lamontagne, C., Seto, D. and Smith, T. J. (2014). National contributions to observed global warming. *Environmental Research Letters*, 9(1), p. 014010.

McGee, J., Phelan, L. and Wenta, J. (2014). Writing the fine print: Developing regional insurance for climate change adaptation in the Pacific. *Melbourne Journal of International Law*, 15(2), pp. 444–472.

Mitchell, D., Heaviside, C., Vardoulakis, S., Huntingford, C., Masato, G., Guillod, B. P., Frumhoff, P., Bowery, A., Wallom, D. and Allen, M. (2016). Attributing human mortality during extreme heat waves to anthropogenic climate change. *Environmental Research Letters*, 11(7), p. 074006.

New, M., Dorbor, S., Maslo, D. and Odoulami, R. C. (2020). Attribution of anthropogenic climate influence on drought insurance risk and premiums, *Nature*, (under review).

Osuteye, E., Johnson, C. and Brown, D. (2017). The data gap: An analysis of data availability on disaster losses in sub-Saharan African cities. *International Journal of Disaster Risk Reduction*, 26, pp. 24–33. doi: https://doi.org/10.1016/j.ijdrr.2017.09.026.

Phelan, L., Taplin, R., Henderson-Sellers, A. and Albrecht, G. (2011). Ecological viability or liability? Insurance system responses to climate risk. *Environmental Policy and Governance*, 21(2), pp. 112–130. doi: 10.1002/eet.565.

Reeves, J. (2017). *The Wrong Model for Resilience: How G7-Backed Drought Insurance Failed Malawi, and What We Must Learn from It*. Johannesburg: ActionAid, 28. Available at: https://actionaid.org/sites/default/files/the_wrong_model_for_resilience_final_230517.pdf [Accessed January 2020].

Rosenzweig, C. and Neofotis, P. (2013). Detection and attribution of anthropogenic climate change impacts. *WIREs Climate Change*, 4(2), pp. 121–150. doi: 10.1002/wcc.209.

Schiermeier, Q. (2018). Climate as culprit: Weather forecasters will soon provide instant assessments of global warming's influence on heatwaves and floods. *Nature*, 560, pp. 21–22.

Schlemmer, L. and Rinehart-Smit, K. (2020). *What we've Learnt About the Risk Protection Gap in Sub-Saharan Africa from Finscope Consumer Data*. Cape Town: Cenfri. Available at: https://cenfri.org/articles/what-we-learnt-about-the-risk-protection-gap-in-sub-saharan-africa-by-engaging-with-finscope-consumer-data/ [Accessed 6 March 2020].

Singh, P. and Agrawal, G. (2019). Efficacy of weather index insurance for mitigation of weather risks in agriculture: An integrative review. *International Journal of Ethics and Systems*, 35(4), pp. 584–616. doi: 10.1108/IJOES-09-2018-0132.

South African Insurance Association (SAIA). (2019). Building Resilience and Reducing the Risk Protection Gap. [News Bulletin] May. Available at: https://saia. co.za/saia-news/2019/06/07/building-resilience [Accessed March 2020].

Stott, P. A., Christidis, N., Otto, F. E. L., Sun, Y., Vanderlinden, J.-P., van Oldenborgh, G. J., Vautard, R., von Storch, H., Walton, P., Yiou, P. and Zwiers, F. W. (2016). Attribution of extreme weather and climate-related events. *Wiley Interdisciplinary Reviews: Climate Change*, 7(1), pp. 23–41.

Stott, P. A., Gillett, N. P., Hegerl, G. C., Karoly, D. J., Stone, D. A., Zhang, X. and Zwiers, F. (2010). Detection and attribution of climate change: A regional perspective. *WIREs Climate Change*, 1(2), pp. 192–211.

Taylor, K. E., Stouffer R. J. and Meehl, G. A. (2012). An overview of CMIP5 and the experiment design. *Bulletin of the American Meteorological Society*, 93(4), pp. 485–498. doi: 10.1175/bams-d-11-00094.1.

United Nations Framework Convention on Climate Change (UNFCCC). (2015). Paris Agreement, in United Nations Framework Convention on Climate Change, COP Report No. 21, Addendum, at 21, U.N. Doc. FCCC/CP/2015/10/Add, 1.

United Nations General Assembly. (1994). United Nations Framework Convention on Climate Change. *United Nations, Treaty Series*, vol. 1771, p. 107.

United Nations International Strategy for Disaster Reduction (UNISDR). (2017). UNISDR Terminology on Disaster Risk Reduction. United Nations International Strategy for Disaster Reduction. Available at: https://www.preventionweb.net/ files/50683_oiewgreportenglish.pdf [Accessed February 2020].

World Food Programme (WFP). (2018). *ARC Replica: WFP's Partnership With the African Risk Capacity (ARC) for the Expansion of Climate Risk Insurance.* Rome: World Food Programme. Available at: https://docs.wfp.org/api/documents/ WFP-0000063792/download [Accessed December 2019].

Index